UNCUT

PRESENTS

HISTORY OF

ROCK

IN THE

1970s

THIS IS A CARLTON BOOK

Published by Carlton Books Ltd
20 Mortimer Street
London W1T 3JW

Text © 2017 Time Inc (UK) LTD

Design © 2017 Carlton Books Ltd

ISBN 978-1-78097-984-7

Editor: Chris Mitchell
Design: Russell Knowles and James Pople
Production: Emily Noto
Picture Research: Steve Behan

A CIP catalogue for this book is available from the British Library

Printed in Dubai

10 9 8 7 6 5 4 3 2 1

PRESENTS

HISTORY OF

ROCK

IN THE

1970s

THE COMPLETE STORY OF A MOMENTOUS
MUSICAL DECADE

FROM THE ARCHIVES OF
MELODY MAKER & NME

CARLTON
BOOKS

▶ An understated, but still
mesmerising, post-Ziggy Stardust
David Bowie, performing during the
Diamond Dogs tour in 1974

Introduction

John Mulvey
Editor, *Uncut*

The 1970s did not, by most measures, get off to a promising start. In April 1970, Paul McCartney formally announced that he had left The Beatles, leaving many observers wondering what a music world would look like without its most dominant, most fearless and most experimental band. Would the radical advances of the '60s be sustained? Would the masses remain transfixed? Or would rock be revealed, like so many other scenes before it, to be a mere passing fad, destined to wither away after a decade or two?

Intimations of doom, of course, turned out to be short-lived. As this hefty volume illustrates, rock's wild and unpredictable development only intensified through the 1970s. Bands became bigger, louder and more decadent, as the likes of Led Zeppelin, The Rolling Stones, The Who and Queen flourished in stadiums and arenas across the world. David Bowie ushered in a flamboyant cadre of glam rockers, while their bookish brothers and sisters ensured that prog would open up a world of extravagant and complicated new possibilities for rock. Over in the States, the hippies evolved into rootsy singer-songwriters, and a rough-and-ready guy from New Jersey called Bruce Springsteen was beginning to create street corner symphonies for dreamers across America and beyond.

Soon enough, rock would be subjected to another seismic upheaval, as the marauding hordes of punk, led by the Sex Pistols and The Clash, would try and change music forever. By the end of the decade, a transient music scene had proved itself to be amazingly resilient, able to not only endure radical changes but be made stronger by them. Rock had become an essential, indestructible part of our culture.

Through this turbulent time, the valiant journalists of *NME* and *Melody Maker* were the first to every story that mattered. They were at every concert and party worth attending, had the first and most respected opinions on every record that was released, and enjoyed a now unimaginable degree of access to stars who seem, at this remove, so remote and untouchable. The *History Of Rock In The 1970s* compiles the very best stories from those inky pages, as an encyclopaedic compendium of an extraordinary decade.

From "Ziggy Stardust" to "God Save The Queen", "Stairway To Heaven" to "Wuthering Heights", "Dark Side Of The Moon" to "Saturday Night Fever", it's a heroic yarn, told by the most stylish writers of their time... "Carry me back, baby, where I come from!"

Enjoy the trip!

▲ Keith Richards and Mick Jagger of The Rolling Stones pose for photographer Michael Putland in 1978.

The Beatles // Crosby, Stills, Nash & Young
Eric Clapton // Jimi Hendrix // Jimmy Page
Joni Mitchell // Led Zeppelin // Nico
Paul McCartney // Roger Daltrey

1970

The Beatles' story – in many ways the story of the Sixties – is coming to an end, and who knows what the new decade will bring? The electric blues of Eric Clapton and the Stones provides some continuity, and the biggest heavy rockers of them all emerge as Led Zeppelin conquer the stadium circuit.

Rock music's most spectacular guitar hero Jimi Hendrix wows them at the Isle of Wight, only to die just weeks later. Meanwhile the gentler West Coast sound of Joni Mitchell and Crosby, Stills, Nash & Young calms nerves while we wait for the next big thing... T. Rex?

14

"It's not easy to do this"

But when she arrives in London, JONI MITCHELL wows everyone she meets. Easy definition (as folk singer, celebrity girlfriend) is something she seeks to elude. Her songs and performance do just that. "I want my music to get more involved and sophisticated," she says.

CANADIAN FOLK SINGER Joni Mitchell this week denied rumours that she would be retiring after her Royal Festival Hall concert on January 17. But Joni, who can scarcely be described as a folk singer any more and has no current connections with Canada either, will be a good deal more withdrawn in the future.

She flew to London from Los Angeles last week, and at a Warner Reprise reception she told *Melody Maker (MM)*, "It's true I've postponed all bookings indefinitely, but that's just to catch my breath. I really need to get some new material together, and I also want to learn to play more instruments, and find time to do some painting."

So Joni, far from taking things easy, is going to have her time cut out in the next few months. She made it quite apparent that she is going through a transitional stage in her career, expressing herself through a wider range of media, but at the same time delving deeper into her own distinctive musical bag.

"I've got a hard core of fans who follow me around from one concert to another, and it's for them I feel I ought to produce some new songs. I come from Saskatoon, Canada originally, and I'll probably move back there, but at this point in my life I would rather live in Los Angeles as it's right in the middle of change, and therefore far more stimulating. There are a lot of artists in LA at the moment, and the exchange between artists is tremendous."

Joni took a trip back to her previous two visits to England. The first she remembers specifically as her first taste of English folk clubs, and the second for her appearance at the Festival of Contemporary Song in September 1968, with Al Stewart, Jackson C Frank and The Johnstons. It was this concert that really established her as a major artist in Britain, and she is still more than enthusiastic about that concert. "I'd sure like to meet The Johnstons again while I'm here," she added.

◄ Canadian Joni Mitchell sings to a homeland crowd in the city of Toronto, after the success of "Big Yellow Taxi"

▲ Joni Mitchell performing on stage at the Isle of Wight Festival, August 29, 1970, the biggest of its kind ever seen in Great Britain

But songs like "Chelsea Morning", "Marcie" and "Both Sides Now", which acted as her springboard, have now made way for slightly more complex numbers, perhaps brought about by the change of environment.

"I want my music to get more involved and more sophisticated. Right now I'm learning how to play a lot of new instruments. In the last month I've managed to write three new songs, including a couple of Christmas songs. I've also written a song for a film score that hasn't been used, and 'Woodstock', which is the next Crosby, Stills, Nash & Young single."

Joni emphasised that she will not be playing any folk clubs while in Britain. She will make only one concert appearance, and will be tele-recording a guest spot on the Tom Jones show. "I shall then take a couple of weeks' holiday in Britain before returning. I want to get out into the country, and in particular to Scotland."

Country and city life both play prominent but entirely different roles in Joni Mitchell's life. And it is the latter that is currently influencing her writing. "I've a feeling that America may suddenly get very strange. In Los Angeles the air is very bad, and it's not good to breathe city air all the time. But it's not just this environment that influences me. Any kind of music that moves me in any way has some effect on my writing."

Joni is more than enthusiastic about her next album, which is almost completed. A couple of tunes she picked out for special attention: "They Paved Paradise And Put Up A Parking Lot" and "He Played Real Good For Free", the latter being about a sidewalk musician. **MM**

GIG REVIEW

The Walls Were Shaking

JANUARY 17 · ROYAL FESTIVAL HALL, LONDON

Joni is captivating at the modernist concert hall beside the Thames.

JONI MITCHELL MUST love England to the same extent that England loves Joni Mitchell. This fact was implicit throughout the whole of her two-hour concert at the Festival Hall on Saturday. The walls were still shaking 10 minutes after Joni had taken her second encore. Such was the greed and expectation, that hardly a person had left the hall when she finally returned for a farewell acknowledgement, and the audience rose en masse.

With great warmth and presence, the Canadian songstress appeared for the first set in a long red dress, her voice soaring and plummeting over that aggressive and characteristically open-tuned guitar. After three numbers Joni moved to the piano and captured the audience completely by the nature of "He Played Real Good For Free", a recent composition, which reflects her environmental change. She closed a well-balanced first-half repertoire with the famous "Both Sides Now".

Next Joni appeared in blue and embarked on a much longer set which included "Galleries", "Marcie" and "Michael From Mountains", and with each song she drew the audience further into her. An outstanding Richard Farina-style rock number, "They Paved Paradise And Put Up A Parking Lot", and the next Crosby, Stills, Nash & Young single, "Woodstock", prefaced the finale, which was an event in itself – Dino Valente's great song about brotherhood. **MM**

"Is this the A-side?"

MAY 16

Roger Daltrey picks the winners among the new singles and album tracks.

Aretha Franklin "Let It Be"
Only one person it could be... and I ain't trying to guess. It's no improvement on The Beatles. It's Aretha Franklin. I heard some of her album tracks recently and they were a lot better than this. The tenor solo was a downer – it just doesn't get off the ground. Not one of her best performances. Can I hear it again? Definitely not a single – it doesn't come up enough.

Free "All Right Now"
Are you sure this is the A-side? Ha ha! Good voice, though the tune is a bit meaningless. It sounds like a B-side. Haven't a clue who it is. Liberace? I can't imagine anybody releasing that as an A-side. Let's turn it over. It must be Fleetwood Mac. Oh dear, I'm really not interested and I don't care!

Arrival "I Will Survive"
The Arrival? It's the sort of group you see on the box. They are refreshing, but definitely not a hit. It just wanders all over the place. They are good at what they do and have a nice, easy-listening image. Can I listen to the B-side? That's better – the chick is a good singer. This is what they are all about. For an English band they have an incredible sound.

Ben E King "Goodbye My Old Girl"
Jesus Christ – it's Mario Lanza! No thoughts on that one. It'll be a No 1 in the Darby & Joan clubs. I'm not going to ask who it is – I'm not interested. That must be a record-company thing where they had to put something out. It may have been alright for 1959, but not for today. I'll play you one of Towshend's new songs to cheer you up!

Mary Johnson "So Glad You Chose Me"
Don't like it. It's that Atlantic/Motown soul sound, and definitely not a good song, although he's a good singer. What can you say about a rubbish song? I can't see the guy singing liking it even.

Elvis Presley "Kentucky Rain"
Horrible. Presley, ennit? Nothing much to say about that. I thought he had it in the bag, and he goes back to this kind of stuff. But it will probably be a hit. If he'd put out a good old funky rock'n'roll record, I'd buy it. **MM**

"We build it and polish it like a jewel"

Films. Music. "The movement". CROSBY, STILLS, NASH & YOUNG talk (and talk) a good game, but ambition is at the heart of their group. What they achieve together is one thing; what they achieve on their own is important also.

"**D**ON'T BUILD ME UP into a pop star. I'm no different from you or anybody else. It's just that, because I'm a musician, I can put music to people's thoughts."

Stephen Stills, talking about his position in society. Like many of his generation growing up inside the terror of the Great American Dream gone broke, Stills talks music and politico-sociology with equal ease. To him, they are indivisible.

"But music is not the be-all and end-all," he says. "It's a fulcrum around which the movement exists, because it sets people's heads to music and perhaps sometimes says things that they feel inside but can't articulate. It's very scary in the States at the moment. Did you read that the cops busted into a couple of houses in Chicago and Los

▶ Portrait of Graham Nash by photographer Michael Putland, while the singer was being interviewed in London, October 28,1970

◀ Left to right: Neil Young, Graham Nash, David Crosby and Stephen Stills rehearsing backstage before a concert in July 1970

Angeles a few days ago and mowed down the Black Panthers? Wow...

"That's why I want to stay in England for a while. It's more... civilised, plus there are a few people I want to play with. I stood up in front of a lot of people during the Vietnam Moratorium in San Francisco recently and read a poem. So if there's a list, I'm on it."

Can he see the seeds of an alternative culture emerging in America?

"Yeah, it's going through its birth-pains. The young people have got to find a new way to live, and they're getting there because history shows that no revolution that has come from the people has ever failed, even if it's had to take a couple of generations to get through. Right from the time of Alexander The Great, that's been a fact. Of course, people are in varying stages of preparing for it. The leaders... well, we're not getting quite as high these days."

This situation will be reflected in Crosby, Stills, Nash & Young's first movie, a full feature-length picture to be called *Wooden Ships*, and based loosely on the words of that song from their first album.

"We're getting Theodore Sturgeon to write the screenplay; he's a science-fiction writer and I'm pretty sure that it's suitable for him. That should be ready pretty soon."

Briefly, the story centres round the survivors of a nuclear holocaust, who meet up with a South American tribe (I think) and sail off in wooden ships in search of an uncontaminated area where they can begin to build a new civilisation. Steve says that they're trying to get Stanley Kubrick (of *2001* fame) to direct the film.

"It won't be an Arthur C Clarke screenplay, so it won't have the same cold feeling as *2001* – I hope it will be more like Kubrick's earlier films, with the characters laid out so well. It's got to be done properly. If it's too serious you blow it, and if it's too funny you blow it. You've got to strike a balance."

Perhaps we in Britain don't realise just how big CSNY are in America. They've already done 25 concerts in cities which include Chicago (twice), Houston, New York, Dallas, Los Angeles, Salt Lake City and San Francisco.

"We've averaged 14,000 people a concert," says Steve. "Some of the concerts have been in the open air, in football parks, but we're not doing any more of those. You get so many people there it's ridiculous. That essential intimate feeling is lost in a football park, and we're going to concentrate on playing halls with a capacity between 10,000–14,000."

Possibly a large percentage of their success can be ascribed to the variety they project throughout their concerts, with four such diverse talents to call on. "We play for two hours, the first hour acoustic and the second half with electronic equipment. Just as people think they're listening to a folk concert, we plug in and WHAM! We're a rock band!"

When I put forward my pet theory, that country-rock hasn't broken big over here because basically country music is a particularly American form, Steve replied, "Well, it all goes back to Elizabethan music and so forth. It may not have been this year's music, but next year. Anyway, I couldn't restrict myself to country music, just as I couldn't restrict myself to the blues. I want to be able to cover it all, to play it all, and I don't see why I shouldn't." **MM**

▲ Neil Young on stage in Denmark as part of Crosby, Stills, Nash & Young, in January 1970

Lengthy and Often Enjoyable

JANUARY 6 · ROYAL ALBERT HALL, LONDON

CSNY rock, perhaps too gently.

CROSBY, STILLS, NASH, YOUNG AND OLD gave a lengthy and often enjoyable concert at London's Royal Albert Hall last week. "The Old" was the age-old problem of untutored musicians having to devote much time to tuning their instruments on stage.

But while Neil Young emerged as an exceptional talent with superb compositions and the only voice of distinction, and Dallas Taylor rocked up a storm on drums, the two-hour show often verged dangerously into the realms of tedium.

Dave Crosby brightened the intermissions between numbers with dry and droll remarks, but the silence which often prevailed was so intense I could distinctly hear a man scratch the stubble on his chin and at one point I dozed off, having spent a hectic night before digging Roland Kirk, now in a season at Ronnie Scott's.

The first half was devoted to gentle acoustic music, which was agreeable enough, and each member had a chance to take a solo spot or work with the partner of his choice. Opening with "Suite: Judy Blue Eyes", they moved on to "Triad" by Dave Crosby and "Our House" by our old mate Graham Nash on piano.

Steve Stills' piano solo received an ovation, although he had difficulty keeping time and seemed restricted to approximately three chords. After this bring-down, the electrification of the rhythm section was a welcome relief, and Dallas Taylor leaping about on drums brightened proceedings considerably. Undoubtedly, Neil Young's haunted lonesome voice, with just the right amount of vibrato on the "The Loner" and "Down By The River", was the high spot.

While CSN&Y did not deserve the critical pasting they received in some quarters, they could improve themselves by being a little less self-indulgent, and knowing when to stop. *MM*

1970

▶ Left to right: John Bonham, John Paul Jones, Jimmy Page and Robert Plant in London, 1970

"There is a powerful astrological force"

**How else to account for the success of
LED ZEPPELIN? An in-depth encounter with
JIMMY PAGE reveals plenty. "It's been
quite a year…"**

WHEN A BAND ACHIEVES Led Zeppelin's kind of success in such a short time, there are bound to be whispered accusations in the corridors of pop. In recent years, fans have become more aware of "The Business". Far from blindly accepting new trends and groups, there is a tendency towards cynicism, especially among those who interest themselves in progressive rock.

They have learned the meaning of the slang word "hype", which hints at hyperbole and hypocrisy, and neatly sums up the process of falsely exaggerating the popularity and earning power of an artist. The situation has been largely brought upon pop by the policy of management in building up groups with advance publicity which later fails to fulfil its promise – rather like general election campaigns.

Fans eagerly await a performance or album and are disappointed by a display of careless indifference. "Hype" – goes up the cry. Now there is cynical backlash where groups, teenybop or underground, are suspect if they gain too much BREAD and publicity.

Zeppelin are one of the groups who have experienced sniping, at home and abroad. Says Jimmy Page, "Before they saw us in America there was a blast of publicity and they heard all about the money

Turn It Up!

NOVEMBER 7

The increasing trend among groups like Led Zeppelin or the Flying Burrito Brothers towards quiet, acoustic music is a bad one. Many of these groups say rock is getting stale and stereotyped, and is also too loud: and that their music offers a fresh alternative. However, acoustic guitar means, almost inevitably, folk-style music.

However pleasant and "easy on the ear" this is, it is a very limited medium which is a cul-de-sac as far as musical development goes; admittedly many rock groups are stale and stereotyped, but there is, in the long run, far more potential for progression in rock music than in folk.

It lies with the rock and jazz-rock groups to get music out of its present stagnant pool – not the acoustic groups, who are trying much too hard just to be different.

N MAYFIELD, 5 Pytte House West, Clyst St George, Exeter, Devon. **MM**

being advanced to us by the record company. So the reaction was – 'Ah, a capitalist group.' They realised we weren't when they saw us playing a three-hour non-stop show every night.

"And the reason why we played that long was because when we started a year ago we had worked out a one-hour set and onstage this naturally expanded to an hour and a half. As we put in other numbers, this became two hours. In America they wanted encores and it expanded to three hours with the extra material from the second album.

"We enjoy ourselves and that shows in our playing. If somebody wants to hype a group, they only suffer in the end because people understand the economics of bands, especially in the States where it is the fashion to ask who is getting what out of what.

"I'm sure that when Hendrix played a West Coast festival, people knew he was being paid 100,000 dollars. There were a lot of snide remarks, and afterwards he seemed to drop in popularity. If we play at a university, kids say, 'Hey, you're getting £1,000 tonight.' So what? They think £1,000 is a lot of money, but it's not in relation to the expenses of a band with road managers, airfares and hotel bills. But really, money has nothing to do with it. You can tell when a band is being hyped, by their manner. You can tell from the vibrations. I can tell, so I'm sure everyone else can."

Have Zeppelin received much criticism of their music?

"The only criticism came after our Albert Hall concert in London, recently. One reviewer said we got off to a slow start. Well, I don't know if the guy had seen us before, but the idea is to start off with recognisable Zeppelin things, then go much quieter and use acoustic guitar, which is always well received. Then we build it up again.

"You can't possibly have a climax all the way. We like to play a cross-section of styles. We're not a rabble-rousing group. We are trying to play some music. One has to remember, at the Royal Albert Hall concerts, all the tickets were sold out in a day, so they must have been Zeppelin people in the audience who knew what we play."

Did Jimmy think there was a danger of too much being written and said about the "rock revolution"? Isn't it all getting out of hand?

"There shouldn't be a lot more written about it, because pop is going through a very revolutionary stage at the moment. I saw the Jack Bruce film on TV and I was quite amazed. He was tremendous. The whole message was – just listen to the music. That's what it's all about.

"Many classical people listen to pop music. They realise pop is not just a joke. Critics like Tony Palmer in the Sunday newspapers have helped it all to an incredible extent. It's strange, but I never saw the Cream and I had never seen Jack Bruce until his Lyceum concert. I've started going to concerts because I never saw any when I was working so hard touring. You have to be quick these days to see a group before they split up. I never saw Hendrix or the Cream while we were working in the States, or any other groups unless they were on the same bill as us.

"This has been my first real break in years, although we are working on the third album. We have to keep working all the time. We are working on a film. I don't know if it will ever be shown, really, but we filmed the Albert Hall concert and it will be a documentary on what has been going on with the band.

"Everything's been slowed up with Robert's accident. That was a horrific scene. The police came banging at the door with flashlights

and asked me if I knew a Mr Robert Plant. When they advised me to call him at Kidderminster Hospital I knew it had got to be serious. I was really worried, wondering if he had the baby in the car. He's still in a bad way and we had to cancel some work, although he said he would appear on stage in a wheelchair. He can't lift his arm above his shoulder and he has a cut over his eye.

"We've got a lot of recording to do. On the first album, we were finding out about each other. On the second, I really thought John Paul Jones came through strongly. We can feel each other much more.

"I've prepared a lot of acoustic stuff for the next album. It's just a matter of getting into a studio. They are all fully booked – it's incredible. We all do a bit of writing in the group and make tape recordings of ideas for songs. I like to get a basic construction together and a number grows from that."

What did Jimmy think of the trend towards jazz-rock?

"I don't like it, personally. I never liked Blood, Sweat & Tears. I'm all for a fusion of ideas, but this is just not my cup of tea, and has not been as well accepted as classical rock. Jazz-rock all rests on the brass players waiting for the chance to play as fast as possible at 78rpm. To me, it represents cacophony. I like and understand Eric Dolphy and John Coltrane. But when you get Fred Bloggs blowing away – it doesn't come off.

"The things Dick Heckstall-Smith plays with Colosseum are good and valid, and they make sense. When it doesn't make sense – I can't be bothered. I was never convinced by Blood, Sweat & Tears, yet lots of people think it's the epitome of pop today. What didn't I like about them? The arrangements and the singer. I couldn't believe that

singer. Everything sounds so false after one or two listens. The most progressive groups today are the Pink Floyd and Moody Blues."

Are Led Zeppelin a progressive group?

"I've been asking myself if we were progressive. In fact, I've been waiting for somebody to ask me that. I don't know. What we have done is to present rock in a different package. We are not a band like the Floyd, who are really progressive. Maybe our next album will be progressive – for us. People tend to say Pink Floyd are still just a 1967 flower-power group, but they are not. They sound fresh and beautiful."

To ward off the effects of heavy rock interviewing, Jimmy tottered off in search of a few aspirins.

"It's been quite a year," he said on his return. "I can hardly believe how much has happened – four tours of the States and two platinum albums. It sounds like a lot of old bull, but I can't really believe it sometimes. It's like looking at somebody else's career.

"There is a very powerful astrological force at work within the band, which I am sure had a lot to do with our success. Robert is a Leo, which makes him a perfect leader, with two Capricorns on either side and a Gemini behind. Leo is always a leader, like Ginger Baker, Keith Moon and Mick Jagger. I'm a Capricorn, which speaks for itself – very stubborn with a split personality." **MM**

◀ Jimmy Page performing with Zeppelin at the KB Hallen venue in Copenhagen, Denmark, February 21, 1970

▲ Led Zeppelin backstage at the Bath Festival of Blues and Progressive Music, June 28, 1970

◀ Plant and Page in action – with "Bonzo" Bonham behind the drum kit – at a Led Zeppelin date in Copenhagen, February 28, 1970

"Nobody knows me"

NICO is a woman alone. On a visit to London, she explains her relationship with music ("I wanted to be an opera singer") and with Andy Warhol ("He could never get me to take my clothes off").

THE SLEEVE OF The Velvet Underground's first album was dead right when it read "Nico: chanteuse". Not just "singer", because Nico is more than that, and the word "chanteuse" contains just the right registrations of the European tradition of chanson. For me, she is a logical extension of Marlene Dietrich singing "Falling In Love Again" in the Blue Angel bar; and yet, while her singing has that feeling of age and tradition behind it, it is also beyond tomorrow, way ahead of all those other lady singers who are still into "interpretation".

Those who have her Elektra album *The Marble Index* will already know what I'm saying. The LP is a journey through a landscape not unlike Berlin, where she lived as a child: desolate and wind-blown, scarred yet futuristic.

She is in London just now, attempting to make another LP, but has met only disillusionment and loneliness. Her friends from the old days – Keith Richards and Anita Pallenberg, Paul McCartney and Linda Eastman – were too busy with their new lives to help her, and record-company executives were uniformly uncooperative.

▲ Pop artist Andy Warhol (far right) and associate Gerard Malanga (wielding a whip) with Velvet Underground members John Cale (left) and Nico (centre right). NYC, 1966

◀ Nico and Sterling Morrison on stage at the The Delmonico Hotel, New York, January 13, 1966

"I can't stand the thought of going to New York, so I'm flying to Ibiza"

She played one gig, an implosion night at the Roundhouse, but when I asked her if she had been invited to do any more, she replied, in the deep Wagnerian accent, "No, who should ask me? I have a reputation for not turning up to sing. It's something I want very badly to get rid of."

But to get back to the beginning, a brief history: Nico, born of a Polish mother and a father who died in the concentration camps, was a top Parisian cover girl before she met the Stones. About four years ago Brian Jones took her to Andy Warhol's Factory in New York, and she joined The Velvet Underground, the group that was part of Warhol's Exploding Plastic Inevitable – the pioneering multi-media troupe which used dancers plus the first-ever light show.

GIG REVIEW

Difficult, Desolate

MARCH 21 · ROUNDHOUSE, LONDON

Nico's capital concert.

"I THOUGHT THIS was a rock and roll place," said Nico, smiling between numbers at the Roundhouse last Sunday. She was right, but she contrived to transcend barriers of taste and finally left the stage to warm applause.

Hers is difficult music. It's tonal range circumscribed by the sound of the harmonium she played and her intensely personal, desolate delivery. The emotional range of these interior monologues is, however, unlimited, and among the most memorable of the songs were "My Empty Pages", "No-one Is There" and a new song, "In Her Native German". *MM*

With them she sang at the Dom in New York, cut an album for Verve, travelled across the States to Los Angeles in a bus (she and Sterling Morrison took turns driving), and played the Fillmore West to the accompaniment of some bad scenes with Bill Graham. After about a year she left the group to sing on her own, starting at the Balloon Farm (upstairs from the Dom). Her accompanists changed every week, but the main ones were Lou Reed and John Cale from the Velvets and Jackson Browne, a young guitarist and singer from Orange County.

The upshot was that three of Browne's songs were on her first, badly produced album (for Verve), alongside Bob Dylan's "I'll Keep It With Mine", which legend says the master wrote for Nico, but of which she simply declares, "I don't know about that. He just gave it to me."

That album, *Chelsea Girl*, was titled after a Warhol movie in which she appeared. She made another one with him, which he has never shown – "Maybe it wasn't dirty enough for old New York. He could never get me to take my clothes off."

There followed a long silence, broken a year ago by the appearance of *The Marble Index*, which is one of those records which just might, in 10 or 20 years' time, be regarded as some sort of milestone.

Since then she's spent a lot of time in Italy, and has made part of a film called *La Cicatrice Intérieure* with the French director Philippe Garelle – "He's really one of the best movie-makers. He's directed five films, but he's never let them be released. This new one is very important to me. It's so powerful. We did part of it in the American desert and part of it in the Egyptian desert... I don't know when we'll finish it. It doesn't matter; there's no hurry because it's a very timeless thing."

But the most vital thing at the moment is to make a record, a task which amazingly defeated her in London. She accompanies herself on a very small Indian harmonium, and has 15 or 20 songs of her own that she wants to record. She started composing a couple of years ago, and bought the harmonium at just about the same time. She had no lessons ("Just singing lessons – I wanted to be an opera singer since I was a very little girl") and plays the instrument in a uniquely delicate style, based on modes rather than chords.

"I don't want to play in any more clubs," she says. "I'd like to do concerts, and maybe colleges would be good. But I don't have a manager, and nobody knows me here. In New York all the young people know me... I have a lot of friends... but I hate New York. Maybe I should get a manager. I wouldn't mind all the hassling if somebody else could go through it for me."

She was planning to fly to New York later the day that I saw her, possibly to take up the option on her Elektra contract. But a couple of hours after we'd parted she rang to say that she'd changed her mind. "I can't stand the thought of going to New York, so I'm flying to Ibiza. It's my favourite place, and I think I'll die there."

So perhaps those 15 beautiful songs will never be heard. But somehow I think there's hope yet, even if London isn't ready for it. *MM*

"I'm out of my depth!"

JUNE 27

Eric Clapton reviews the latest sounds.

Fred McDowell "61 Highway" and "Big Mama" from the LP *When I Lay My Burden Down*

Is that LP called *I Ain't Gonna Play No Rock And Roll*? Yeah – Fred McDowell. He's fantastic. He's using a slide guitar, probably tuned open, but not down too much. I've never seen him "live" – but I'd love to. I thought it might be Son House for a minute. It sounds like it might be recorded in the '50s. [**MM**: It was recorded at Fred's home in Mississippi in 1969.] It almost sounds like an electric guitar, doesn't it? He's from Mississippi – great.

Bill Evans and Jim Hall "My Funny Valentine" from the LP *Undercurrent*

(Sings along) Are they young musicians? Is it Kenny Burrell? It sounds ageless. I would have thought it's Larry Coryell, but I've no idea, I'll guess Barney Kessel. Tal Farlow. Joe Pass? Who is it? – Jim Hall? You realise I am out of my depth. What do you mean "yes"!

I liked this very much. I would have been anti-jazz a few years ago. It's a special kind of school, and something I wish I could… you know (plays imaginary guitar). Have you got any records by Charlie Christian? This one is beautiful.

Smiley Lewis "Shame, Shame, Shame" from the LP *Shame, Shame, Shame*

It's very familiar – Joe Turner? Beautiful – is it Ray Charles' band backing the singer? Who is it? Smiley Lewis? You're kidding. Can I see the cover? Sounds back to the '50s again. When I was first buying records this would have been too jazzy for me. It's not now, but I used to be a purist.

Miles Davis "Bitches Brew" from the LP *Bitches Brew*

It's either Miles Davis or Dr John! Is this "Bitches Brew"? I like this – no, I haven't heard it before, I've been waiting to hear it. Who's the drummer? Tony Williams? Can I see the cover? I'd like to have a go at playing with Miles – it would be an incredible challenge. But I have tried to back out of it a couple of times, because I don't know if I am up to it. I don't think I'm good enough. It's the kind of music that avoids the obvious, and I've had a few plays like that with Steve when we were forming Blind Faith. We played for five hours at a time – absolute madness.

Canned Heat "That's All Right Mama" from the LP *Canned Heat '70 Concert*

BB? I'll have to try and guess by the accents – Canned Heat? It's not fair – you're not giving me enough volume. This is a Big Boy Arthur Crudup number – have they given him a credit on the album? That's good. Alan Wilson flattens me the most. This track sounds pretty hairy. Our band will be getting more into the blues on our club dates, I expect. I'm split half down the middle. Half of me is black and half is white. I started out digging Buddy Holly songs, and we'll be doing some of his in country fashion. I liked this a lot. *MM*

Q: Is Lennon/ McCartney still a partnership? A: "No"

His solo debut is out, so PAUL McCARTNEY interviews himself – and breaks up THE BEATLES.

PAUL McCARTNEY SPEAKS... or rather sends out his words via a printed sheet which we reproduce below, just as he sent it out. That way we cannot get anything wrong, something Paul accuses the press of doing from time to time! Paul has used the time-honoured *NME* Question-Time format to put his message over, writing the questions and giving the answers himself.

You'll find what he thinks of Lennon; and Allen Klein; how he made his new album; who gets the composing credits; if he missed other Beatles and George Martin on the sessions; and what he wants to do in the future. Here is what he has to say...

Question: Why did you decide to make a solo album?
Answer: Because I got a Studer four-track recording machine at home – practised on it (playing all instruments) – liked the result, and decided to make it into an album.

Q: Were you influenced by John's adventures with the Plastic Ono Band and Ringo's solo LP?
A: Sort of but not really.

Q: Are all the songs by Paul McCartney alone?
A: Yes sir.

Q: Will they be so credited: McCartney?
A: It's a bit daft for them to be Lennon/McCartney credited, so "McCartney" it is.

Q: Did you enjoy working as a solo?
A: Very much. I only had me to ask for a decision, and I agreed with me. Remember Linda's on it too, so it's really a double act.

Q: What is Linda's contribution?
A: Strictly speaking she harmonises, but of course, it's more than that because she is a shoulder to lean on, a second opinion, and a photographer of renown. More than all this, she believes in me – constantly.

Q: Where was the album recorded?
A: At home, at EMI (No 2 studio) and at Morgan Studios (WILLESDEN!)

Q: What is your home equipment? (in some detail).
A: Studer four-track machine. I only had, however, one mic, and, as Mr Pender, Mr Sweatenham and others only managed to take six months or so (slight delay) I worked without VU meters or a mixer, which meant that everything had to be listened to first (for distortion, etc...) then recorded. So the Answer: STUDER. ONE MIC. And nerve.

Q: Why did you choose to work in the studios you chose?
A: They were available. EMI is technically good, and Morgan is cosy.

Q: The album was not known about until it was nearly completed. Was this deliberate?
A: Yes, because normally an album is old before it comes out. (Aside) Witness *Get Back*.

▶ January 5, 1970: The McCartneys on their farm in Scotland, the day after Paul started High Court proceedings to disband The Beatles

Dear Mailbag

MAY 2

Who does Paul McCartney think he is? We don't see anything of him for a year, and then out he pops from his mysterious hermit-like existence, advertising his new record in a publicity-crazed manner. Does he really think we'll believe that he played all the instruments? Let's face it, Mailbag, we're not suckers. It's obvious George Martin had a lot to do with it. In fact if you listen carefully to the end of the third track played backwards, you can almost hear him whistling.

PAUL McCARTNEY

Q: Why?
A: I've always wanted to buy a Beatles album like "people" do and be as surprised as they must be. So this was the next best thing. Linda and I are the only two who will be sick of it by the release date. We love it really.

Q: Are you able to describe the texture or feel or the theme of the album in a few words?
A: Home, Family, Love.

Q: How long did it take to complete – from when to when?
A: From just before (I think) Xmas, until now. "The Lovely Linda" was the first thing I recorded at home, and was originally to test the equipment. That was around Xmas.

Q: Assuming all the songs are new to the public, how new are they to you? Are they recent?
A: One was 1959 ("Hot As Sun"). Two from India, "Junk", "Teddy Boy", and the rest are pretty recent. "Valentine Day", "Momma Miss America" and "Oo You" were ad-libbed on the spot.

Q: Which instruments have you played on the album?
A: Bass, drums, acoustic guitar, lead guitar, piano and organ-mellotron, toy xylophone, bow and arrow.

Q: Have you played all these instruments on earlier recordings?
A: Yes, drums being the one that I wouldn't normally do.

Q: Why did you do all the instruments yourself?
A: I think I'm pretty good.

Q: Will Linda be heard on all future records?
A: Could be; we love singing together, and have plenty of opportunity for practice.

Q: Will Paul and Linda become a John and Yoko?
A: No, they will become Paul and Linda.

Q: Are you pleased with your work?
A: Yes.

Q: Will the other Beatles receive the first copies?
A: Wait and see.

Q: What has recording along taught you?
A: That to make your own decisions about what you do is easy, and playing with yourself is difficult, but satisfying.

Q: Who has done the artwork?
A: Linda has taken all the photos, and she and I designed the package.

Q: Is it true that neither Allen Klein nor ABKCO have been nor will be in any way involved with the production, manufacturing, distribution or promotion of this new album?
A: Not if I can help it.

Q: Did you miss the other Beatles and George Martin? Was there a moment, eg, when you thought: "Wish Ringo was here for this break?"
A: No.

Q: Assuming this is a very big album, will you do another?
A: Even if it isn't, I will continue to do what I want – when I want to.

Q: Are you planning a new album or single with The Beatles?
A: No.

Q: Is this album a rest away from Beatles, or start of solo career?
A: Time will tell. Being a solo album means it's "the start of a solo career"... and not being done with The Beatles means it's a rest. So, it's both.

Q: Is your break with The Beatles temporary or permanent; due to personal differences or musical ones?
A: Personal differences, business differences, musical differences, but most of all because I have a better time with my family. Temporary or permanent? I don't know.

Dear Mailbag

AUGUST 29

In order to put out of its misery the limping dog of a news story which has been dragging itself across your pages for the past year, my answer to the question, "Will The Beatles get together again?"... is no.

PAUL McCARTNEY

▲ Paul and Linda McCartney in October 1970, with their children Mary (left) and Heather (right)

Q: Do you foresee a time when Lennon-McCartney becomes an active songwriting partnership again?

A: No.

Q: Does it please you to hear views on John's possible band names? The Plastic Ono Band? Giving Back The MBE? Yoko's Influence? Yoko?

A: I love John and respect what he does – it doesn't give me any pleasure.

Q: Were any of the songs on the album originally written with The Beatles in mind?

A: The older ones were. "Junk" was intended for *Abbey Road*, but something happened. "Teddy Boy" was for *Get Back* but something happened.

Q: Were you pleased with *Abbey Road*? Was it musically restricting?

A: It was a good album (No 1 for a long time).

Q: What is your relationship with Klein?

A: It isn't. I am not in contact with him, and he does not represent me in ANY way.

Q: What is your relationship with Apple?

A: It is the office of a company which I part own with the other three Beatles. I don't go there because I don't like offices or businesses, especially when I'm on holiday.

Q: Have you any plans to set up an Independent Production Company?

A: McCartney Productions.

Q: What sort of music has influenced you on this album?

A: Light and loose.

Q: Are you writing more prolifically now? Or less so?

A: About the same. I have a queue waiting to be recorded.

Q: What are your plans now? A holiday? A musical? A movie? Retirement?

A: My only plan is to grow up. *NME*

"A question I cannot answer"

What is happening with THE BEATLES, the *Maker* asks?

How long is it since The Beatles – all four of them – actually played together?

Apple: The last time was during the recording of the *Abbey Road* album, which was in the late summer of 1969. Various members of the group have since recorded together on individual sessions. George has been on Ringo's sessions and vice versa, but all four have never actually played together since summer 1969. That's about a year ago.

Is there any recorded material still unreleased?

Apple: No. Even if there was it would never be issued. The group are always very conscious of keeping up with the current tastes.

Are any of the individual members working on solo albums at present?

Apple: Ringo has completed his country album in Nashville and it will probably be released in September. George is nearing the completion of his new album but we don't know when it will be released. This will be very different from his solo albums. The other two have not been in the recording studios but I would presume they have not been idle during the summer. It is not their nature to sit and do nothing.

Why has John Lennon been in Los Angeles all this year?

Apple: He is living very quietly over there. There have been no press reports about his activities, so I assume he is living quietly. He has

◀ John Lennon performing "'Instant Karma!" on BBC TV's *Top of the Pops*; February 11, 1970

▲ The original interview "with" Paul McCartney, as it appeared on page 2 of the *NME* on April 18, 1970

rented a house there. There is a lot of building going on at his house in Ascot. I have no idea when he will be back.

Where are the other three Beatles at the moment?

Apple: Paul is at his farm in Scotland. I have no idea when he will return to London. George and Ringo are both at their homes.

Are there any plans for any kind of performance whatsoever?

Apple: None at all. There are no plans for any shows or tours.

What, if any, plans do the individual members of the group have for the future?

Apple: I don't think any of them have any long-term plans. This isn't unusual because they have never made long-term plans, even in their touring days. George is increasing his success at writing his own songs. He has developed as a composer and will probably continue this. Ringo is exploring different things. He may do more films and may do more comedy, singing and acting.

Have The Beatles finished as a group?

Apple: That is a question I cannot answer. There is no harm in anyone discussing it, but it is a futile discussion for people who are not involved in it. I don't think they will ever lose their Beatles tag, even though they may never work together again.

LETTERS Come Untogether

SEPTEMBER 12

I once thought Paul McCartney was God. My! How things have changed, though I have yet to discover whether it is myself who has outgrown him or he who has become so conceited that he really thinks the average pop fan is really concerned with whether he and the other Beatles will ever play together again.

No, we've all grown out of that by now, the heartache we once felt has gone, leaving only a little scar which reminds us that one Beatle broke away, leaving the others to wonder why.

Paul is obviously too bound up in his own self-importance to notice that no one cares any more.
MISS S SAPWORTH, 38 Stafford Place, Peterlee, Co. Durham. **MM**

"Dear Mailbag", wrote the great McCartney. I agree, being a fan since '63, he is brilliant. But as a person with feelings and someone who shows consideration he is sadly lacking.

He's become terribly arrogant since all his beloved fans helped him grab his millions. He hasn't thought about those who realise that no other group can ever hope to replace The Beatles.

Paul, the one who's taking the part of the spoiled brat and the one who wants everything his way.
S SELKIRK, 136 Colston Street, Newcastle Upon Tyne. **MM**

So, once again Paul McCartney has roared. It's a pity. A great many people had hoped that he would have put aside his anger, or disenchantment, or whatever, and say that, yes, he would come together with the other Beatles to put out some more music into this not-too-happy and altogether imperfect world.

If, however, Paul is not to be persuaded, then perhaps get together with Billy Preston, with whom they have made beautiful music in the past.
C ALEXANDER BROWN, Darums Capricornus Musicus Company, 113 Valley Woods Road, Townhouse, 93 Don Mills 401, Ontario, Canada. **MM**

Was *Let It Be* the last Beatles album, as it appeared to be from the way it was packaged?

Apple: That way it was packaged did not mean it was the final album. The art work was planned long before all the publicity about the group breaking up. It may have looked like that but it wasn't meant to.

Does the fact that there are no plans for the future mean there is no future for The Beatles?

Apple: No. The fact that there are no plans doesn't mean anything. The group have never planned things much. It is not essential to make plans with the Beatles. **MM**

◀ Jimi Hendrix in action on the closing day of the Isle of Wight Festival, Sunday August 30, 1970

"Ready for the next trip"

JIMI HENDRIX comes to Britain to play the third ISLE OF WIGHT FESTIVAL. *MM* doesn't only draw deep insight from the musician – it despatches a writer to rough it with "the kids". "I suspected my colleagues' commiserations were not genuine," he reports.

JIMI HENDRIX, THE MAN with the misleading reputation that had mothers locking away young daughters when he was in town, is talking again. After six months of hiding in corners, crawling into cracks when people were around, and generally locking himself away from the world, our Jimi is back in business, and his mind is six months' pregnant with ideas.

For Jimi, the first long trip has come to an end. It's time to go back home, feed himself until he's fat again, and then set out on trip number two, which will be a longer trip, and intrepid exploration, and for Jimi a new experience.

"It's all turned full circle, I'm back right now to where I started. I've given this era of music everything. I still sound the same, my music's the same, and I can't think of anything new to add to it in its present state," Jimi told me as he sat tending an English cold in a lavish London Park Lane hotel.

"When the last American tour finished earlier this year, I just wanted to go away a while, and forget everything. I wanted to just do recording, and see if I could write something. Then I started

"We will paint pictures of Earth and space. It will open minds"

thinking. Thinking about the future. Thinking that this era of music – sparked off by The Beatles – had come to an end. Something new has got to come, and Jimi Hendrix will be there.

"I want a big band; I don't mean three harps and 14 violins. I mean a big band full of competent musicians that I can conduct and write for. And with the music we will paint pictures of Earth and space, so that the listener can be taken somewhere. It's going to be something that will open up a new sense in people's minds. They are getting their minds ready now. Like me, they are going back home, getting fat, and making themselves ready for the next trip."

"You see, music is so important. I don't any longer dig the pop and politics crap. That's old fashioned. It was somebody's personal opinion. But politics is old hat. Anyone can go round shaking babies by the hand, and kissing the mothers, and saying that it was groovy. But you see, you can't do this in music. Music doesn't lie. I agree it can be misinterpreted, but it cannot lie.

"When there are vast changes in the way the world goes, it's usually something like art and music that changes it. Music is going to change the world next time."

Jimi couldn't fully explain what his new music would be like, but he put forward his visions of how the next music form would be born.

▲ Hendrix on stage at the KB Hallen, Copenhagen, Denmark, September 3, 1970

▶ January 29, 1970: Jimi Hendrix backstage at the Winter Concert for Peace held at Madison Square Garden, New York City

"We are going to stand still for a while, and gather everything we've learned musically in the last 30 years, and we are going to blend all the ideas that worked into a new form of classical music. It's going to take some doing to figure out all the things that worked, but it's going to be done.

"I dig Strauss and Wagner – those cats are good, and I think that they are going to form the background of my music. Floating in the sky about it will be blues –I've still got plenty of blues – and then there will be Western sky music, and sweet opium music [you'll have to bring your own opium] and these will be mixed together to form one.

"You know the drug scene came to a big head. It was opening up things in people's minds, giving them things that they just couldn't handle. Well, music can do that, you know, and you don't need any drugs.

"The term 'blowing someone's mind' is valid. People like you to blow their minds, but then we are going to give them something that will blow their mind, and while it's blown, there will be something there to fill the gap. It's going to be a complete form of music. It will be really druggy music. Yes, I agree it could be something on similar lines to what Pink Floyd are tackling. They don't know it, you know, but people like Pink Floyd are the mad scientists of this day and age.

"While I was doing my vanishing act in the States I got this feeling that I was completely blown out of England. I thought that they had forgotten me over here. I'd given them everything I'd got, I thought maybe they didn't want me any more, because they had a nice set of bands. Maybe they were saying, 'Oh, we've had Hendrix, yeah, he was OK.' I really thought I was completely through here."

About his future big band Jimi had talked a lot. But he was also eager to talk about thoughts on the three-piece outfit, which he believed could go on forever. "It was fun, it was the greatest fun. It was good, exciting and I enjoyed it. But the main thing that used to bug me was that people wanted too many visual things from me. I never wanted it to be so much of a visual thing. When I didn't do it, people thought I was being moody, but I can only freak when I really feel like doing so. I can't do it just for the back and close their eyes, and know exactly what was going on, without caring a damn what we were doing while we were on stage."

Could Jimi give any indication when he would start to form the big band? "I don't know, but it won't be very long. Isle of Wight might be the last, or second to last. But if the kids really enjoyed it, then it might carry on a little longer. But I will only carry on that way if I am useful; you know you have got to have a purpose in life."

His hair is a little tamer now. Did he feel he was a tamer person, a changing person?

"No, I don't think so, although I feel as though I get little sparks of maturity every now and then. I think of tunes, I think of riffs. I can hum them. Then there's another melody comes into my head, and then a bass melody, and then another one. On guitar I just can't get them out.

"I think I'm a better guitarist than I was. I've learned a lot. But I've got to learn more about music, because there's a lot in this hair of mine that's got to get out.

"With the bigger band, I don't want to be playing as much guitar; I want other musicians to play my stuff. I want to be a good writer. I

Beyond Replacement

SEPTEMBER 12

It is perhaps just that Jimi Hendrix should die in England. We took him into our heads, and our hearts – and probably launched him into the beginning of what was to be the cause of the end.

He was a "child of God," a minstrel of our time. The world won't miss him, but we will. I shall never forget him.
P IVES, 2a Tyndall's, Hindhead, Surrey. **MM**

The death of Jimi Hendrix is a great shock to me and a huge loss to the Music World!

Jimi was undoubtedly the most inventive rock guitarist in the world, with a tremendous potential which will never now be realised.

Hendrix may have been musically mixed up of late, but his playing could show a beautiful fluidity and sensitivity, as on the highly underrated "Up From The Skies" off the *Axis...* LP and "Red House" from the first album.

There's no point in squabbling over who is the best rock guitarist now, we've just lost him. And who can take his place?
TONY NEALE, 29 Kensington Gardens Square, Queensway, London. **MM**

Jimi Hendrix, who crashed his way to fame in 1966 with "Hey Joe", has departed just as suddenly. Music just can't be the same, he is beyond replacement.

The only three-piece ever to compete with Noel, Mitch and Jimi was Cream, and all that's left of both is records – sadly not enough. His plans for a new music, which never reached maturity, I'm sure, would have resulted in further proof of his supremacy.

He said that when he died he wanted everyone to carry on listening to his records and remember him. So please all go out and buy *Band Of Gypsys* and say "Farewell" as we said "Hello" by making him No 1.
GEOFF BULL, 2 Church Hill Street. **MM**

still can't figure out what direction my writing is going at the moment, but it'll find a way.

"I won't be doing many live gigs, because I'm going to develop the sound, and then put a film out with it. It's so exciting, it's going to be an audio-visual thing that you sit down and plug into and really take in through your ears and eyes. I'm happy, it's gonna be good." **MM**

Phenomenal

SEPTEMBER 18

RIP, Jimi.

JIMI HENDRIX WAS KNOWN AS the wild man of pop and he certainly earned that reputation on stage. But in private life, among his close friends, he had a polite, almost shy, manner. The opposite of the impression he gave on stage. The immense loss that his sad, untimely death will mean to music is beyond doubt and his legion of devoted fans throughout the world have been joined in sadness and mourning by legions of musicians who respected Jimi's work.

He was a brilliant, perhaps phenomenal, guitarist and his writing was extremely original. His songs are immediately identifiable with the writer; nobody else could quite capture the essence of excitement and perception that Jimi had. Jim's rise to fame was meteoric. Former Animal Chas Chandler found him playing in a New York nightclub and brought him to London. It took only a few short weeks for Jimi to become the idol of millions.

His stage act was talked about as being obscene, but this as all part of his music – raw and alive, filled with the problems that confront everyone and, at the same time, sympathetic and releasing.

When Jimi signed with Track records, I worked for him during a period of about three months. It was difficult to get to know him personally as he rarely spoke of anything but his music. He was devoted to it and spent long hours without sleep composing. That, plus the stresses and strains of the hard-working life that had been forced upon him, eventually led to nervous tension. Even when he wanted to be alone, he was rarely allowed to relax.

A series of hit records and massive sell-out concert tours made Jimi the subject of adulation almost everywhere. The Jimi Hendrix Experience became one of the world's highest-paid groups. Jimi, Noel Redding and Mitch Mitchell lived in style. Noel suffered a series of breakdowns before he eventually quit the group to form Fat Mattress, and Mitch was often taken ill too, owing to the demanding schedules of playing and travelling. But it was Jimi who felt the effects most. He sought a release of a kind through drugs, but it is useless to pretend that this is anything new

for musicians. Jimi just seemed to be the one who got the most publicity.

Just as plans were being made to re-form the original trio, Jimi died at the ridiculously early age of 24 [sic: in fact 27]. His body is being flown back to Seattle for burial within the next few days. All those who knew Jimi are still sad and numb. They have lost a friend.

It is hard, too, for the fans who will never be able to see him again. Only his memory and his music live on as an everlasting monument to a truly great man of music and person. **NME**

David Bowie // Isaac Hayes // Jim Morrison
John Bonham // Joni Mitchell // Led Zeppelin
Marc Bolan // Mick Jagger // Pete Townshend
The Rolling Stones // T. Rex // The Who

1971

The biggest stars of the previous decade are locked in verbal conflict. John Lennon presents a song called "How Do You Sleep?", apparently addressed to Paul McCartney ("or maybe it's about some old chick..."). Meanwhile, McCartney can't stop himself unpicking The Beatles' disputes – even when he's meant to be promoting his new band.

Elsewhere, though, the heaviness of the previous year has been tempered with a new sense of fun. Elton John is doing handstands on his piano keyboard, while Marc Bolan's T. Rex are creating the kind of fan pandemonium unseen since The Beatles.

"I want to do something fresh"

ISAAC HAYES, once a jobbing songwriter, has devised a magnificent, symphonic take on soul. Not everyone digs (one US critic calls it "black muzak"), but those who understand know a quiet revolution is underway. "What we're doing just reflects what is happening in the black world generally," says Hayes.

ISAAC HAYES IS already a giant of black music. Yet three albums ago he was little more than one half of a very fine songwriting team that churned out hits for Sam & Dave, Carla Thomas, and other Stax acts. Neither Hayes, nor his partner David Porter, looked like potential superstar material.

But Ike has made it, and how. Those three albums – *Hot Buttered Soul*, *The Isaac Hayes Movement* and *To Be Continued* – have sold millions of copies, topping the American pop, R&B and jazz charts for months on end. Right now, he's one of the hottest contenders around.

The man himself is something of an enigma, at least to outsiders. His publicity pictures have him looking mean, moody and mysterious, bare-torsoed and hung with stark, symbolic chains, head aesthetically shaven, omnipotent. But when you meet him, he's charming to a degree.

He approves of his image of inaccessibility, though, and doesn't deny that he's known to surround himself with heavies. He doesn't intend to go the route of so many exploited black artists, and he's prepared to defend himself in that cause.

His office is phenomenal, the talk of the company. Reclining behind his long desk, he's surrounded by good hi-fi, a small colour TV, wild printed walls, fringed carpets and sci-fi lighting, plus a womb-like chair with speakers in the headrest. It's so freaky that, on my way out, I actually had to enquire which particular panel was the door.

How did you arrive at the idea of extended songs, like "...Phoenix"?

Well, it wasn't really an idea; I just felt that to get the tune over the way I wanted to, it had to be a long version. I was given the opportunity to arrange and cut it as I saw fit, so I did it with no pressure. At the completion everybody said, "Yeah, it's hip, but it might be too long", but I took the selfish attitude that if it doesn't sell a copy I'm satisfied with the arrangement and the performance. When I was cutting it I wasn't conscious of the time; I didn't even think about that.

Did you do it in one take?

"...Phoenix" was, yeah. I just started. I was sitting at the organ and we had kind of a rough time mixing it down because of the bleed from the organ onto the vocal track. I just started rapping and then went on into the song.

I wondered if maybe the idea came from the old style of gospel preaching?

Looking at it afterwards it's kind of in that style, but I didn't think about it like that... I felt I had to do it to sell the tune, especially to get it over to the black market. It had been introduced to the pop and country & western markets, recorded by quite a few other artists, but it hadn't really gone over big black. So I took it on down to Soulsville, with a story that they could identify with.

Is everything you do aimed in terms of the black market?

Yes, I guess... one reason is because of me being black, and the other reason is my approach to the songs. A large percentage of the sales on all my albums are black, but it's beginning to spread over to other markets; there's an almost immediate response on the jazz market.

How do you feel about going on the jazz chart?

Well, when I was younger my understanding of jazz was a tune being improvised... chords, progressions, things like that, and also

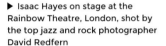

▲ Released in November 1970, Isaac Hayes' fourth studio album ... *To Be Continued*, which hit #11 in the American *Billboard 200*

▶ Isaac Hayes on stage at the Rainbow Theatre, London, shot by the top jazz and rock photographer David Redfern

improvising even from a vocal performance. When I was rated as "jazz" I was in a sense embarrassed; I didn't consider myself a jazz artist. Sure I play with arrangements, and I like to get off into an idea musically, but when you get greats that I had admired for years, the acknowledged great musicians of jazz, and I beat them on polls and things, I get scared. But they rate me, and I accept it as long as someone is accepting what I'm doing.

Were you surprised by all the success?

Yes I was, just by a lot of people saying it was a good album but it wouldn't make it because it's too long. I just accepted the fact that it wouldn't be a hit, but like I say I was well pleased with the performance and everything, and when it started to sell I was... surprised.

So, how did you approach the second album, in the light of this success?

Same way. I didn't do any pre-planning... I feel as if you would pre-plan something like that it might not come out right with a natural feel, so I just waited until I felt it. A lot of times I'd get into the studio, producing other acts, and I'd work myself up, getting really keyed up and in a studio mood, and then ideas would just come. I'd think of a tune and say, "OK, let's cut it", and when I'd cut it I'd listen to the track and when I'm in the mood I'd put my vocal on. It all comes in moods... I'd get in a mood to put the strings and horns on, and then I'd get in a mood to call Dale Warren, my co-arranger, and I'd convey my ideas to him and he'd get them down on paper.

Do you write or read music?

No, I can't. I can play the parts and give him the voicing of the orchestration. I hum the lines, and sometimes I put it on cassette, humming along with the track, and he writes it out and we iron out

the bugs at the actual session. When that's done I give it to Pat Lewis, one of the singers, and she puts in the vocal background. Sometimes I inject some ideas that I might have, but basically I give it to her and she has a beautiful imagination for back-up singing, and when she's through all we do is mix.

One writer put down *To Be Continued* as "black muzak". How do you react to that?

I read it. I was surprised, but I just chalked it up to ignorance of what I'm doing, of what I'm all about. You see, some writers when they don't understand a thing they attack it, and he doesn't see where I'm coming from. Like he says, a man who's written songs for Sam & Dave and people like that... sure, I can also sing like that. David and I at one time contemplated going into a duo, but that has been done, that has been proven. So I want to do something different, something fresh to the people.

It can't be so bad when you've got gold to prove it... it must be saying something that somebody wants to hear. But whenever something different comes along you're going to get criticism as well as acceptance, so I was ready for that the moment it happened. Everybody has a right to do what they want to do as far as music is concerned, because music is free and that's the way I did it. I feel that there should be no restrictions in music and arrangement, even in message. Music is the universal language – that's what keeps society together when nothing else will work.

He said it was a gimmick on "Our Day Will Come", the sound of crickets and that, but that was no gimmick – it was to try and give a clear picture of what was happening on the front end of that tune, and I've had letters from fans saying that they're in a similar situation, that it gives them something to hang on to. If it means something to somebody it's no gimmick. It's something that I feel. That critic made an ass of himself – he's no god to say what's what, and neither am I. I just do what I feel and if people don't accept it I don't try to force it on them. **MM**

1971

"It's a pretty dress…"

A big house. Vintage cars. A growing songwriting empire… DAVID BOWIE is enjoying life post-"Space Oddity", and has a new sound to present. So what if his new flamboyant look earns him threats in the street? "I thought the dress was beautiful," he says.

WHEN DAVID "BANGERS" Bowie came to meet me from the 2.40 from Blackfriars to Beckenham in Kent, I unguardedly climbed into his incredibly ancient mad old Riley. And as the car ambled casually from the station's yard, I remarked that David's appearance had changed considerably since his brief days of glory with his single "Space Oddity". His hair has grown longer and he was wearing blue velvet trousers with a woolly blue dressing gown-cum-coat.

We stopped briefly to pick up some shopping in the town and jammed a sixpence in the engine to keep it turning over. Then we bombed off again. I held on to the door as it appeared to be on the point of dropping off. "It won't come off," I was assured. "It's just a bit loose. And if you think this is old, you wait till you see the house and the rest of my old cars."

David and his lady live in a beautiful Victorian house which even has turrets on the roof and a gallery running around the first floor inside the house. It overlooks a kind of banqueting hall. There's also a huge garden, the domain of a very lazy King Charles spaniel.

Spread out on the floor of one room were numerous tapes of songs from an album to be released here in April, called *The Man Who Sold The World*. It's already selling well in the States, where Three Dog Night have covered three of the tracks. Bowie also has material for a new album he is working on and demos of songs he has sold to other artists.

Herman's next solo single, "Oh! You Pretty Things", was written by him, as were other tracks bought by producer Mickie Most, a song for the Sir Douglas Quintet and one for Gene Vincent. "It's funny how I suddenly seem to have taken off as a songwriter, but this is what living down here has done for me. I'm wrapped up in my friends and include them in the songs. One of my songs, 'Rupert The Riley', is about the car."

The Riley is one of four cars, in various stages of working order, including an enormous old wedding car with plush velvet seats which is soon to have a stereo system installed.

As well as looking after his own album career, David is producing two solo singers and a group called Arnold Corns, who were signed up to B&C Records just as I sat listening to their demo single, "Moonage Daydream". It really is incredible and bodes well for an album they hope to do soon. Three of the band are schoolboys and the lead singer calls himself Rudolph Valentino.

David is also producing and writing for a solo singer called Geoff Alexander, who sounds rather like The Band's Robbie Robertson, and also has an old friend from art college, Calvin James, who designed the sleeves for the first T. Rex album and Gentle Giant. James' single is out on Bell next month.

Since "Space Oddity", David has left the singles market himself to concentrate on albums. "I became disillusioned after 'Space Oddity'. The album was released at the same time and did absolutely nothing. No one even bothered to review it, and I'm personally convinced that some of the tracks were really good. I just decided to leave London and come to live down here. In fact, the only thing that gave me faith again was being asked to go across to America. If I'm into making it in records, I'll have to go and live there."

David has just returned from a three-month stay in America. As he didn't have a work permit, he couldn't do any gigs, but went round some universities talking to students about the album and doing interviews for radio stations.

"In America, although you might not believe it, I'm regarded as an underground artist. They know nothing about my singles and see 'Space Oddity' as just as an LP track. But in America, music is a communicating force; people all relate to it. Besides, there isn't much bread to be made here at the moment."

A frenzied search of the house for a copy of the new LP was fruitless, but David talked about the talent of the two musicians who played on it. They are Mick Ronson and Woody Woodmansey, from a blues band in Hull. Although they felt they could make it if they teamed up as a permanent band, they returned to their group at home.

The songs are much heavier than one would expect and David thinks they were using a Moog long before many of the groups who use them now. The LP was actually recorded a year ago, so David has rather lost interest in it now, and legal hassles delayed its release here. An American review of the album mentions a tinge of bitterness, but David disagrees.

"I'm not bitter. I was disillusioned at first, but all that went long ago. I'd like to become an album artist in this country, but really I'm very happy."

I could see why as we walked round the garden, inspecting the gazebo. The country has been the means of David having time to write his songs. Although he has strong feelings about politics, he never includes them in his numbers. "Britain just doesn't know what revolution is. The people should be fighting against the Common Market, but they won't until it's too late."

It was getting late, and it seemed only fitting that the accelerator should fall out of the car as David drove me to the station. *DISC*

◄ David Bowie and his wife Angie at their home, Haddon Hall, in Beckenham, UK: April 20, 1971

▶ January 1971; David Bowie jamming at a party thrown by the rock publicist and DJ Rodney Bingenheimer, in Los Angeles

"There are no plans"

The ROLLING STONES enter tax exile in France, and meet the press to promote – after a fashion – *Sticky Fingers*. The swish engagement offers insightful glances at business-minded Mick Jagger and also at Keith Richards, who remembers a 1963 meeting with *NME*. "You made us have our picture taken," he cackles. "Ugh!"

CANNES IS A strange place. It sits on the Côte D'Azur beckoning the rich to part with their dollars, pounds and francs in glorious sunshine. If France conjures up a picture of bearded revolutionaries, visit Cannes, where anyone in blue jeans is an "'ippi", where gigantic sailing yachts litter the harbour with pennants from all over the globe and where a hotel without chandeliers is like a pub with no beer.

It is years out of date, where paunchy balding men with fat cigars, blue blazers, white shirts and baggy grey trousers covering sandals can reflect on how life used to be. Duchesses with lorgnettes mingle with the trendy debutantes to whom a season wouldn't be a season without a fortnight in Cannes.

An odd choice, perhaps, for the Rolling Stones to make their home. If tax-dodging was their motive, they obviously aren't the only ones with the same idea. But I detect a change in yer scruffy Stones. At any rate there's a change in their colourful lead singer. The old Mick who perpetually stuck two fingers at society is now well on the way to becoming part of that society. The hair is shorter, neater and well groomed, his jacket is superbly tailored velvet and a handmade shirt replaces the vest. The angry young man is not so angry as he used to be. He may still gyrate wildly onstage, but offstage a suave and confident young man stands before us.

He stood before the music press last weekend with the rest of the group in their new surroundings. The Stones don't come to you; you go to them. And if that means flying to Nice and back via Geneva, it makes no difference. They've just signed a recording contract which will make them very rich indeed – and if that isn't something to shout about, what is?

So it was that I found myself aboard flight Air France 950 on Friday bound for the sunny Riviera, which turned out to be cold and cloudy. Mick and his men had taken over a restaurant for the evening for the kind of press conference befitting a property like the Rolling Stones…

We've been there two hours and it's approaching midnight when a hustle at the door turns our heads. "Jagger's here," someone says

urgently and we look round. Mick strides in with his beautiful lady on one arm. He makes for the food table and 20 photographers gather round. He smiles and poses and the flashbulbs pop. A persistent cameraman annoys Mick. Mick covers him in wine.

Photographers persist and Mick composes himself. This is what the party is for, anyway. Publicist Les Perrin and other Stones drag him to one side and talk. Then Perrin tells us Mick will be over to our table soon, just as soon as he's got a drink.

But it's much, much later when he does, and in the meantime the rest arrive. Mick Taylor in denims and Bill Wyman in stripes. Charlie arrives with an entourage which appears to include Stephen Stills and Ahmet Ertegun, boss of Atlantic Records, and the heaviest guy there.

Flashbulbs pop in all directions now, and rather than talk to Mick senior, I decide on a chat with Mick junior, who is hiding from the cameras with his lady in a corner. "I've rented my house here for six months," he says. "Bill and I are at Grasse, Charlie is over in the Camargue and Keith is way over the other side of Nice. What's happening in London?"

On to the new album. "I haven't written any of the songs on it," says Mick. "But we all contribute in the studio. We take the lead guitar, Keith and me, depending on the number. It's about 50-50. I am writing some stuff of my own, though, but whether the group will play it remains to be seen. We're going to build a recording studio down here as soon as we can so we can rehearse whenever we want. It's a good place to live. The weather's lousy today but the past fortnight has been great."

I keep looking around to see if Jagger has started talking at the English-speaking table. He's there, and I pick up the conversation midway through some chat about the Rolling Stones' new label. "We

▶ Keith Richards with his girlfriend Anita Pallenberg (far left) in Cannes, South of France, May 20, 197

"It's a pity the people that tape
the group can pick a bad night"

can record what we want on it, really," he said. "If we like a group we can put them on our label, and we may make solo albums, but there are no definite plans. I don't know what mine would be like, probably songs like 'Wild Horses', with Keith playing acoustic guitar or something."

Mick runs through the tracks on the new album, with a few comments on each one. "Bitch" was written for dog lovers, he says. "There's no real change of direction musically for the group, but we all think it's the best album we have done," he smiles.

I ask him about *Stone Age*, the album rush-released by Decca following their departure from the label. "I was so mad when it came out," he says. "That was why I spent all that money on the ads in the papers. When we left Decca we knew they had tapes of us which hadn't been released and which they were entitled to put out. But we had a verbal agreement that if they did, they would contact us first. We turn our back and they put one out without telling us at all. The tracks aren't up to the standard of the group's current music and it's

▶ The Rolling Stones at a recording studio mixing desk with (centre, left to right) Keith Richards, Mick Jagger and Charlie Watts

wrong for the fans. Maybe they could have put it out on a budget label. They can do it again and again, just taking tracks from various albums and repackaging them."

Keith Richards arrives in a white silk jacket and looking more like a gypsy than ever. Earrings hang from his ears, his spiky hair stands on end and his eyes look strangely dark. He lunges forward to greet Mick, who obviously wants to bring our little chat to an end. There's one more question I want to ask: what about all the bootlegs? "I don't mind them, really. You can't stop them doing it. They're everywhere. It's a pity that they are too expensive and the people that tape the group can pick a bad night."

That's it. Mick's lady is tired of having no arm to cling on to and he wants to talk with Keith. The photographers persist until they get the whole group together, and then there's an enormous shot of the group with all the Kinney people, and with the Atlantic boss, and with all the Stones people, and with the girlfriends.

It's rather like a wedding reception where the two sides – Stones and recording company – all want the various combinations of the active personnel pictured together. Well, Kinney do even if the Stones don't.

Around two the party starts to break up. Mick says he's going to the casino and breezes out. *MM*

"The bride was attended by local police"

MAY 12

The marriage of Mr Mick Jagger and Miss Bianca Perez Morena de Macia.

THE WEDDING TOOK place at St Anne's, St Tropez, France last week, of Mr Michael Phillip Jagger (27), musician, son of Mr and Mrs J Jagger, of Dartford, Kent, and Miss Bianca Perez Morena de Macias (21), unemployed, of Nicaragua.

The bride, who was given away, was attended by the local police. She wore a delicately spun white flapper suit, with matching white hat and roses on the top. The bridegroom, whose hobbies include singing with a beat group and amateur dramatics, wore a subtle white two-piece, pumps and no socks. Mr Jagger's father is a physical training instructor.

The couple, who met at a dance, plan to live in France, and are travelling for their honeymoon at "a secret destination". Guests at the reception included Mr Paul McCartney, formerly of The Beatles pop group, Mr William Wyman, Mr Richard Starkey, Mr Stephen Stills and many notables from the entertainment world. Music was supplied by Mr Freddie Notes & The Rudies. *MM*

▶ May 12, 1971: Mick and Bianca Jagger, just after their wedding ceremony in the French resort of St.Tropez

Joni Mitchell *Blue*

JUNE 22

YES, IT'S ALL here: the plangent guitar, the moody, swirling piano, the wistful, yearning songs, the beautiful blue sleeve with the brooding cult-image portrait. Everything we need for another volume of vicarious heartache.

Guess that's a pretty sound way to begin a review of what, in many ways, is Joni's most perfect album. But then her songs have come to mean so much to me over the years that my reactions to this album are hopelessly subjective and ambivalent. The problem, I suppose, is one of empathy. Her songs are autobiographical and one's reaction to them depends to a large extent on how far one can relate to the experiences she describes. On her previous albums she has dealt with the joys and sorrows of love; the communication has been direct and often (particularly on her first album, which dealt with the aftermath of her unhappy marriage) sharply poignant.

But now, as they say, the scene changes. The success of those songs has made her a rock star, a member of the new elite, able to fly on a whim from Laurel Canyon to Amsterdam or Spain or the Aegean Islands. The songs here reflect the hang-ups of such an existence and, for me at least, it's hard to relate to them. There is little pain or passion here: where once she

described the nightmare of city life in "Nathan La Franeer", she now muses on the sweet dilemma of being stuck in Paris when she wants to be in California.

It's an inevitable process, and one which has already affected artists like James Taylor, Neil Young and Van Morrison. We elect our heroes because they tell us truths about life, but their very success divorces them from our field of experience. We go on digging them only by becoming, in effect, vicarious rock stars.

None of it is Joni's fault, of course. Her songs continue to reflect her own reality, but where once the truths she distilled were universal, the songs here tend to be inward-looking. The slightly claustrophobic atmosphere is underlined by the cosy presence of Messrs Stephen Stills and James Taylor.

But if her lyrics are less satisfying, her songs are musically (and in particular, melodically) stronger and more assured than ever. Each song seems not to have been worked out but to have been born whole and perfect and complete with shining guitar and velvety piano. The songs are concerned with the men ("All I Want", "My Old Man", "A Case Of You") and places ("California") or both ("Carey") in her restless life and several express an underlying theme: a love/hate relationship with the rock milieu, voiced in these lines from "A Case Of You": *"I'm frightened of the Devil and I'm drawn to those that aren't afraid"*. Her singing is more adventurous than ever, soaring and swooping in the space of a single syllable in a way that recalls Laura Nyro.

It is, perhaps, as a singer of richly contoured, beautifully singable songs, rather than anything more profound, that she now has her greatest strength. All I know is that despite everything I've said above, this LP hasn't been off my turntable in five days. **MM**

"I'm 26. I've seen and done it all"

From the "My Generation" spokesman for rebellious youth to a place in *Who's Who* as composer of the first rock opera, PETE TOWNSHEND's come a long way. Now, in their mid-20s, THE WHO are telling us they "Won't Get Fooled Again."

EVEN WHEN THEY bomb out with relative flops like "The Seeker" and "Dogs", a Who single is invariably something a little special. I suppose it's a hangover from those amazing Who classics "My Generation", "Substitute", "I'm A Boy" – singles that as mouthpieces of a particular generation's muddied but angry refusal to be slapped down rank on a par with the best of the social compositions of Chuck Berry. For a work like "My Generation" alone, The Who's place in rock's hall of fame is already secured.

▶ The Who during the UK press launch party for the release of their album *Who's Next*: July 15, 1971

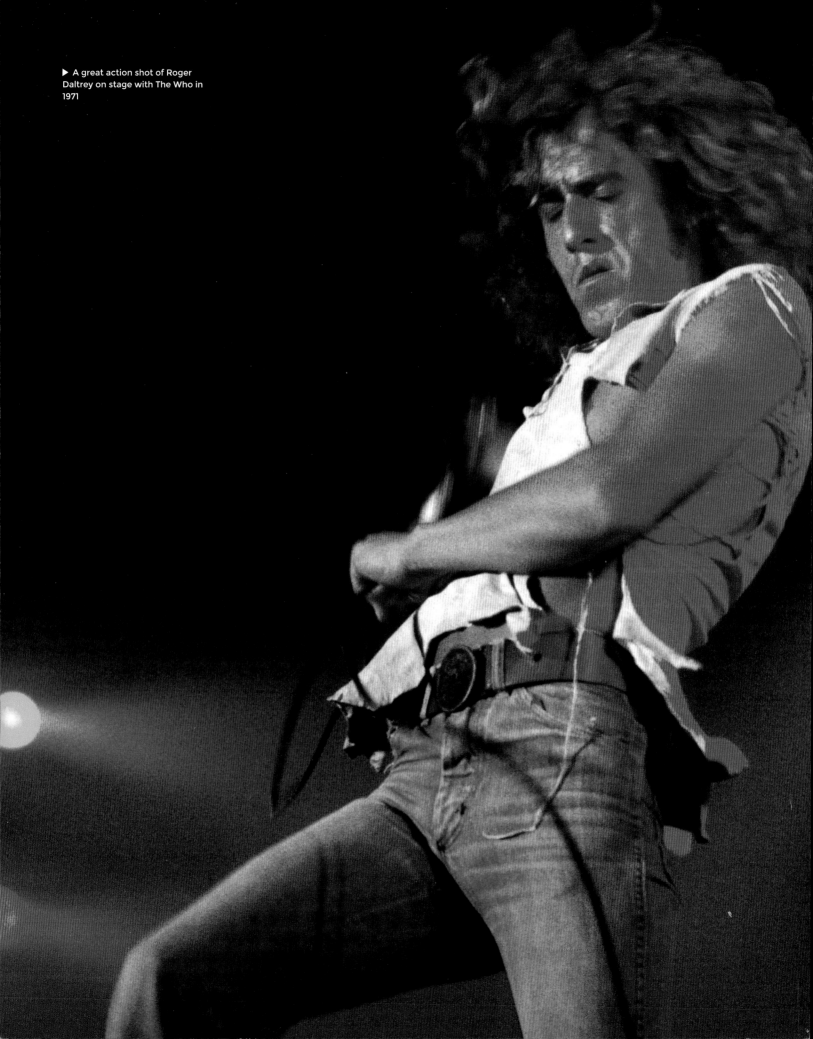

▶ A great action shot of Roger Daltrey on stage with The Who in 1971

Personally, news of each forthcoming Who single has me hoping that Pete Townshend once again will direct himself with the same special insight at today's generation. Widening the view, it seems a shame that a number with the potency of Lennon's "Power To The People" is the exception rather than the rule and that, while musically rock mirrors social change, lyrically it seems reluctant to take up the challenge.

As far as singles are concerned, Townshend says he finds it difficult today to compose for The Who. "I'm thinking of putting out an album of demos of singles," he smiles. "I was listening to some of them through the other day and I thought, 'Christ, aren't some of these bloody lyrics banal?' I think that's one of the reasons I find it so hard to write something which could be a single these days."

The writer now honoured with a listing in American *Who's Who* as composer of the first rock opera leans forward in his chair and grins: "I mean, I'm trying so desperately these days to be a classy composer. What it all boils down to is that all I really am is the

▼ The Who in an outdoor concert held at the Oval Cricket Ground in London on September 18, 1971

▶ A serious-looking Pete Townshend, with an acoustic guitar rather than his usual electric model in Twickenham, West London, in 1971

songwriter for The Who. Like, it means nothing to be the spokesman for The Who or the guitarist for The Who – mainly because there isn't another guitarist alive who couldn't wipe the floor with me. The Who is bigger as a total thing, if you see what I mean, so maybe it would then be far better if I concentrated on singles. The point is really: where is the audience for singles today? They're not our audiences. I suppose we were a singles band when we made things like 'My Generation' and 'Substitute'."

They were great singles...

"They were really worked out as singles. Even 'Anywhere Anyhow Anywhere' – they were all worked out as pop singles with as much happening in two minutes 30 seconds as possible, which is still the way I likes singles to be."

"Won't Get Fooled Again", the group's current single – and already much more successful than some of its recent predecessors – does go some way towards a return to the quality of "My Generation".

"It's really a bit of a weird song," says Townshend when I bring up the subject of the lyric content. "The first verse sounds like a revolution song and the second like somebody getting tired of it. Basically it's the same vein as 'We're Not Gonna Take It' [on the *Tommy* album]. It is an angry anti... not anti-establishment song... more an anti- anti- song. It's anti people who are negative.

"A song against the revolution because the revolution is only a revolution and a revolution is not going to change anything at all in the long run, and a lot of people are going to get hurt.

"When I wrote 'We're Not Gonna Take It', it was really we're not going to take fascism. 'Won't Get Fooled Again' I wrote at a time when I was getting barraged by people at the Eel Pie Island commune. They live opposite me. There was like a love affair going on between me and them. They dug me because I was like a figurehead... I was in a group... and I dug them because I could see what was going on over there.

"At one point there was an amazing scene where the commune was really working, but then the acid started flowing and I got on the end of some psychotic conversations and I just thought, 'Oh, f--- it.' I call it 'The Glastonbury Syndrome'. It's not where I'm at; this isn't really what I want to be involved in. I don't really want to be talking to people about things flying around in space. I'm very old-fashioned. I'm 26, I've seen and done it all in a lot of ways, and I've come back full circle to being right in the middle of the road.

"And that's not as boring as it sounds. It's, like, terribly exciting. Like a revelation to find that there is a middle of the road which is stable. A lot of people find this incredibly frustrating. It makes me angry when people insist that I have a responsibility to do what they think I should do."

"Won't Get Fooled Again", an extended version with organ fed through a synthesizer, is also on the next Who album, cunningly entitled *Who's Next* and released next week, as the closing cut.

The guitarist – we met up at Track before the group left for the States – volunteered a run-through of the rest of the material, after explaining that initially they recorded enough material for two LPs, then left producer Glynn Johns to programme the selections into one set. *NME*

"I had a rough script"

AUGUST 14

Pete Townshend goes track by track through studio album five, *Who's Next*, and explains how it derived from a recent live/film experiment at London's Young Vic theatre.

Baba O'Riley

This was a number I wrote while I was doing these experiments with tapes on the synthesizer. Among my plans for the concert and film of the concert at the Young Vic was to take a person out of the audience and feed information – height, weight, astrological details, beliefs and behaviour, etc. – about that person into the synthesizer.

The synthesizer would then select notes from the pattern of that person. It would be like translating a person into music. On this particular track I programmed details about the life of Meher Baba, and that provides the backing for the number.

Love Ain't For Keeping

That is the current set opener, one that we did on acoustic guitars.

Bargain

One of the best numbers on the album.

My Wife

A John Entwistle song. It's a really good number. I don't know whether I should say this, but it's much better than a lot of the stuff on John's own album. There's more meat in it. It became quite clear when we were doing this album how much experience John has gained from doing his own album. He did the horn parts in half an hour, whereas before it used to take him days.

The Song Is Over

This would originally have come at the end of the film. I had a rough script where all the Young Vic audience would dance and dance and all freak out, and then disappear. Then you would have heard this song. Nicky Hopkins plays piano here.

Getting In Tune

Also features Nicky Hopkins and is another stage number.

Going Mobile

Again connected with the script. I've got this big Dodge bus which we use to travel round in, and this is just about the joys of travelling in it. We did this with acoustic bass and drums and I did the vocal because the words are real tongue twisters.

Behind Blue Eyes

Really the one that is the least Who-like. It was going to be the single but we thought it was too much out of character. *NME*

► A bearded Jimmy Page playing a twin-necked guitar at a Zeppelin gig at the Wembley Empire Pool in London; November 23, 1971

LUDWIG

"The next stage..."

LED ZEPPELIN drummer JOHN BONHAM returns from tour to address Zep split rumours – and give the lowdown on the group's new fourth LP. "My personal view," he says, "is that it's the best thing we've ever done."

LED ZEPPELIN? NEVER 'eard of yer!" And John Bonham chuckles heartily. "Oh, you still get it," he says, downing a tankard, still fresh from his travels to Japan and America.

Jim Public may be a little vague on the subject of the world's ace rock band, but the heads are with them – all the way from Hiroshima to the Empire Pool, Wembley. Led Zeppelin have created quite a mystery in recent months. No tours, no gigs, no albums. What was happening?

John their power-house drummer, one of the finest in rock, explained it all as he thundered into London this week. First he described his impressions of Japan, where John, Robert, Jimmy and John Paul made their first visit recently. "It was a fantastic place to play. Rock music has only just started to happen there in the last two years, but it is now the second-biggest market in the world for rock records. The people were so friendly and we had the best rock promoter in the world there looking after us.

"It turned out that 'Immigrant Song' is one of our biggest songs in Japan and it's the number with which we always open the act. So the audiences went potty! It's a strange scene there. A lot of big groups are going in now, but they don't have a rock station on the radio. There's only the US Forces stuff.

"The American tour we did was good, in actual fact. It was quite strange because we hadn't been to America for almost a year. To be perfectly honest – I was really scared. But we played really well and had some great things happen.

"They said I was leaving to join George Harrison. I never met the guy"

"The Los Angeles Forum sold out in one day, so we did another concert there, and we really didn't expect such a demand. I think I enjoyed it more than any other tour of America.

"You see – we had a lot of time at home to think, and we grew a lot closer together. We kept seeing stories 'Zeppelin are breaking up'. But really, we have never been closer together! We all came out of ourselves and everybody played well, and we are really happy!"

He warmed to his theme: "These 'breaking up' rumours are always cropping up. I don't know their source, but they are forever saying that so-and-so is leaving. There was an unbelievable one about a year ago. They said I was leaving to join George Harrison. Well, I've never even met the guy. That's how much I know him. I'd like to meet him."

▲ September 1, 1971: Left to right, John Paul Jones, Robert Plant and Jimmy Page onstage at the Honolulu Civic Auditorium, Hawaii

But what caused that massive lay-off that led to the fears of a split?

"We did three tours last year and finished off feeling, 'We've just about had enough'. We had done so much in such a short space of time, we were drained. We had offers to go everywhere – France, America – and we could have done them. But what would be the point? We were tired. We had worked hard and Peter had probably worked harder than any of us.

"We enjoyed working, but we needed the break before we got stale. We spent the time – six months – at home and writing songs. Then we said, 'Right, we're ready to go.' During the break, we did a lot of recording and wrote a lot and improved. We didn't do any gigs, but there was absolutely no inclination to split up, and I'm not

▶ Robert Plant arriving for some Led Zeppelin dates in Japan: Haneda Airport, Tokyo, September 1971

旅客到着口
ARRIVALS

2

ALBUM REVIEW

Led Zeppelin
Led Zeppelin IV

NOVEMBER 8

TAKE A DEEP BREATH. Robert Plant does this just before "Going To California". It is their fourth and not their "best" or their "worst". It is a fine new album by a group who can now take a step outside the environment of controversy that expands around the newly successful.

Heated discussion in terms of comparison can end here. Page, Plant, Bonham and Jones are the band, and they have deliberately left their work untitled. It is not a denial of the past but a springboard to better things. Not all tracks are brilliant.

"Four Sticks" is not a riff that knocks me out overmuch. So it is not a perfect album, but there is a thread of consistency that winds through all the music and there is a bond between the players that reveals strength and a sense of direction not so apparent on their last album.

The sound of Zeppelin in full cry is most satisfying, and "Black Dog", the opener, is a beefy stomp, with Robert throwing his head back at some point midway between speakers and the Page guitar and Bonham drums marching on triumphant.

"Rock And Roll" is just that, and winds up the tempo to feature Jimmy in a looping, exultant solo while John Paul's piano clinks in the time-honoured fashion. Sandy Denny makes a welcome guest appearance on the attractive "Battle Of Evermore", and sings a pretty but lusty duet with Bob over a choir of mandolin and acoustic guitars. To complete the goodies on Side One is "Stairway To Heaven", one of the band's best songs, and another splendid performance by Robert.

It's back to the best on "Misty Mountain Hop", and it is here the strange contrast between songs becomes most apparent. There is a cliff-hanging sensation from the soft moods of "Stairway" to the drive of "Hop", which jumps in all directions with good country cheer.

"Four Sticks" is a powerful piece and features Bonham using four drumsticks. But the repetitive riff Jimmy employs here is not particularly inventive. "Going To California" gives Robert another opportunity to sing in his lower register, which he does so well.

"When The Levee Breaks", their final statement, is a good example of the full band in action. Taken at mid-tempo, it has a hypnotic effect as Bonham's bass drum drops bombs into the cellar. *MM*

bullshitting. We've all got ideas and things we want to do.

"John Paul Jones is incredible. He comes along to the studio and he's always got a new instrument he wants to play. I don't do much writing myself, but I appreciate what they write and I can enjoy playing it. I'm not governed by them in what I play. They ask me how a drum thing should be played, and that's the way we all work."

How was John's playing these days?

"I've never tried consciously to be one of the best drummers and I don't think I want to be. A lot of kids come up to me and say, 'There are a lot better drummers than you,' or something. But I enjoy playing, to the best of my ability, and that's why I'm here doing it. I don't claim to be 'more exciting than Buddy Rich'. But I don't play what I don't like. I'm a simple, straight-ahead drummer and I don't try to pretend to be anything better than I am. I love playing the drums and I practise a bit. There is always something another drummer can play that will knock me out. I watch all the drummers in groups and I always learn from them."

▶ The Zep in full flight at London's Wembley Arena, October 1971

How did he dig the new LP?

"A-ha! The new LP, he scribbles. The cover [it's wordless] means whatever people want to read into it. For me it means 'I'd rather live in an old house than a block of flats.' My personal view is that the album is the best thing we've ever done. But that's strictly my personal view. I love it. It's the fourth album and it's the next stage we were in at the time of recording. All the albums have been different, and to my mind this is the best we have done and Jimmy is like… mint!"

What was the meaning of the runes on the inner sleeve? There is no information on the cover at all.

"The runes are symbols that simply apply to each of us – I wouldn't like to state what they mean. We each picked one…"

I tried to guess which symbol represented which member of the group. And according to Bonzo – got them right. Three strong circles represent Bonham, a feather in a circle for Robert, linked ovals for John Paul and artistic lettering for Jimmy. Guest artist Sandy Denny was symbolised with three inverted pyramids.

And the reason for the delay in release?

"Oh, we had problems, or rather the printer had problems. But it's an album we can honestly say we are proud of. All the guys are looking forward to the tour. A lot of kids have called us an American group or even a Japanese group. But we are going to do four gigs a week here until the end of January. I hate it when they start slagging us!"

How would Zeppelin music sound in the future?

"Oh, he's come out with a gem! I knew it! Bloody hard to say. I can't say what we are going to sound like in the future and I don't really want to know. If I could tell you what we're going to sound like in two years' time, it would ruin it anyway. We might be on top next year. Or I might be back on the buildings." *MM*

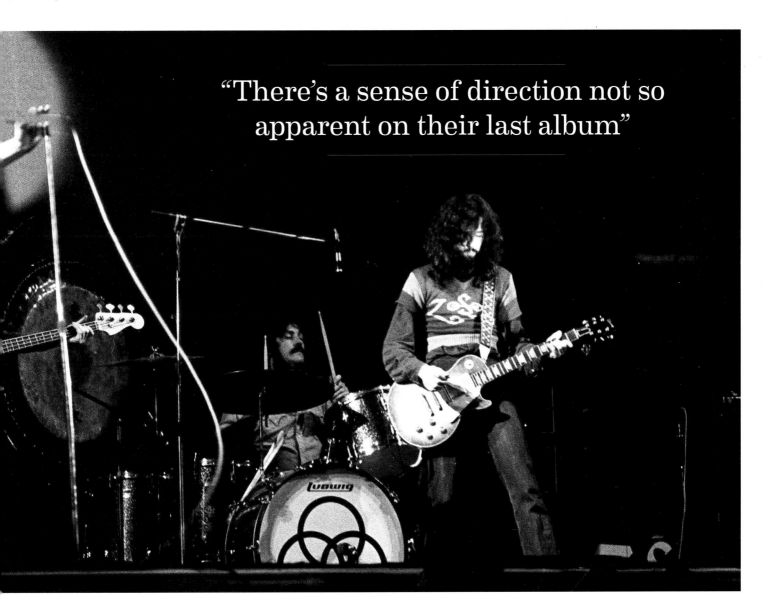

"There's a sense of direction not so apparent on their last album"

"We did get all that Beatlemania stuff"

As MARC BOLAN and band round off a year of phenomenal success, young crowds run riot during the winter tour. "Marc gives the kids strength," says tour compère Bob Harris, and Marc does not disagree. "The revolution has come," he says. "It is here."

O NCE UPON A time, there was a little monster all of a half-dozen rejected singles and four moderately received albums high. Across the land the little monster loped spryly with a song for whoever would listen, a little sad but not dejected that few spared him their time, until one day the tiny beastie discovered destiny and the magic power of electricity and proceeded to grow and grow, lumbering devastatingly out of its Notting Hill lair to wreak its mighty will upon the nation. *"Get it on"*, roared the monster, swelling like a mountain, *"bang a gong... Hot love, ooh-ooh-ee"*.

I mean, it's really approaching a phenomenon how, in the space of 12 months, the former Tyrannosaurus Rex, darlings of cross-legged highbrow floor squatters, has escaped its minority-interest pigeon hole and ballooned into the colossus T. Rex, conquering the airwaves and setting the nation's teenage hearts a-flutter in a manner long thought dead and gone.

And if that piece of whimsy fails to impress upon you the extent of T. Rex's domination, here are the facts 'n' figures to supply the substance: from last December to this, the four T. Rex singles have occupied placings in the *NME* Chart for 42 weeks out of 52.

It doesn't seem so long ago that Marc Bolan and I were sitting in his Notting Hill attic – "Penthouse, please," he interrupts – with the Tyrannosaurus Rex leader despairing over the "intellectual barrier" the public and media appeared to have erected against his band, allowing their records far short of the unprejudiced hearing he felt they deserved.

And here we are, some good few months later, in the front room of the Bolans' Little Venice house surrounded by a dazzling array of lighting, sound and camera equipment property of ATV, who are filming our interview for a television documentary. With a touch of irony, a nice case of the mountain coming to Mohammed's front room.

▲ Marc Bolan, from elfin folkie to glam rock superstar, photographed in London in 1971

That's some transformation of status, I note, as we sit in front of the cameras and lights, solaced by June Bolan's home-made red wine and trying hard to ignore the army of black polo necks weaving around us.

"We had a period when we didn't get played on the radio, basically because the music wasn't conventional enough," Bolan rejoined after a smile at my comparison.

"What happened was that, after doing the Tyrannosaurus Rex thing for two and a half years, things were slowing down. I wasn't getting bored; I just wasn't happy with the response to the music.

"I decided to clear my head and get down to playing electric. I shortened the name to T. Rex, too, and the whole thing had a nice fresh feel to it. There were obviously hundreds of people out there who had never heard of us. We did 'White Swan', then we did a TV show, and that was it. From then it has been a very strange year for us. The strangest thing is that we started the year as a minority band and have become, at the end of it, the biggest media band."

And the intellectual barrier? That obviously went somewhere along the way.

"I hope so, because you write for people. You don't write for intellectual reviewers. Basically, at the beginning, I wrote for myself. But the emotions began gradually to come through more and more, where they were possibly screened off before. Music is such a personal thing. It just gets my rocks off. It has been a groovy year and the next will be even more interesting."

In many ways, though, the really phenomenal part of the T. Rex phenomenon didn't become apparent until the band went on the tour of Britain that finished last month. That is, the band's elevation to a "teen idol" status reminiscent of the mid-'60s peak of fan idolatry.

"You mean like Cliff Bolan?" smiled Marc, adjusting his cross-legged position on the settee to concur with the producer's demands. "It has been an exciting year, and I suppose the tour was the capper. For a long time kids have wanted to boogie at concerts. I know that, because that's what I wanted to do. The mood of the country has been right for it. I certainly dig those kinds of concerts.

"We did get all that Beatlemania stuff, I accept that, but I was really just being myself and I would rather it was happening to me than some plastic Ricky Steele. It's surely nice that people warm to you in that way, and in my own way I have integrity. We don't have any cigar-smoking dudes behind us. It is down to me what happens, and I find that exciting and stimulating.

"Lots of funky things happened on the tour, cars being smashed up. And a lot of frightening things. We were in Newcastle stuck in a car with kids banging on the roof. You could see it caving in and it was a bit frightening, but then these five little faces came over the top and they all looked like me. They all had Marc Bolan T-shirts and corkscrew hair. It was really weird, but it was nice that they were getting involved in a way. We found out afterwards there were hairdressers doing the Marc Bolan cut."

◀ On the T Rex US tour, 1971: Marc Bolan in the back of a limousine with his wife June Child

"We did 'White Swan', then a TV show... and that was it"

The camera whirs into silence. Technical hitch.

"Can you come in on that again?" requests polo neck of Marc.

"One of the nicest things I really flashed on," Marc is telling me later in the kitchen when we get a break from the filming, "is people like Lennon, McCartney and Ringo saying nice things about us. I am not assuming we are the new Beatles, but if we were totally lame they might be uptight.

"I think there is a new phase beginning. Because the revolution has come, it is here. Like five years ago the whole T. Rex thing would not have happened without an entourage of showbusiness people behind us. We didn't have any of that. The next record we put out will be on our own label."

Back on camera, after Marc had again gone through several changes of posture to satisfy the continuity department, I asked if he felt he had now turned his back on old Tyrannosaurus Rex followers, or if they had turned their backs on him.

"I have never had any evidence apart from a few letters in the music press, and if you look at them they all come from the same handful of people. The progressive thing was decided on album-selling qualities, and *Electric Warrior* has been in the charts for three months. Taking your audience seriously... that, for me, was what the underground was all about, and that I still do. People talk about how I move about on stage, but it is very hard to wiggle when you are sitting on the floor.

"Then again, someone came up on tour and said why don't you do stuff like *Beard Of Stars* any more? Well, *Beard Of Stars* was primarily electric. On another occasion, some little guy of around nine came up and asked why we didn't play acoustic. That night I had done a 40-minute acoustic spot. The changes in the music have been so gradual.

"I mean, Elton John is a good example of somebody who has had to put up with that sort of jive. It is very easy for people to rip you to pieces. There seems to be a group of people like that, a little group who look around for someone to knock. I remember reading an interview where Rod Stewart said that if 'Maggie May' was big he wanted to avoid that knocking. Four weeks later he had exactly the same thing. It was his turn then, and they backed off me for a few months."

With sound recording over now and the crew using film only, and between requests to turn first this way and then that way a little more, I ask Bolan how he reacted to the side of the new-found T. Rex appreciation that has seen his face spread across a thousand teenage girls' bedroom walls.

▲ When Tyrannosaurus Rex became T Rex: Marc Bolan and musical partner Mickey Finn, 1971

He goes silent for a minute.

"Is it not nice for people to care for you? Do you not think so?"

And after further reflection: "I don't know. The most unexpected thing was the sexual overtones that have gone down. But isn't it nice that someone can be concerned enough to put you on their walls? I mean, in my music room upstairs I have pictures of Lennon and Hendrix and Salvador Dali. Better that it be me than Shane Fenton. Surely it is funkier for you to interview me, someone who has something to say."

"It is really down to credibility. Dylan suddenly made The Beatles seem more important. He gave them respect for themselves. I always had that, and because I had that, and basically because of the history of the band, it has made me a credible person. I really think people were pleased that we made it."

Filming over, we flee from the chaos to Marc's music room, where I'm played a tape Bolan has just acquired of him making a demo at 15 – strongly influenced by Dylan but the T. Rex feel was well developed even then – and then brought up to date with a play through of the four new tracks under consideration for the band's next single.

"After seven years of trying to do something," muses Bolan, "having actually done it is a very strange feeling." *NME*

Sexual. Brooding. Misunderstood.

JULY 3

RIP, Jim Morrison.

AMERICA DIDN'T HAVE a Jagger. It did have Jim Morrison: the first major American male sex symbol since James Dean. The American dream has always held a morbid fascination for its deceased cult heroes, and like Dean – and Valentino before him – the untimely passing of James Douglas Morrison has guaranteed his immortality.

Morrison, the leather-clad Lizard King, was the epitome of the Big, Bad Guy: sexual, brooding, misunderstood. Morrison's mystique was much maligned. His sanity, not to mention his motives, were constantly questioned. "Pretentious" was a word often levelled at him. "Acid Evangelist," his devotees yelled in defence of their symbolic superstar.

Like him or not, Jim Morrison was a superstar of the first order, and the rest of The Doors – Ray Manzarek, John Densmore and Robbie Krieger – his electric disciples.

In 1968, the *Saturday Evening Post* described them thus: "The Doors are the Norman Mailer of the Top 40. Missionaries of apocalyptic sex, their music insists that love is sex, and sex is death, and therein lies salvation." To which Morrison replied, "We are erotic politicians."

Morrison was both the singer and the song, and his songs revealed the recurring symbolism of snakes, Oedipus' relationship, sexual tragedy and death.

Attired in tight black leather pants, the man his friends called Jimbo was the kind of guy you wouldn't want your sister to date. No doubt, however, she would have squirmed with ecstatic delight at the mere suggestion.

The Doors forte was the Theatre of Rock. With dramatic menace in their music, Morrison would take up his familiar stance... right foot resting on the microphone base while both his hands caressed the head. With agonised expressions contorting his classic features, he sang and enacted each song in a deadpan monotone. Suddenly, he would throw back his head – a scream of pain would come from deep within his throat – Morrison would collapse as if machine-gunned or kicked in the groin. He was the dying "Unknown Soldier", the

Oedipus slaughterer in "The End". The impact: completely hypnotic.

Constantly attacked for his overt sexuality, Morrison was arrested and charged with giving obscene performances on at least two separate occasions, though there are legends of more outrageous happenings. Morrison enjoyed his juice to the point of overindulgence, and though he died through natural causes, there is no doubt that it was his undenied continued misuse of alcohol and drugs which in the end aggravated his failing health, changed his appearance, and brought about his sudden death at the age of 27.

Morrison and The Doors had terminated their association at the beginning of this year and Morrison had made it clear that he had completely forsaken stage appearance in order to concentrate on creative writing. *NME*

"With agonised expressions, he sang and enacted each song"

David Bowie // Faces // The Jackson 5
John Lennon // Lou Reed // MC5
Neil Young // New York Dolls
The Osmonds // Wings

1972

There's the smell of revolution in the air, with Sixties rebels MC5 still manning the barricades, and the New York Dolls hinting at more glamorous changes to come – which they do, straight from Mars, in the sequined form of Bowie's Ziggy Stardust.

Rod Stewart and the Faces, on the other hand, are out to convince us that plain old rock 'n' roll isn't dead yet, as Transformer man Lou Reed also testifies. And in New York City, John Lennon admits he's enjoying a spot of self-indulgence – with Yoko ever-present – in his self-imposed exile.

"A battle cry for the kids in America"

American revolutionaries the MC5 arrive in London. On the agenda: "reality vibration", future shock, love, and even music. "We're not interested in making it big like Led Zeppelin," says Fred Smith. "There are more important things to do."

THE MC5 DON'T WANT to be stars, if you can dig that. The reason that they are there with you is to fill the air with vibrations, to take control of the air molecules and fill them with sensitivity. You see they are still very much into politics, although it is more subtle now and not just a matter of "Kick Out The Jams".

You have to progress, and they make a point of putting over the fact that they are now into reality. Tuned into reality because rock'n'roll is a force that can put people back into a feeling of security. It's a high-level energy trip that can give people something they need.

But at the same time when stars become stars they lose that high-level energy and reality because instead of them thinking of the people, they become a machine that thinks of tax returns. And money prevails. At least that's how the MC5 see it.

"I think the political side of rock'n'roll is still there, but like a lot of other people, it is not just slogans. Political music is moving into reality," says guitarist Fred "Sonic" Smith. "It's more tuned into a reality vibration."

◀ November 23, 1972: One of the final gigs by the MC5 before they split at the end of the year

▲ Only Kramer and Smith remained of the original MC5 lineup when they played the Beat Forum in Gladsaxe, near Copenhagen, Denmark

"It's a high-energy release," added Wayne Kramer, the band's second guitarist.

Outside their hotel room, across the road, children played during their lunch hour, shouting and letting off all the energy they could. If everything in the world is too cool it is up to them to make it so. But they point out that the natural loving instinct in children is stifled from the day they are born. Parents teach children to love them only, the brothers and sisters a little bit less, and to be careful of everything else around them. It's all to do with possessiveness and sexuality, the band point out.

"It is to do with the way you approach living," said vocalist Rob Tyner. "You can approach it living and loving everything like children, or you can approach it from a personal thing like in America. Children are brought up in such a way that they are afraid to love.

"When you are young you are willing to love anybody, but your parents close that sensitive door. They close it so that you love them only. I have a child myself. I try to help it as much as I can, because I know what happened to me when I was a kid. God knows what I would have been like if I had not been repressed at home and at school, and in religion. I'm bizarre enough now, but I don't know what I would be like if I had been left to grow up in my own way."

"Religion," says Wayne "is particularly repressive. Just take the title, which comes from the Latin word *religio*, which means to follow a dogma. It has nothing to do with turning this planet around and changing it."

The phrase "future shock" crops up with Wayne as he stresses a point about people's closeness to their own way of life. Future shock has caused a lot of people to crack, people who can't keep up with the use of change. That, he says, accounts for the weird behaviour of people who become involved in senseless violence that has become a pattern of life in the western world, especially America.

So where does rock'n'roll come in to this pattern of future shock? How can rock'n'roll save the world from going to the dogs?

Well, it can change because it is a powerful force. People read books, stresses Wayne, but they only read them once and then put them on a shelf or leave them in a plane or something. Films you can only see once, and he dismisses TV.

"People play records a lot. They are part of a lifestyle. People listen to rock'n'roll throughout the day, and they keep playing their records. But mainly they listen to it when they do anything. In a sense, rock'n'roll is the most powerful medium we have at the moment," said Wayne.

Rock'n'roll has a different, anarchistic lifestyle too, and that, Fred thinks, is important. But most important of all, he feels that people have to be re-sensitised. We need change. People need to change their lifestyles, and lifestyles have been changing with rock'n'roll. With rock'n'roll, the most important thing is to have sensitivity to airspace, to treat the air molecules with respect.

Rock'n'roll has escaped from the rigid musical traditions that have prevailed in music for thousands of years. If rock can do that, then people can escape from the structures that have tied them for thousands of years. Look at the States, they say; the ideal behind the democratic government goes back to Greece and Rome.

To find ideals they are looking for in life, the MC5 are thinking of moving their operations to London, because things are cooler here and because they feel that it is the centre of European art. Anyway, there are lots of people they want to get to know, especially science-fiction writers they admire and musicians they want to dig out and get to know.

But the main thing with the MC5 when you get underneath all their political ideals is that they are open and honest. Unlike the vast majority of radicals who want to replace what we have now with equally restrictive governments, they are as mixed up as anybody. That is an important thing when they talk politics.

They are talking from a human level, a level that they themselves have found. Anarchy, they feel, is the thing, but anarchy that allows people to feel free to move in their own direction instead of those laid down by the powers that be. *MM*

"Children are brought up in such a way that they are afraid to love"

NEWS

Fan hysteria on a massive level

OCTOBER 28

Two of the three biggest US pop stars, The Jackson 5 and The Osmonds, are set to arrive in Britain.

THE BIG SCREAM is on its way back to Britain – and the biggest scream of all is due to fill the skies around London's Heathrow Airport this Sunday morning when The Jackson 5 and The Osmond Brothers touch down within hours of each other. It's doubtful whether Heathrow will have played host to such a fan gathering since the days when The Beatles returned triumphant from their American tours. For accompanying the Jacksons and Osmonds is the biggest wave of fan worship since Beatlemania.

First to arrive are The Jackson 5. Their plane, Pan Am Flight Number 106, is due to arrive at Terminal 3 at 7.20am. The Osmonds arrive at Terminal 3 at 10.30am. Arrangements have been made for The Osmonds to drive in front of Terminal 2.

Together with David Cassidy, the Jacksons and the Osmonds make up a trio of American acts that have brought back fan hysteria on a massive level. Record sales for The Osmonds alone are toppling records set by The Beatles at the height of their touring days. In Britain alone, The Jackson 5 have sold two million singles and 100,000 albums for Tamla Motown in two years, counting recordings by the group and lead singer Michael Jackson.

First-to-arrive Jacksons will spend the Sunday at rehearsals for the Royal Variety Performance at the London Palladium, which takes place the next day. Following concerts on the Continent, the group play two shows at Birmingham Odeon on November 9, Belle Vue, Manchester (10), Liverpool Empire... two shows (11) and they wind up with a massive concert at the Wembley Empire Pool on November 12.

The Osmonds will be driven from the airport to their central London hotel for an afternoon press reception. They will play concerts at London's Rainbow Theatre (November 4), Manchester Free Trade Hall (6) and Birmingham Town Hall (7). All the concerts have sold out. Concerts follow in France, Germany and Scandinavia. *MM*

▶ The Jackson 5 playing basketball at their Hollywood Hills home in 1972. Left to right, Michael, Randy (not a member of the group) Jackie, Tito, Jermaine and Marlon

NEWS

"We'll definitely be electric in January"

JUNE 10

Back in good health, Neil Young plans his return.

NEIL YOUNG IS PLANNING a major British tour – and now that he is in good physical condition after a spinal operation, he will be playing electric guitar. On his last British concert, at London's Royal Festival Hall in 1970, Neil confined himself to acoustic work because it was less strenuous.

"I've wanted to do a proper tour with electric and now my back's OK we can go ahead." Neil told *MM* editor Ray Coleman in Hollywood last week: "So we'll definitely be electric in January in England. I've had back trouble for two years, so I've not been able to strain myself and it's been frustrating. It should be a new dimension for me next time in England."

Neil said he would be accompanied on the tour by the musicians who were featured on the *Harvest* album. "I'd like to do a free concert in Hyde Park – that really appeals to me. But we'll be coming at the wrong time of the year. It will be freezing in England in January and I can't play with gloves on!"

He added that the idea of doing a Hyde Park show was still not being dismissed. Neil and his manager David Geffen stressed that the British tour – a week playing the major cities – would be planned with low prices for seats. "We feel strongly that audiences should not be robbed," said Geffen. "Neil's fans deserve a really good deal and that's what they'll get." The British visit will be part of Neil's first major European tour. *MM*

Neil Young
Harvest   FEBRUARY 1

THE MONA LISA has nothing on Neil Young. Enigmatic is probably too precise a work for a man whose songs defy any attempt to pin him down. He is all things to all men: loner, martyr, Christ-figure, poet, mystic. The archetypal, all-purpose outsider, with whom any screwed-up, alienated kid can identify and through whom countless more can wallow in sweet, vicarious sadness.

He is also one of rock's greatest song-writers, wrapping up small nuggets of truth and pain and beauty in melodies which have the haunting simplicity of songs half-remembered from childhood and lyrics which, like the best songs of Dylan and Lennon, can be interpreted on many different levels.

It is the elusiveness of many of Young's songs that makes them so precious. Because they are not explicit, each listener can interpret them in a way which is meaningful to him or her. Listening to the songs on this album, I find it impossible to set down on paper what many of them are really about. Yet meaning is there, to be divined instinctively.

A few of the songs, superficially at least, are more explicit than others. "The Needle And The Damage Done", recorded live at the UCLA, California, is a quietly poignant lament for a dead addict. "Alabama" seems to continue the theme of "Southern Man" on his previous album, albeit more obliquely. "A Man Needs A Maid" is about the pain of love, of being involved, and the impossibility of living without it: "To give a love, you gotta live a love/To live a love, you gotta be 'part of'".

The other songs are harder to pin down. They tell of joy, sorrow, love, old age, half-described incidents and meetings – all expressed in oblique, fragmented lyrics which create an indefinable atmosphere of regret and nostalgia for a simpler, happier way of life which probably never existed.

Musically, the songs here hold few surprises, except for "A Man Needs A Maid" and "There's A World", which were recorded with the London Symphony Orchestra at London's Barking Town Hall, with some majestic string arrangements by Jack Nitzsche. The rest feature the fairly familiar mixture of plangent rhythm guitar, wood-chopping drums, stinging lead guitar and touches of steel, harmonica and piano.

Melodically, Young's songs seem to have been getting gradually simpler, and some of the songs here, notably "Heart Of Gold" and "Are You Ready For The Country", are simple to the point of being facile.

And yet... he makes them work. That desolate, vulnerable, painful voice compels you to listen. And when the voice, the song and the arrangement come together as they do on "A Man Needs A Maid" the result is... frightening. *MM*

◄ Portrait of Neil Young in 1971 by photographer Henry Diltz

▲ Neil Young photographed at his north California ranch in June, 1971

"We knew we had PIZZAZZ!"

Something unusual is happening in New York City. *MM*'s reporter sits down with the spectacular, self-confident NEW YORK DOLLS. "We were just flawless," says guitarist Johnny Thunders. "We were rock'n'roll"…

THEY MIGHT JUST BE the best rock'n'roll band in the world. And whether you believe that or not, you're going to have to take notice of them… The New York Dolls. Musically, they hurt, because they don't have any manners. They can't play very well. They pout, and swank, and shake their bums with the hellish rhythm thrown up by their drummer, who wears driving gloves and smacks about like a madman.

The singer, a lovely young replica of Mick Jagger, shouts as though each word were a swear word, and the rock-a-boogie swears on to meet its evil end. These are young New Yorkers, seemingly unimpressed with the switches and swatches of progressive music – as is their growing audience. Not for them any boring, endless singer-songwriters; not for them any polite sobering up in the quality of rock.

Not for them any attention to what old men are flogging off as hip. No class, little discussion, just stuff wild and unsubtle. And it makes

▶ The New York Dolls in 1972: (left to right) David Johansen, Sylvain Sylvain, Johnny Thunders, Arthur Kane and Jerry Nolan

wholesome sense. The New York Dolls are a five-piece with no manager, no record company, no publicity unit, and precious little equipment, and yet their quest must be logged.

For in them, and their kind, lies the rebellion needed to crush the languid cloud of nothingness that rolls out from the rock establishment, and falls like endless drizzle on the ears. They are growing up within the hot swathe cut by Alice Cooper. They have picked up on the remnants of things that have been misused. They sound like a cross between The Deviants, Pretty Things and very early Rolling Stones.

In other words, the circle has indeed turned. The need for wildness and arrogance is back again, as much as it was during the '50s. A need to enjoy without inhibition. The Dolls are one of the possibly many bands – mostly very young – who are crawling out of the shadows cast by their elders and, with sneaky cheek and brash egos, pulling notes of scorn against the establishment.

Their music may sound like drivel, but whatever it is, it is indeed alive – and you can see an audience dance themselves dead and blur their minds crazy to it. A rock musician may be likened to a footballer. He's at his best when young. The mature years over 25 meet for more stylish eclectic play – the sting in the tail becomes a wise glow in the eye. After 28, the style begins to dim, and then even being wise cannot match the impact of youth.

And rock must be young.

"We don't try and offend people, but somehow we do offend"

Being wise also fails to throw up any sort of ugly, but fiery, ego. Confidence becomes a substitute for that character, but egos, no matter how sickening with their arrogance, make for colour. The Dolls and their like have colour, the colour that is now being lightly painted in pastel shades by their elders. The youngsters paint with blood.

It's rather like changing one's hobby from cock-fighting to chess – growing old, that is. The music follows suit – watching the New York Dolls is like watching not just a cock-fight, but a dog-fight – in drag.

They don't have anything to say of importance offstage. They aren't talkers, they don't have any amazing concepts to drawl on about, they just want to play what the people want to hear. Really, it's as simple as that.

The first time I saw them was at Greenwich Village's Mercer Arts Centre, and they did everything right. They played Bo Diddley's "Pills" in a very brash way, dressed in a variety of clothes, women's shoes and vampy makeup.

Guitarists Johnny Thunders and Sylvain Sylvain were high on treble and big, fast chords – few riffs, just rock and blues, nicely out of tune in places, and evil. It owed nothing to the respect electric guitar has got over the past few years.

Singer David Johansen is a young, bubbling spot of Jagger, but instead of straight copying, he just camps naturally, and shouts like a bitch. Then there was strange, supine bassist Arthur Kane, blond, and with white makeup, tights, high-heeled shoes, and a mouth full of surly posing. He struck loud patterns, while drummer Billy Murcia drew savage percussion.

You hear this band for a minute, and there's one thought in your head – you want to dance.

And the people at Mercer leapt up and down, sideways and went well crazy on the floor as The Dolls' music got louder, and sawed about the room. It's simple music, just rock and blues, but it's played right, and played with monster arrogance.

They look young too. No lazy, bored 30-year-old in jeans, picking notes and their noses, but kids having a great time, playing heavy rock like it had just been discovered. They're going to make great singles, are The Dolls. Now they live in an attic, just on the Bowery,

◀ The New York Dolls playing the Mercer Arts Center, New York, in 1972

▲ Image-wise, the New York Dolls were a cross between Glam Rock and Punk Rock, which would emerge later in the decade

in a dimly lit, seedy area, where activity consists of pool rooms, and standing with little or totally lost ambition on street corners. Bo Diddley was on the stereo, and a couple of big dogs filled the stale air in the attic with doggy smells.

A couple of ladies are busy in dark corners, and the toilet is a sink. For the Dolls, money is hard come by, but even with a little, luxuries like cans of Budweiser can be bought.

They were formed in January of this year. "Three of us knew each other, two of us didn't," said Johansen. Their first gig was a political benefit party – they don't know what politics were involved – but an ad in the *Village Voice*, plus a shoddy picture, launched them. There was something about the "ad" – a little magic maybe.

"I think we all felt something was lacking in music. It wasn't exciting any more to us. Everyone was hanging about on stage, being morose as well... We didn't dig that. We reckoned what bands were lacking was PIZZAZZ. We knew we had PIZZAZZ, we knew what we wanted to do. We wanted to play rock," said Johansen.

Being young, what had they picked up on; in other words, what were their roots? "Well, we picked up on anybody that was really good. The Stones, Kinks, Pretty Things, Pink Fairies. Oh, and James Brown. And so our music has a lot to do with the way we were brought up. The time is right for some good rock again... Some good things are going to happen."

Did they ever imagine that people would actually like what they played? "No, not really, what has happened has been pretty amazing. I mean we haven't even got any equipment, except guitars and harmonicas."

A few weeks ago somebody described the Dolls as "subterranean sleazoid flash", which is maybe getting quite close to the core.

"I think that, on a social level, we try to be inoffensive – but it doesn't work. We don't try and offend people, but somehow we do offend.

"You see, we don't want nobody laying down any rules. We don't want to get involved with corporate enterprise. At the moment that makes for hard living. Where do we get money? Well, basically we hassle. We've been picking up about five dollars for the gigs at the Mercer."

Five dollars?

"Yeah, and sometimes less," said Johansen.

"Alice Cooper is possibly the better of the top bands, but really the music scene to us didn't have much going for it – except money. Sure, there was money, but there was no vitality. I know if I was 13, I'd be off on Alice Cooper like crazy. Alice to me would be the greatest."

Offers have been pouring in from all angles to sign the band. "We haven't accepted any. We're waiting to hear the whole situation on everything. What's a good record label?"

Thunders cuts in. "Yeah, nice people being interested – the more the merrier. You should have seen us last night, we were just flawless. You know, everyone was dancing. Rather than have them sit there

listening, we want them dancing on the floor, we want them getting off to us. We're rock'n'roll.

"Sure, we have few technicalities about our music, but, my God, we have feel. We don't attempt to be a type of Segovia with guitar work, but when we play, everyone casts their shackles aside and dances. We're playthings; kids want to have us."

Johansen: "The thing about rock today is that you have to impress somebody, have to relate to them. It lost a lot when it became just like that. They forgot that you also have to entertain people."

And with a couple of gigs a week, the Dolls are entertaining. "Is it a crime to fall in love with Frankenstein?" is a line from "Personality Crisis", one of their self-penned items. "The lyrics are high," Johansen tells us.

New York, says Johansen, has a lot of good musicians. "But they somehow find difficulty in playing together – in a group. We didn't have any trouble at all. We were a group from the start – a proper group. It's got to the state where it's all we want to do."

So the next week down the Mercer, the crowd was twice as big and there were twice as many people dancing. The Dolls are making it in an old-fashioned way. There's no hype – they're just the best new, young band I've ever seen. Yes, young. *MM*

◀ The 'Dolls had a Tuesday night residency at the Mercer Arts Center from the summer of 1972, that lasted almost a year

▼ Guitarist Johnny Thunders, with the New York Dolls at the Wembley Festival of Music, London, October 29, 1972

"Nothing to do with drugs"

DECEMBER 2

The new Wings single gets banned – this time for "sexy" content.

PAUL MCCARTNEY – WHOSE "Give Ireland Back To The Irish" was banned by the BBC last February – has again fallen foul of the Beeb. His latest single, out tomorrow (Friday), has been banned by Radios One and Two. Title of the piece, written by Paul and his wife Linda, is "Hi, Hi, Hi", by Wings.

BBC publicity officer Rodney Collins told the *MM*: "The ban has nothing to do with drugs. We thought the record unfit for broadcasting because of the lyric. Part of it goes: 'I want you to lie on the bed and get you ready for my body, gon' do it, do it, do it to you'.

"Another part goes: 'Like a rabbit I'm going to grab it and do it till the night is done'."

"Hi, Hi, Hi" was broadcast by Tony Blackburn once last week, but this was a "mistake", say the BBC. *MM*

▶ Portrait of David Bowie taken in London in June 1972, in his full regalia as his alter ego Ziggy Stardust

Flourishing Theatricatility

JUNE 6

Bowie's songs of self-transformation assessed.

David Bowie *The Rise And Fall Of Ziggy Stardust And The Spiders From Mars*

THE COVER OF Bowie's new album has a picture of him in a telephone booth looking every inch the stylish poseur. Style and content have now become inextricably tangled in Bowie's case. Campness has become built-in to his public persona. I mean that, however, in a far from derogatory sense. The main preoccupation of David's work is not directly gay sexuality, though that element is there, as with a flourishing theatricality and dramatic sense.

On *Ziggy Stardust* this is apparent even with a song like "Five Years". Ostensibly about the death of the world, Bowie turns it into a "performance" by virtue of his gift for artful mannerism and by creating a convincing *mise-en-scène* (a cop kneels at the feet of a priest and a soldier is run over by a car after it is announced on the news that the Earth has five years left). It would also go some way towards explaining why this album has such a conceptual-sounding title.

There is no well-defined storyline, as there is in *Tommy*, say, but there are odd songs and references to the business of being a pop star that overall add up to a strong sense of biographical drama. On one track, "Star", he sings about playing "the wild mutation of a rock'n'roll star/I'd send my photograph to my honey/And I'd come on like a regular superstar"). Then "Ziggy Stardust", the title track, is about a guitar superhero who "took it all too far". ("Making love with his ego, Ziggy sucked up into his mind".)

The final track is simply called "Rock'n'Roll Suicide" – it speaks for itself. In the space of three songs he thus suggests the ascent and decline of a big rock figure, but leaves the listener to fill in his own details, and in the process he's also referring obliquely to his own role as a rock star and sending it up. There are many layers to Bowie the artist, but he has this uncanny knack of turning a whole album or stage performance into a torch song.

Ziggy Stardust is a little less instantly appealing than *Hunky Dory*, basically because that album was written with the intention of being commercial. This one rocks more, though, and the paradox is that it will be much more commercially successful than the last, because Bowie's bid for stardom is accelerating at lightning speed. **MM**

With most of his material either dealing with the flashier style of city living or looking far into the future, Bowie must rate as our most futuristic songwriter. Sometimes what he sees is just a little scary, and perhaps there's a bit more pessimism here than on previous releases, but they're still fine songs.

Like the first track, "Five Years", about the imminent death of a decaying world, is a real downer to start with, but Bowie brings a new approach to the rather overworked theme.

Certainly all the tracks, written by Bowie with the exception of Ron Davies' "It Ain't Easy", are never less than entertaining. "Soul Love" features some withdrawn sax from Mick Ronson [sic], "Ziggy Stardust" deals with the destruction of a rock star, while "Hang Onto Yourself" is a real little sexual gem. Also included is Bowie's current single, "Starman".

Mick Ronson (guitar), Trevor Bolder (bass) and Mick Woodmansey (drums) handle the backing all through.

Of course, there's nothing Bowie would like more than to be a glittery superstar, and it could still come to pass. By now everybody ought to know he's tremendous and this latest chunk of fantasy can only enhance his reputation further. **NME**

"Bowie has this uncanny knack of turning a whole album into a torch song"

Q&G
REVIEW

"He left the stage a giant"

JUNE 21 · **CIVIC HALL, DUNSTABLE**

Throughout the summer, David Bowie inspires adulation with his Ziggy show – becoming the authentic star many in the press suggested he might be.

IT WAS RAINING the night Jim met Phil. They were total strangers to each other, but Phil had asked Jim for a cigarette, and well... one thing led to another. They've become very good friends. Phil still recalls how Jim's hands had trembled, though.

They'd gone along to see David Bowie in Dunstable. Great fans of Bowie they were, and Jim had almost to pinch himself when he first heard such a grand person was actually coming to that place. He hated it there. Privately, his mother confided that he found it difficult to make friends at work.

That Wednesday night he was there, though, clutching his copy of the new David Bowie album, *The Rise And Fall Of Ziggy Stardust*, which he hoped David would autograph after the show. He was wearing his red scarf, flung nonchalantly over his shoulder, and his red platform boots. His hair was long down the back but cropped fairly short on top so that it stuck up when he brushed his fingers through it. He hated that it was dark brown. He'd promised himself that when he eventually split to London he'd have it done bright blond. He was just turned 19.

Phil was one of the first to arrive at the Civic Hall. He'd stood in the queue for an hour and a half to get a ticket, so when he was inside he rushed quickly to the front and stood beneath the stage. He waited patiently while the Flamin' Groovies went through their set. He was to say later, in fact, that they were quite super, but after all, he'd really gone to see Dave, hadn't he?

He was so excited, Phil can't remember exactly what Bowie came out wearing, but towards the end of the performance it was certain that the outfit was white satin shirt and trousers, the legs tucked into glistening, thick-soled white boots. He looked like *Vogue*'s idea of what the well-dressed astronaut should be wearing. Dare it be said? A delicious space oddity.

A lesser hunk of glamour might have been upstaged by guitarist Mick Ronson with his maroon sequinned jacket, red lipstick and hair dyed peroxide as a '50s starlet, but though oohs and aaahs were directed his way, teenage hearts went fluttering out to David; for can anything dim the splendour of this ravishing creature whom all Britain is learning to love?

The newspapers were to report subsequently that this performance was one of the major turning points in David Bowie's incredible success story. The man from United Artists Records, who knows what he likes, was quite sure of that. He said afterwards that DB was definitely the biggest thing around.

To those who had seen his act before this year, the format was not new. That's to say he started the set rockin' like a bitch before cooling down somewhat with "Changes", a song of mixed tempos, and then the darkling, apocalyptic message of "Five Years", which owes something lyrically to Lou Reed ("I think I saw you in an ice-cream parlour /Drinking milkshakes cold and long"). And then the acoustic passages with Mick Ronson ("Space Oddity" and "Andy Warhol"), culminating in a solo version of "Amsterdam", a febrile account of rough trade, as delightfully coarse as navy-blue serge.

"Now some golden oldies for you." He announced the number as written by Jack Bruce and Pete Brown. All his fans, of course, needed no telling. "I Feel Free" ripped out of the stereo PA system, choreographed by the flickering strobe lighting; it's not what you do, it's the way you do it. My, how they clapped and whistled.

The band returned for an encore. It was "I'm Waiting For The Man". But something rather strange was happening up there on stage. During the instrumental break, Bowie began chasing Ronson around the stage, hustling him, trying to press his body close. The attendants at the exits looked twice to see if they could believe their eyes. The teenage chickies stared in bewilderment. The men knew but the little girls didn't understand. Jeees – us! It had happened.

It should be recorded that the first act of fellatio on a musical instrument in the British Isles took place at Dunstable Civic Hall. How do you top that? You don't. You get off stage.

After the show was over, scores of people were still milling around. Over the loudspeaker system *Hunky Dory* was playing. The autograph hunters were crowding round the dressing-room door, but he wasn't seen to emerge. Moist-eyed boys still hung around. After a while, Jim and Phil left the place together. **MM**

"Can anything dim the splendour of this ravishing creature?"

▶ David Bowie on the first date of
the Ziggy Stardust tour at the
Borough Assembly Hall, Aylesbury,
UK on January 29, 1972

▶ Lou Reed relaxes between shows in Amsterdam, during a September 1972 visit to the Netherlands

"I just like rock'n'roll"

Recalling the groundbreaking Velvet Underground back in 1967, LOU REED reflects on how they were the inspiration for the glam rock outrage of Bowie and Roxy Music; and, like a true prima donna, he has to complain about the dressing rooms.

"ALICE COOPER REALLY DOESN'T make it as a drag queen," says Lou Reed. "I mean he's so ugly. Iggy, now Iggy's really very beautiful, and so's David, but Alice…"

The former mastermind of The Velvet Underground shuddered delicately and inspected his maroon fingernails, which were chipped around the edges. Talk to Lou Reed, they said. Since his outward appearance was rather forbidding, and two previous encounters had proved slightly less than productive, the idea had been that, instead of a formal interview, a sumptuous lunch with plentiful alcohol would induce the saturnine, taciturn Lou Reed to give forth with intimate revelations concerning his lifestyle and music.

What actually happened was that we all got pissed.

"When he's not being troubled by things around him, he's a very generous person with time and conversation," was what David Bowie had said of Reed, and with these words ringing in my ears, we went out to lunch at a plush Italian restaurant. Lou had just bought some clothes at Liberty's, and was enthusing about his "new drag". "Isn't it heaven?" he drawled.

Once ensconced at a comfortable table by the window with RCA's genial Geoff Thorn to act as referee and pay the bill, things moved into high gear. Reed was determined that we would get into the liquors, and get into them we did. It is only recently that the songs Lou Reed wrote five years ago for The Velvet Underground have become noticeably influential. David Bowie and Roxy Music have paid their dues to Lou, and the tortured, violent guitars of Reed and Sterling Morrison have taught many to extend the boundaries of their instruments.

"I never keep to things...
I'm really very inconsistent"

◄ Portrait of Lou Reed taken by
photographer Michael Putland in
London, January 1972

▲ Lou Reed live on stage at the Carre Theatre
in Amsterdam, September 30, 1972

"What I was writing about was just what was going on around me," says Reed. "I didn't realise it was a whole new world for everybody else. Everybody else is now at the point I was in 1967. Makes me wonder where they'll be in five years' time. Come to that, makes me wonder where I'm at now."

One of Lou's best known is "Venus in Furs" from the Velvet Underground & Nico album. "I saw the book (by Leonard Sacher-Masoch) and just thought it would be a great idea for a song. Now everybody thinks I invented masochism."

Despite the ads, Reed is not going to return to Kingsound – the King's Cross rock venue. He didn't like the hall, and found the dressing rooms cramped and crowded.

"You're in there trying to find a place to change into your drag and put on your makeup and people keep coming up to you and offering you joints and rapping to you, and it's just intolerable."

Lou's girlfriend is coming over from the States soon, and he's looking forward to seeing her, because things are getting a mite chaotic at his Wimbledon residence. Seems that some of his friends began smashing up the house but his landlady didn't mind. She thought he put some life into the place.

As the meal grew progressively more and more bizarre, we switched to grappa, using chablis as a chaser. Lou recalled the time when, as a hitchhiker, he turned to desperate measures and lay down across the centre of the road. The first car to stop was a police van, and far from getting his lift, he got busted. "If it'd been me in the car, I would have kept right on going," he said. "They'd never catch me, and the experience of running somebody over…"

I pointed out that on the Velvets' live album, Lou told the audience they didn't play "Heroin" any more, but that he played it at King's Cross.

"Oh, we just didn't feel like doing it that night. Besides, I never mean what I say." What? "Oh, I never keep to things unless I actually promise. I told some journalist that I was very hung up on cowboys. If I saw him today I'd probably tell him I was really aggressive and that all cowboys are a bunch of assholes. I'm really very inconsistent."

After that, an almost total disintegration sets in. I remember Reed drawling that Englishmen were really sexy because they didn't have hair on their chest, and Geoff Thorn opened his shirt to prove the contrary.

Unlike at the Dorchester with Ziggy, Lou's outrageous clothes and painted fingernails left the waiters at the restaurant rather cold, but then they weren't Lou's type anyway. The following day I was still drunk. A lot of people have learned a lot of things from Lou Reed, and there's a strong possibility that they can still learn a whole lot more. His new single "Walk It And Talk It" is a remixed version of a track from his album, and wouldn't it be a gas to see that on *Top of the Pops*?

If Ziggy isn't too outrageous for the BBC, then it's about time we saw Lou. After all, he was the man who started that brand of outrage way back in the swinging '60s. We may even see where everybody else will be at in five years. *NME*

▶ Lou with his 1972 backing band The Tots, comprising Vinny Laporta and Eddie Reynolds on guitars, Bobby Resigno on bass, and drummer Scottie Clark

The Most Gifted Writer in Rock

NOVEMBER 8

Reed's second solo LP, under the VU microscope.

Lou Reed *Transformer*

IS KNOWLEDGE NECESSARILY beneficial? That's the question this album poses for me. If "Walk On The Wild Side" had been cut in '66, when I didn't have a clue that "Jackie" is Jackie Curtis and "Candy" is Candy Darling, would I have been as helplessly beguiled as I was then (and still am) by "All Tomorrow's Parties" and "I'll Be Your Mirror"? This is no longer the first Polaroid print from the New World: nowadays, we've all got maps.

But Lou Reed is still the most gifted, personal writer in rock, and anything he does is necessarily of great interest. Transformer has its ups and downs, and I'd say that the general level is rather lower than his initial RCA solo album, but it obviously does its appointed task of reflecting where Lou's brain has travelled during the past year or so. "Upfront" is the key phrase this time: nothing needs to be shrouded in metaphor or obliquely alluded to. If Lou wants to write a gay-lib song, as he does with "Make Up", he can be completely explicit: "We're coming out, out of our closets". The result is heightened by the use of carefully crafted arrangements (using strings, voices, tuba, Dixieland band, etc.), and some may think that the settings are, indeed, too neat and precise. "White Light/White Heat" was so surprising because art was couched inside a matrix of rock, whereas now he's taken the Bowie route and gone all out to create art-rock. They're two very different things. Nothing much against Bowie ("Jean Genie" is terrific), but whatever else he may have achieved, he's never proved himself capable of making really satisfying rock'n'roll; all too often he simply titillates, and the Bowie/Ronson production work here lures Reed into the same trap.

Lou is a rocker and the role now chosen ill becomes him, however liberating he may find the new surroundings. The beat tracks here are "Andy's Chest", which has a lot of the old mystery and menace, a really cutting vocal, and a fade-out ("Swoop, swoop... Oh baby, rock, rock") which is the album's finest moment; "Satellite Of Love", a very humorous '50s-style group song which reminds me of an old doo-wop classic called "Guided Missiles (To Your Heart)"; and "Walk On The Wild Side", a beautifully controlled production number (here, the "gimmicks" like the string bass and baritonic sax solos coalesce in a valid way).

I'm unhappiest about the rockers: "Vicious" is a parody of former glory, while "Hangin' Round", "Wagon Wheel" and "I'm So Free" simply never take off – oh for Clem Cattini or Les Hurdle! "New York Telephone Conversation" is, at 1.31, an amusing skit on the behaviour of the girls who frequent the back room at Max's; "Perfect Day" is pretty and nothing more and "Goodnight Ladies" attempts to come on like Kurt Weill or Cabaret but ends up plain boring. Of course, you should buy *Transformer* – after all, it's still the second-best Lou Reed album of 1972 (not counting the Velvets' live LP). But it seems to me to be an album for two kinds of people: David Bowie fans and those who heard about Lou this year (sorry, maybe that's one kind of person). Anyone who's heard "Heroin", or "Femme Fatale", or "Here She Comes", or "I'm Set Free", or "Rock And Roll", or "New Age" knows that he can – and will – achieve something of greater worth than this, whatever he might be thinking at the moment. **MM**

"We'll show Marc Bolan a few tricks"

The FACES continue their American campaign, with an eye on the state of things back home. Their unrehearsed approach continues to yield results.

"'**A**NG ON. I'LL WAKE UP in a minute," says Ian McLagan for the fourth time. It's 3.30 in the afternoon and Mac's struggling through an interview. As a rule, he's something of a talker, but right now he's only been out of bed half an hour and his mind's a little foggy.

The night before, the Faces had been down at the studios, doing nothing in particular, just trying out a few possible ideas for their next album. In fact, it isn't due to be recorded until after the band's next American tour, when they'll get down to making the finished product in Los Angeles. But still McLagan thinks working on odd bits and pieces is a valuable exercise.

Now though, this afternoon, his eyes spell "hangover" in big letters. He blinks out of the kitchen door at the bright sunshine, makes some coffee, takes some pills of a mildly rejuvenating nature and tries to think clearly. We stick to fairly simple stuff.

"The thing is, we've never rehearsed for recordings before, 'never even considered it," he says, talking of the recent sessions in the studios. "It's bad really, 'cos when you think of it they're more important than gigs, because they're going to be confronting your ears the whole time. We thought we'd go down to the studios with

▶ Rod Stewart posing for a portrait during a recording session for his album *Never A Dull Moment*: May 15, 1972, Miami, Florida

an open frame of mind to see what we could do and what would come out. If we got bored with an idea after five minutes, we'd drop it and move on to something else. In fact, the number of ideas we came up with was amazing.

"We should have used this system to start every album. Sometimes, in the past, things have been a little too forced. There's too much pressure if you start thinking you've got to make numbers that have got to be Number One hits..."

The results, according to Mac, were more ideas than actual tracks, but a few numbers had been kicked around, like the old Impressions number "Fall For You" which Mac said he "would like to stick in somewhere". Also, he thought the overall feel of the album would be rock'n'roll. But that was hardly world-shattering information. What were the other albums, then?

"Well, I suppose the last one was rock'n'roll," he replied, "but I don't think the first two had any kind of overall feel. They were really just bits and pieces. Basically we have just two types of numbers – the rockers that steam along and are good for stage, and then the low-down, quiet sort of things. On *Nod*, the rock side dominated, and I think it will on the next – I hope it will, at least."

Mac is gradually warming up, becoming more articulate. Gradually we get on to talking about Rod Stewart, and I mention the recent suggestion that Stewart's singing is better on his solo albums than on those with the Faces. He half agrees: "I think his own albums definitely bring out the best in his voice. It's natural really, simply because they are his own albums. They don't necessarily make him a better singer, but I think he's a bit of a folkie at heart and we're a rock'n'roll band, if you like.

"If everything fell apart tomorrow I could almost see Rod down at the Crown Folk Club in Twickenham doing the old acoustic guitar bit, staring up at the ceiling... Well, perhaps not, but I don't think he's satisfied just singing rock'n'roll. He's been singing that for quite a long time, and before that he was singing a bit of the old folk.

"Like in the band, I don't think any of our musical tastes have changed that much, but with Rod maybe they've reverted a bit to his original ideas – a bit Jack Elliott and all that. I like to hear him sing rock'n'roll, but his voice has got so much subtlety as well. People knock it and say it sounds like an old rusty gatepost or something... and, well, it's true, but that's his voice. The way he uses it can be very subtle; there's a lot of innuendo – if that's the right word."

With so much attention paid to Stewart, and with Mac along with Kenney Jones seemingly the quieter in the group, I wondered if he ever felt a little left in the background. "Yeah, I do now and again, but it suits me quite well. I mean it's all fair; Rod can do what he can do. Like there was a similar idea with Steve [Marriott] when I was with the Small Faces. A lot of emphasis was put on Steve and in a way it did him in the same way it can do Rod in. At the same time, Rod is very level-headed and it ain't going to go to his head... I don't want to say like Steve... but he was younger and Rod's been through a lot more.

"Of course Steve's been through a lot more now as well, but in the old days it used to cause a bit of friction. And I think it's good that Rod's got his own thing going, doing his own albums, and that's one of the reasons the set-up works so well. Like, if I had so much going in me the best thing would be to split from the band and do my own album or something... but Rod can do it, at the same time realising that it's the band which is what it's all really about. Without the band, Rod wouldn't get to sing his solo stuff onstage; it's a great set-up."

Continuing on the same theme of the Small Faces, he pointed out: "I've been with Kenney and Ronnie for seven years now and I always celebrate on November the first, 'cos that's the date I first joined them. A few bottles are opened. Rod and Ron have been together just as long, and even now, it helps. It's good to play with the same people for such a long time, because you can rely on certain musical things happening. Also, we know each other's jokes."

As for Steve Marriott, though, Mac says he hasn't seen him for a long, long time. "I'd like to," he says. "I still feel close to him. A lot of his musical influences are the same as mine, but then at the same time there's nothing much to say. It's a load of water under the bridge really."

At this point he decides it's time for another coffee and also brings his portable stereo down to the kitchen. He plays a few records and talks a bit about some Chuck Berry sessions he was playing on recently. One of the things that impressed him about Berry, apart from his music, was his total disregard for the ways of the music scene as a whole... the way he thinks of "Chuck Berry only" and doesn't bother himself with any kind of trends. I suggest that it's been a bit the same for the Faces.

Mac agrees. "If we concerned ourselves with what other bands were doing when we started, we would have gone well under," he says. "A big thing was made of the drink thing with the Faces, and I think it made a change because all the other bands would be smoking and would go onstage in a kind of euphoric state. Drink isn't so introspective. I mean, I tend to be a bit introspective myself, but a few drinks soon loosen me up."

On gigs as a whole, I suggest, their sets tend to vary in quality to a greater extent than most bands.

"I'm on the inside and it's difficult to tell," he replies, "but I wouldn't have thought so. It's a fair comment but it doesn't seem like that to me. If it comes across that way I can only put it down to creative genius... Oh no, what am I saying?" He breaks into a smile.

"But to me, all gigs seem much the same. I'm not saying I'm bored or anything, but we always put as much into each one. The one thing that really pisses me off, though, are encores. I'd like to rub them out forever. It's like you do a whole set and you get nice applause and then you say it's the last number and everybody gets on their feet and starts screamin'. It's like... for fuck's sake... if they'd done that earlier we would have had more fun out of the whole set.

"I don't want to get into a big thing about 'the overwhelming feedback, man' or that waffle, but we do tend to rely quite a lot on the excitement. Hey, would ya like another coffee?"

Well yeah, why not... **NME**

◀ Rod Stewart singing with The Faces at the Rainbow Theatre, London in 1972

▶ The Faces live on stage in Bristol,
April 8, 1972: Left to right, Ronnie
Wood, Rod Stewart, Kenney Jones,
Ronnie Lane, and Ian McLagan

"People say I'm self-indulgent"

JOHN LENNON delights in telling how he's been influenced by Yoko, and vice versa. And contemplating the media madness surrounding the likes of Bolan and Bowie, he recalls the heady days of Beatlemania, when it was easy to slip out of touch with reality.

"THE BEATLES HAD A standard to live up to," admits John Lennon, lighting up yet another four-inch link in an endless chain of battered cigarettes. "And for that reason, when The Beatles went into the studio, they had to stay in for at least six months. Today, I just couldn't stand to be locked up in a studio for that length of time."

Lennon's reason is as simple as it is short: "I don't want a standard to live up to."

"You know," he tells me that muggy night in New York, "when the Beatles cartoons come on the TV every Sunday, I still get a kick outta watching them... It's just like leaving home – after that you automatically get on with your parents."

I bring us back to the present and ask: How much has Yoko influenced John, and how much has John influenced Yoko? Lennon displays obvious pleasure at the subject. "She," he begins with an affectionate smile at Yoko, "changed my life completely. Not just physically... the only way I can describe it is that Yoko was like an

◀ October 1972: John Lennon sits on a bench in the back porch of the New York apartment, at 105 Bank Street, he shared with his wife Yoko Ono

acid trip or the first time you got drunk. It was that big a change, and that's just about it. I can't really describe it to this day."

I put it to them that an example would be appreciated and they both choose their new album, Sometime In New York City, as an illustration. Again, it's John who leads off: "If you really wanna know, Yoko writes all her own chords and music completely. If I can get in a riff or something, then I'm lucky. A lot of people don't know this, but Yoko was classically trained from the age of four, and that, as you know, has its rewards and its disadvantages, in the same way of any training. It's always hard to hit upon specific details, but for instance, the idea for a song like "Imagine" came out of Yoko's influence regardless of what the format of that song was. Half the way I'm thinking, musically, philosophically and every other way is her influence both as a woman and an artist. Her influence is so overwhelming that it was big enough not only for me to change my life with The Beatles, but also my private life, which has nothing to do with how sexually attractive we are to each other."

For Lennon it's time for another cigarette, for Yoko a chance to offer her observations.

"Naturally, my life also changed. Mainly what we give each other is energy, because we're both energetic people and when we're in the company of other people who we might feel are less energetic, then we have to give more. For instance, if we're on stage and John is reading a song really good, and I have to come after him, then that means that I've got to do my very best. So then I do a screaming piece

or something, and then John does a screaming piece after that, and then he has to stop me. That's precisely what was happening during our concert at Madison Square Garden. Many of our close friends noticed we were really sparking off each other."

John interjects with his own interpretation: "I mean, I got up from the piano in one number, and Jeezus, it was like following an act or something. Phew, it was just the same as competing in the Olympics when you've really got to box your best. It was really weird."

Suddenly Lennon stops talking, leans over, and with a teasing growl, roars into Yoko's right ear, "Go on, luv, tell him how I influenced yer."

She laughs nervously, tries to ignore his request. "The thing is..." But she can't complete the sentence as she breaks up in a fit of laughter.

"Alright," she concedes.

"That was the question, remember," says John in an effort to redirect her train of thought.

"OK then, I'll answer it. It's obvious, I think, that these days my songs are all rock..."

"And what were they before?" intrudes Lennon, temporarily taking over the role of interviewer.

"Well, I was mainly doing my voice experiments. You know, screaming and all that, but then I got very interested in the rock beat, because it is like the heartbeat. It's very basic and a very healthy thing. Most music, other than rock, went away from that healthy direction and into perversion. That's the way I feel about it."

John: "Just virtuosity."

Yoko: "Actually, I think the most obvious change has been on my side, which is that my musical style changed. Whereas John is virtually sticking to what he's always done. But I adopted rock."

Yoko's last four words prompt Lennon to enthuse "Yeah... yeah" prior to proudly pointing out to his wife: "But I did that Cambridge thing with you. Now wasn't that an adaptation?"

Yoko, unperturbed: "Rock is a whole new field for me and I get inspired so much that I find that now a lot of songs are coming out of me. Also, I think I was getting to a point where I didn't have too much competition. John was always with boys who were working together and therefore in direct competition. That was his situation. I was far more isolated."

She pauses and Lennon takes over the conversation: "It just came to me – for the two of us it was a question of mutual adjustment, with all the joys and pleasures of marriage on an artistic and musical level. However, it's not just the music, or our lifestyle, or where we're living. The whole change is happening in the space between us.

"Yoko coined a phrase. 'Rock Square'... and I was definitely in that box. I would never have admitted it while it was happening, but nevertheless, it was going on. What happens is that you suddenly become exactly what you didn't like about other forms of music, be it jazz or classical or whatever, and then you have to admit that it should really be like this or that. Now, when someone comes along and says 'no', it can be whatever you want it to be. That's a very big change to go through. But after you experience it, then you loosen. You feel free to do whatever you want."

The facts behind Lennon's candour reveal that at the dizziest heights of Beatlemania he lost contact with reality. "That happened many times, but then a lot of other people go the same way. Just being, quote, 'A Star', or whatever it was that happened, made it a little more unreal. So perhaps the periods lasted just a little bit longer.

"Look, a working guy will get lost for a weekend, get pissed, and forget who he is or dream that he's so-and-so in his car. Well, it was just the same with us. But instead of getting blotto for a weekend, we got blotto for two months, trying to forget whatever it is that everybody tries to forget all the time. Instead of worrying about who is gonna pay the milkman, we worried who was gonna pay whatever it was we'd gone out and spent.

"I think that around the time of *Help!* I began to wonder what the hell was happening, because things were definitely starting to get very weird by then. But then, I can only judge it by *A Hard Day's Night*. At that time, we still had one foot in the backyard."

With Marc Bolan today attempting to Xerox the kind of hysteria amongst Britannia's children that John, Paul, George and Ringo patented a generation earlier, I further enquire if Lennon bleeds in sympathy for today's teenyboppers.

"I dunno if I feel sorry for these people or not. But I do think about it. The first thing that strikes me is the things these stars say in the musical papers changes so often. Yer know what I mean: like when they keep on saying, 'We're the greatest.' I mean, when I read about Dave Bowie bitchin' with Marc Bolan, who is bitchin' with Fred Astaire... Actually, it's a bit of a laugh when you're not doing it yourself.

"I imagine it's all down to the fact of the bigger you become, the more insecure you feel. I'd like to think that people could learn from the mistakes others have made. But they don't. It's like you can't tell anybody

◀ Lennon kisses the cheek of Yoko Ono, at their Bank Street home in Greenwich Village

▲ Lennon explains a point during a recording session in New York City, 1972

nothing, ever. I can't learn myself from other people's mistakes. There's nobody I can think of, where he did that, and that's where he goofed. You can sing about it, because that's your own experience, but you can't expect anyone to think along the lines, 'Oh, so they did that and that happened, so we won't do that.' You can't do it. It never works."

Self-indulgent is a put-down constantly aimed at John Lennon, and his reply to such criticism is explicit.

"When people say I'm self-indulgent, it's only because I'm not doing what they want me to do. Simply because they're still hung up on my past. If you've noticed, when they say such things, they don't usually refer to the music. Actually, I got it down the other day. People talk about not what you do, but how you do it, which is like discussing how you dress or if your hair is long or short. They can say what they want, but the artist knows best, anyway. And when you work at such an energy level, like Yoko and me, then you're doomed to be heavily criticised."

The cigarettes have run out, so has the tape, and we've talked ourselves dry. I have a plane to catch at noon and the Lennons have a live TV show to rehearse. New York City   New York City... *Que pasa*, New York. *Que pasa*, New York. *Que pasa*, John and Yoko? **NME**

The Beatles // Bob Marley and the Wailers
Bruce Springsteen // Captain Beefheart // David Bowie
Eagles // Gram Parsons // Grateful Dead
Led Zeppelin // Pink Floyd // The Rolling Stones

1973

West Coast soft rockers the Eagles claim the secret's in the songwriting, while country rock renegade Gram Parsons meets his end in a California hotel room, aged just 27. Jamaica's Bob Marley and the Wailers are ready to take on the world, and the splendidly eccentric Captain Beefheart contemplates his commercial breakthrough.

While Led Zeppelin and the Rolling Stones both release landmark albums, the uncomfortable responsibility as "the future of rock and roll" had been laid at the door of New Jersey's own Bruce Springsteen. He insists he's not the new Dylan, it's just record company hype – "Every year somethin' comes along."

"Songs are so important"

LA's EAGLES are in London, making album two. They talk about how they all backed Linda Ronstadt at one time or another, a key player in their eventual coming together, and their disdain for bands having to "rely on weird clothes, makeup and stuff" to get their message across.

IT'S A RARE TRIP. You hear a band and turn on to their music straight off. Warm and refreshing or hard-driving, straight-down-the-line rock'n'roll. The music's biting hard and filters into the bloodstream.

First time I heard the Eagles it was like that. I popped their album on the turntable, listened to a couple of bars and was totally immersed in the songs. And it was the songs that caught me before their own unique, relaxed country-rock style brought a new awareness. The songs on the debut album are so strong, each one played and recorded with a feeling of love and care.

In the States, the Eagles are home and dry, their album's been a constant seller since it was released around the middle of last year and in the singles market it's had good mileage. Two Top 10 singles and another, "Peaceful Easy Feeling", just working its way into the Top 20.

Yet here they don't mean a light. The name got around to a few people, the buzz went through the music business when their first album was released, but there was little action.

But by the time they've played two concerts here next month at the Royal Festival Hall, London, and the Hard Rock in Manchester, there'll be enough of a buzz for their name to stick.

At the moment they're in Britain, living in a series of service flats just off the Kings Road while they record their second album at Island Studios.

The Eagles are LA people; it was the catalyst that drew them together. Musically, they ended up there after their own areas had run out of experiences; it's a dragnet that allowed some of the finest American musicians to get together and bounce off one another.

New York gave out driving rock'n'roll and its current bizarre side effects, while in the sunshine, LA took away the tensions and gave us relaxed country-flavoured rock.

Linda Ronstadt brought the Eagles together. All the band had worked backing her at one time or another.

Drummer/vocalist Don Henley – who went to California from Texas with his band Shiloh, which included Al Perkins, now with Manassas – and vocalist/slide guitarist Glenn Frey worked with Linda two years ago. They talked about putting a band together and met bass player Randy Meisner, who was in the original Poco when he filled in for Linda's bass player, who couldn't make a gig in San Francisco.

Don and Glenn stayed with Linda a while, dreaming of getting a band together. Randy split Poco and joined up with Rick Nelson's Stone Canyon Band, a gig that made him quit music for eight months until the Eagles came along.

Circumstance threw the three of them together, they decided on forming a group, and at just the right time Bernie Leadon split from The Flying Burrito Brothers.

"We all knew each other simply because we'd all been playing in the LA music scene," said Glenn Frey. "There must be a pool of about 50 musicians in LA that gravitate between the pure bluegrass music and country pop rock. There's all kinds of people in LA that play music and we got to know one another's music through that scene.

"All of us had played with Linda as part of her band at one time or another. Bernie had played with her three and a half years ago before he joined the Burrito Brothers. Don and I were playing with her when we got together with Randy, and when we heard Bernie was leaving the Burritos we called him up and asked him to have a play with us."

Randy: "It was real nice the way the band came together. It was like things just had to happen."

Glenn: "Putting a band together is real easy, because we were all doing othe=r gigs and meeting people. But finding a band with all the right people who have the ability to shine is another matter. A real band is always growing together and getting each other to play better."

▶ The Eagles photographed in London in 1973.
Left to right, Randy Meisner, Bernie Leadon, Glenn Frey and Don Henley

◀ The Eagles on stage during their European tour, appearing on the *Pop Gala* TV show from Voorburg, Netherlands. March 10, 1973

The Eagles have something really positive in their songs and in their sound, which is tight four-voice harmonies and constructive arrangements. Also, with four singers there are four lead voices, which add a whole new edge to their music. But it is the song consciousness, as Glenn puts it, that is so important with the band. That's why from the first album they were able to get three hit singles out of 10 songs.

"It wasn't a planned move that we would record an album full of singles. But we did set out to put 10 good songs on every album instead of having fillers, where one song is the single because it's so obviously a better song than any other on the album.

"Surely you get song conscious," added Glenn. "In LA, you cannot help but be influenced and affected on some level by the people you meet, like Jackson Browne. The people in The Byrds and Buffalo Springfield above all else were good songwriters.

"Songs are so important. It's like loud rock'n'roll has been done at its best; anything else is a poor relation. It's like long guitar solos, when I hear them, are a poor excuse compared to the things that have gone down before from Clapton and Hendrix.

"But then it's like, are people trying to get better at writing songs, or are they just copping a trip? All musicians tend to confine what they see going on to their own music style. The ultimate in theatre for me was watching Neil Young walk on stage at Carnegie Hall in work boots and denims and the audience just coming to a complete hush. Neil can make that magic work every night. To me that's the get off; that's not just getting real crazy."

Don: "Don't think we're opposed to theatrics, but when you can't play and have to rely on weird clothes, makeup and stuff then that's not valid to me. If you're a good musician, wear what you like, but it seems at the moment there's an awful lot of bands who need all the freakiness to get by.

"It seems that for bands like Alice Cooper and The Sweet the music is secondary to the theatre trip. They try to bash everybody with the body first. For us the music comes first."

"Alice can do what he likes," says Randy, "but don't he step on baby chickens? Is that rock'n'roll?"

Don: "No, man, that's burlesque."

It sounds like sour grapes. In fact that couldn't be further from the truth. There's no malice as they talk about other bands. They can't figure it, but then maybe the other bands can't figure them.

The new album, unlike the first, has a concept running through it. The thread that ties the songs together being an outlaw gang in the Old West – the Doolin-Dalton Gang who cleaned up around Kansas in the 1890s. It draws parallels between outlaws and rock'n'rollers. Both basically are the same is the conclusion. Both living outside the laws of normality. The basic story is that of an outlaw's life told in flashbacks. His discovery of a gun (or guitar) in a shop window, becoming a man, getting drunk for the first time, fighting over an unfaithful woman, making easy money and the final big job (or album), before the final burning. Nothing left.

But the Eagles have a lot left to do before the final job. Looking much like an outlaw himself and prime for a movie part, Glenn Frey says they'll be working a lot yet. "While the going's easy," he says, "you can't stop." **MM**

▼ Don Henley photographed during an interview in London in 1973

Beatles seen in LA

MARCH 17

Voorman to replace Paul?

RUMOURS FLASHED THROUGH Los Angeles this week that three of The Beatles have again teamed up for recording purposes. John Lennon, Ringo Starr and George Harrison are all in Los Angeles with Klaus Voorman, the bassist rumoured to replace Paul McCartney after his departure from the group. Rumours that the four were trying to get together were circulating in New York six months ago, though no visible move has been made until now. *MM*

A love of the blues

MARCH 8

RIP, the Dead's Pigpen.

RON "PIGPEN" MCKERNAN, organist and vocalist with the Grateful Dead, died last week at his San Francisco home. He was 27.

Pigpen had been hospitalised for the last six months, but was allowed home a few days ago. Cause of death was reported to be cirrhosis of the liver, but this has not yet been confirmed. Pigpen – nicknamed after the character in the *Peanuts* strip – inherited a love of the blues piano as a child.

Later he became friendly with Jerry Garcia, then a solo artist, and made his first public appearance at a San Francisco folk club singing blues and playing harmonica backed by Garcia on guitar. He was a founder member of The Warlocks, the San Franciscan band which became the Grateful Dead in 1966.

His organ-playing was an integral part of the Dead's sound. Recently he had been unable to play such an important part in the band's live concerts, missing several gigs through bad health. *MM*

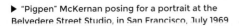 "Pigpen" McKernan posing for a portrait at the Belvedere Street Studio, in San Francisco, July 1969

"In Jamaica, you use your machete or your gun"

"If your record sells good," says BOB MARLEY of his experiences in the Jamaican music business, "the producer pretends he's gone to Nassau." Now he and THE WAILERS have taken control of their affairs and are ready for the world. "I get high," he says, "but I don't like sitting around."

BOB MARLEY, SLIGHTLY BUILT and quiet to the point of diffidence, is a leader. He's the master of reggae, the man who's about to give it that big shove out of its normal cultural confinement and into the rest of the world. The consequences of this action may be drastic for the health of the music. It could be the making of reggae, or could sap its vitality beyond repair. But that won't affect Marley, because for the past seven years he's been making the best music to be heard in Jamaica, and his potential is limitless.

He and his group, The Wailers, have an album called *Catch A Fire* out here next week, on Island's Blue Mountain label. It seems to

◄ Bob Marley photographed at the London offices of Island records

me that this may be the most important reggae record ever made – it's equivalent of Sly's *Dance To The Music* or Marvin Gaye's *What's Going On*.

It has that kind of potential: revitalising the style from which it springs, and introducing it to an entirely new audience. A few years will need to have passed before we'll know for sure, but Marley may even be a genius.

Like many great musicians, he's a different man inside the recording studio. The shyness is stripped away, and he becomes totally as one with the music, controlling it and swaying in sympathy with the extraordinary rhythm patterns he draws from his bassist, Aston "Family Man" Barrett, and his drummer, Family Man's brother Carlton.

Marley's musical assurance comes from a considerable depth of experience. At 28, he's been burned and hassled as badly as most of his Jamaican contemporaries, but unlike a lot of them he's putting the knowledge he's gained to good use.

He can see why and how he got burned, and he's going to make sure it doesn't happen again. What's happened to him already, though, gives him just as much right to sing the blues as Robert Johnson ever had.

He was born in Kingston, Jamaica, the son of a white British Army captain from Liverpool – "I only remember seeing him twice, when I was small" – and a black Jamaican who wrote spirituals and sang in the local Apostolic Church.

Unlike some people with mixed parentage, who violently take one side or another, it's given him an unusually open view of race: "I don't really check people's colour," he says.

Bob sang in church too, but he didn't care for it. "I preferred dancing music. I listened to Ricky Nelson, Elvis, Fats Domino... that kind of thing was popular with Jamaican kids in the '50s. The only English-speaking radio station we heard was from Miami, but we got a lot of Latin stations, mostly from Cuba, before and after Castro."

He began to learn welding as a trade. "But I loved to sing, so I thought I might as well take the chance. Welding was too hard! So I went down to Leslie Kong at Beverley's Records in '64, and made a record on a single-track machine. Jimmy Cliff took me there – he was Beverley's number-one man."

▲ London, 1973: Bob Marley and the Wailers (left to right) Peter Tosh, Aston Barrett, Bob Marley, Earl Lindo, Carlton Barrett and Bunny Wailer.

▶ Bob Marley and the Wailers on the influential BBC TV music show *The Old Grey Whistle Test* in 1973

"Johnny Nash isn't really our idol. That's Otis or Brown or Pickett"

The record was called "One Cup Of Coffee", and the world ignored it. But Marley, undaunted, went back to the woodshed. "My greatest influence at the time was The Drifters – 'Magic Moment', 'Please Stay', those things. So I figured I should get a group together."

He assembled four other kids: Peter Tosh (vocals, piano, organ, guitar) and Bunny Wailer (vocals, congas, congos), who're still with him today, plus a boy named Junior and a girl, Beverley Kelso. He wrote a song called "Simmer Down". They rehearsed it, and went to see producer Coxsone Dodd, who liked and recorded it, putting it out on his Coxsone label.

"It went off like a bullet," says Bob. "But they didn't tell me how much to sell... that's supposed to be the private business of the producer. I don't remember how much I was paid for 'Simmer Down',

because when they give you money, they don't tell you what it's for.

"After we left Coxsone in '69, we got no more royalties – and the songs we did for him are selling ever since. We made 30 or 40 records for him, and most of them sold good."

Among them was the brilliant "Put It On", a shimmering ska classic which surfaced in Britain on Island in 1966, and the gorgeous "Sunday Morning" (on a par with the best of Curtis Mayfield), the B-side to "Love Won't Be Mine" in the same year. If you look hard, you can probably still find them on the secondhand stalls – and if you do, you'll be congratulating yourself for ever.

"We weren't making enough money to share between five, so two of the group left. Junior went to live in America, and Beverley... well, she was kinda slow-like. She didn't have good timing."

▲ Bob Marley live in concert with the Wailers

After they left Coxsone Dodd, Bob and his mother left Jamaica for a while.

"It was hard in Kingston, so we went to live in America, in Wilmington, Delaware. I rehearsed by myself in our basement, where it was nice and quiet, but after a few months I went back to Jamaica, and I thought I might as well continue with The Wailers."

He got Peter and Bunny back together, and they decided to form their own record label. "That's a big move, in Jamaica. Prince Buster was the first to start the revolution by leaving the producers and doing it himself. Then myself, then Lee Perry... and you can't count the rest.

"It's better to know for yourself if your record is a flop than have someone else tell you. And if your record sells good, the producer pretends he's gone to Nassau when you come by the office. In Jamaica, you're expected to use your knife, or your machete, or your gun."

That first label was called Wailin' Soul, but it got off to a bad start when Bunny was jailed for almost a year on a ganja rap – and those who've seen The Harder They Come may understand the Machiavellian implications of frame-up behind that. At that point around '68, American singer Johnny Nash and his manager, Danny Simms, came on the scene. They were looking for talent, saw Bob singing on Jamaican TV, and signed him up.

Bob recorded an album for their JAD label, but from it only one single – "Bend Down Low" – ever saw the light of day, in the States. However, they took Bob's song "Stir It Up", recorded already by The Wailers on Coxsone, and turned it into a worldwide smash for Nash, who also used other Marley songs ("Guava Jelly", "Belly Rub") on his I Can See Clearly Now album.

They even took Marley to Sweden for three months, to help write the music for a film starring Nash which has yet to be released, and over in England they got a single by him out on CBS – "Reggae On Broadway", with which he's far from satisfied because Nash had too much influence on the production.

"He's a hard worker, but he didn't know my music. I don't want to put him down, but reggae isn't really his bag. We knew of Johnny Nash in Jamaica before he arrived, but we didn't love him that much; we appreciated him singing the kind of music he does – he was the first US artist to do reggae – but he isn't really our idol. That's Otis or James Brown or Pickett, the people who work it more hard."

Going to Sweden did Bob's business no good: "When I came back, it was all mash [ruined]. I'm the only one who takes a real interest in it. Jamaica's a place where you sit around and get high. I'm not gonna do that; I get high, but I don't like sitting around too much."

So on his return, in 1970, he started a new label, Tuff Gong, and also a record shop, The Soul Shack on King Street in Kingston. The shop is mostly devoted to selling records by The Wailers and Rita & The Soulettes. Rita Marley is known as Bob's wife, but they aren't actually married – it was just an idea to get some publicity for one of her records. They stock the old Wailers records on Coxsone, their six 45s on Wailin' Soul, and the dozen or so they've released on Tuff Gong, including their biggest hit to date – the fantastic "Trenchtown Rock", which sold about 25,000 and was Jamaica's Number One for three weeks around Christmas 1971, and the recent mind-destroying "Satisfy My Soul (Jah Jah)".

The problem for a small label is getting airplay: "You have to be big friends with the radio disc jockeys, take them out and treat them like family. They make up the radio station charts, and people only buy what's in the charts." Bob is not unduly optimistic about the business side of the Jamaican music scene. "We've hurt the big guys by starting our own labels, because all they've got left is the studios and the pressing plants. But the business will only change when younger guys appear, who'll deal fairly with the artists. The older guys will never get better."

It was Island's Chris Blackwell who gave Bob the chance to use a lot of time and a fair amount of money to make the Catch A Fire album. Advances to Jamaican artists are unknown – but Blackwell saw the potential in Marley, and the two men tacitly decided to trust each other.

The result is the first example of Marley's music which hasn't been hampered by absurdly low budgets. The album has several quite long tracks, maybe the first extended reggae songs, but Bob says, "They're always like that in the studio, and then they get cut down to three minutes or something. Jamaica is a place where the musicians are restricted, going into the studio and just playing the same old thing because they're afraid that anything different might not sell.

"What we need here is people who're not concerned with holding the artists down. But I don't think it'll happen for a long time."

Make no mistake – Marley is potentially a giant figure. **MM**

An Inner Gravity

APRIL 13

The first reggae album to be marketed as a rock record.

The Wailers
Catch a Fire

THE PROBLEM: how to communicate the excitement of this album to people who are already prejudiced against what it represents? I'm taking for granted that most readers of this paper still believe that reggae is a crude form of musical expression, with a complete lack of creative potential, and I can understand that stance because there's been a lot of rubbish put about in the name of Jamaican music. But ever since last autumn, I've been waiting for this album more eagerly than for almost anything within memory, and I'd like to turn you on as well.

This is, for a start, the first reggae-rooted album to be packaged and marketed as if it were by a "name" white rock group; it has a tastefully conceived, expensively produced sleeve, and it's being promoted heavily, particularly in America, where West Indian music is now the object of much curiosity. In keeping with its image, the album's music gives evidence that Bob Marley, The Wailers' leader, is broadening his scope; you'll hear slide guitars and electric keyboards, both sometimes modified by synthesizer, and most of the tracks come in at around four minutes. I don't believe, though, that Marley has compromised the integrity of the music by dressing it up in this way. He retains that lopsided, falling-over-itself rhythm feel, and his songs, both words and music, are simple and direct. The core, in fact, is there, just as Sly Stone is still making blues music despite the trimmings. The album leans heavily on the playing of bassist Family Man and drummer Carlton Barrett, both of whom are utterly brilliant, constantly shifting and blending their rhythms with a natural-born sophistication. There's more than enough subtlety to feed the ears, and you can always, always dance to what they play. Unfortunately, the sleeves don't mention that the beautiful melodic guitar solos are played by Wayne Perkins from Muscle Shoals, and that the synthesizer work is done by Rabbit Bundrick. Keyboards are shared by Rabbit, Marley and Winston Riley.

Marley sings most of the lead, and he's the equal of any black American. His tone is light and airy but has an inner gravity and his phrasing is endlessly fascinating. The back-up chorales are endlessly fascinating: on this new version of "Stir It Up" they sound like soul Beach Boys (to borrow Nick Jones' old phrase), while the care that went into the spiritual-like arrangement of "No More Trouble" is self-evident. Singers Bunny Wailer and Peter Tosh are never stooges: like the Pips with Gladys Knight, they participate fully in the emotional content of each song.

And what songs. "Stir It Up" is slowed right down until it becomes a melting, sensual love song, its synthesizer lines following like cream around Marley's cool, pliable lead. "Slave Driver" is mournful and evocative. "Concrete Jungle" has guitars and "Superstition"-like electric piano poured around it. "Kinky Reggae" is hilariously funny. McIntosh, too, provides one of the best songs, "400 Years", which like much of the album's content refers to the plight of Kingston's ghetto people. In fact, nothing here is less than exceptional and Marley is helped by injecting frequent variations of pace, which should ensure that charges of monotony are redundant. And if you're not moved by "Stir It Up", you must be made of stone. A fabulous and important album. *MM*

"I get happier all the time"

CAPTAIN BEEFHEART wrote his new album in two hours, driving between Harvard and Yale. Could *Clear Spot* finally be his commercial breakthrough? "It's my love album," he confides. "It's for all women." But what will Beefheart say to George Best?

WHEN IN ALL SERIOUSNESS, Captain Beefheart describes Muhammad Ali as his favourite percussionist and talks of him being "probably one of the greatest living musicians", he isn't referring to some previously unpublicised facet of the man's life. This is your Captain speaking specifically about Ali's pugilistic artistry in the ring. But then, the Beefheart view of the world has always differed somewhat from that of us mere mortals – because he then goes on to add the name of Vincent Van Gogh to his personal Hall Of Fame. He explains this bizarre coupling thus: "Everything these gentlemen ever did was done with a great flair for rhythm. You see, one doesn't really have to play an instrument to be a musician... just a musical grace in the creative use of timing and rhythm. And this is a quality that both these men possess."

In Britain it was Mick Jagger, who distributed hundreds of albums, seeking those who would listen, and John Peel, via his innovative *Perfumed Garden* programme on Radio London, who first exposed the music of Captain Beefheart and his Magic Band to impressionable ears.

► Don Van Vliet, aka
Captain Beefheart, poses
for portrait circa 1973 in
Eureka, California

Indeed, amid the heady aroma of incense and dope and the wall-to-wall jangle of beads and bells, the *Safe As Milk* sound was the only new positive energy not transmitting from Pepperland that made sense and made you want to dance in the psychedelic smashed summit of '67. And that, as they say, is owning up.

Yet in spite of Beefheart's stature as the underground cult hero of Antonioni's "Swingin' London" (etc.) and the endorsement of just about anyone whom word was worthy of respect, the band seemed unable to get off and running stateside. Along with Wild Man Fischer, the GTOs and Alice Cooper, the talent of the amiable Captain was misinterpreted as being nothing more than yet another musical clown in Uncle Frank Zappa's nasty little freak show.

When I last paid my respects to the good Captain – almost a year to the day – he impressed upon me: "I've had my fun... now I'm going to make myself far more accessible to the public."

Not that Beefheart intentionally schemed to aim his music over the heads of his audience. But, like most innovators – and make no mistake about it, Beefheart is an innovator – public acceptance can take an awful long time a-coming: "Some people think I'm surreal. Others that I'm a dadaist. Well, I think not. My art is abstract and therefor people have just got to realise that I'm just who I am."

Finally, however, the American public may be coming around to the Captain's way. "They're beginning to dig me at last," he says with a bellow, "but it sure is late for them. They've always been much more hip in Europe. Over here, they still have to rely on their mothers to tell 'em what to like." And, for once, he wasn't talking about Zappa.

Looking back over the last 12 months, he lets out another laugh and continues: "With the *Clear Spot* album, I went completely in reverse, didn't I? Funnily enough, I don't know why I did it." He quickly adds: "Though, of course, I'm glad I did. As everyone knows, I've never been influenced by what record-company people term 'the market'.

"*Clear Spot* wasn't supposed to be a commercial endeavour on my part, though people say it was. My opinion is that anything that sells is commercial. And the only thing commercial about *Clear Spot* is that it's selling more than any of the others."

Beefheart, in fact, is willing to accept a large responsibility for his years of hardship. The fact is, annual visits to Europe aside, the Captain has never hit the road in the States. Only now is he beginning to pack his bags for a coast-to-coast tour of his homeland.

"Sure, we've played a few gigs in this country," he explains. "But we haven't undertaken a tour like this before now simply because I didn't think that anyone really wanted to see us.

"In Europe, audiences knew what to expect when we don't know what to expect because they hadn't heard us. Thankfully, once we've played for them, they seem to enjoy it and embrace the group."

Clear Spot – which the composer affectionately refers to as "my love album", but didn't think it was an appropriate title to have embossed on the clear PVC sleeve – has proved to be the artistic clincher in terms of mass Beefheart acceptance. "In one sentence, what do you most like about *Clear Spot*?" the Captain suddenly springs on me.

It's full of total energy and happiness, I reply off the top of my head.

"You said the magic words, Roy," the maestro says with a laugh. "You see, I'm a lot happier these days, 'cos I've been married to my wife Jan for three years and I just get happier and happier all the time. And it's because of this that my music has gotten even more spontaneous.

"Did you know?" his voice takes on a tone of confidence, "that I wrote all the material for *Clear Spot* in just two and a half hours." He turns and calls out to Jan, who's in another room. "I know it was when we were driving between two college dates, but can you remember where I wrote *Clear Spot*?" There's no reply. "Jan," he bellows. "Where did I write *Clear Spot*?" "Between Harvard and Yale," answers a voice.

"Of course, now I remember. We were driving to Yale in the station wagon when I wrote the songs. So, as you can see, it's a pretty spontaneous little album, perhaps even more than any of the others.

"Like just about everything I do – writing, painting or making music – I like things to be spontaneous. So when I feel that it's time for me to do a new album I always put the material together as quickly as possible, and get it in the stores so as it's reflective of what I'm doing at that point in my career.

"At the moment, I'm putting a new album together – trouble is, I've got at least 50 things I would like to use, but there's just no way I can fit them on one album. I guess I just don't get to do enough albums. When I get inspired I tend to work very quickly, and when I get into the studio I'm one of the least expensive acts to record. So I guess that's some kind of compensation."

You may well ask from what fount of knowledge the amazing Captain derives such inspiration. I ask and I am informed: "Animals. I think I've gotten all my inspiration from watching animals, though I have to admit that the inspiration for *Clear Spot* came from women. I suppose you could say that album is really for all women.

"I thought that women were getting neglected," he elaborates. "I guess up until that album I'd been kinda selfish. You have to understand that before I got married I didn't realise I wasn't the complete artist I thought I was.

"I never was with women." He corrects himself: "I mean, I was with women, but there was never that close relationship, and that makes the big difference. For a man needs a friend to run through life with him. Indeed, there are times when I wonder what I was doing before... you've heard all that stuff that I did."

He laughs and concludes: "What I'm doing now is much nicer."

"I've now realised that the real test of an artist is to make his work accessible to everyone, and that's what I'm now attempting to do. And because of this, I think my band will help a lot of people, and if I make some money, a lot of animals.

"I want to open up an animal park where no one can get in, and let the animals get on with it all by themselves. I think it would be a terrible world if kids grew up without ever seeing an animal in its natural environment."

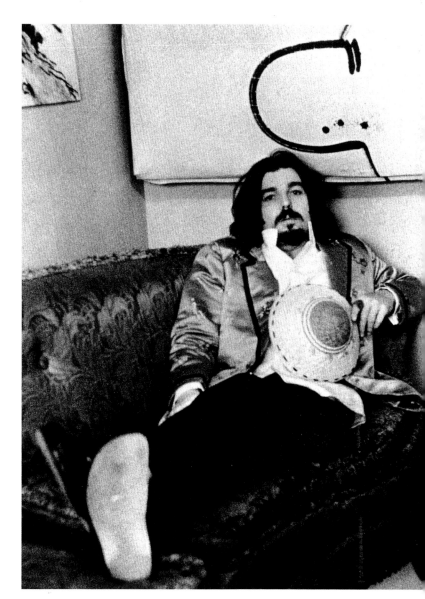

◀ An atmospheric close-up of Captain Beefheart performing live on stage in 1973

▲ The enigmatic musician, singer-songwriter, experimental composer, artist and poet known as Captain Beefheart, California 1973

It's an exacting task to keep up with the Captain. He's prone to redirect his conversation without prior warning. "I'm amused by this new Flash Gordon makeup cult that's suddenly sprung up. I did that over seven years ago in London, when I appeared at the Middle Earth Club wearing blue lipstick and red nail polish."

Well, we all have skeletons in our closets.

"Seems that I've always been ahead of the times," he muses, "but it's only now that the public and I are catching up with each other. But I'm glad I got out of that thing when I did. Today, I'm being realistic in my role as a human being without having to contend with all that bullshit."

As with most conversations with the Captain, he offers an old Beefism: "Remember, it's not worth getting into the bullshit to find out what the bull ate." Ah, but what about the big eyed beans from Venus? **NME**

Led Zeppelin
Houses of the Holy

MARCH 28

WHEN ZEPPELIN ARE roaring on stage, there is hardly another band in the world to beat them. Jimmy Page is one of the all-time greats of rock guitar, the Bonham-Jones rhythm section is a byword for power and invincible drive, while Robert Plant is a singer whose sheer presence and involvement in a song seems larger than life.

Thus it grieves me very much when they allow their own tremendously high standards to slip, when the vital spark that made their first albums timeless seems to flicker, uncertainly. It was with no small pleasure that I approached their fifth album. The unusual dreamlike cover design seemed to indicate that much fresh thinking was afoot and surprises were in store. But after the initial drive of "The Song Remains The Same", when it seemed Zeppelin were about to lift off with renewed brilliance, a malaise began to creep in, reaching a nadir in the sadly indulgent "D'yer Mak'er", a cool pop tune which is not worthy of them. It is intended as a fun track, not intended to be rated overseriously, but after some frankly dull material like "The Rain Song", and listless James Brown-style riffs like "The Crunge", the joke wears thin. The overall effect is that they seem afraid to play what they do best, which is the blues, gut rock. Even Robert's tremendously distinctive voice is twisted and bent by studio techniques, and although they lay back on the beat in firm fashion on "The Ocean", there is not one tune, with the exception of "Song Remains The Same", that has any buzz of excitement.

As they have taken a year to produce this, it would perhaps be a better idea if they were rushed into a studio, told to keep the costs down and get the album out in a week, or else! Nobody expects Zep to be tied to "Communication Breakdown" forever, and they must be free to progress. But the lack of firm direction is all too apparent. The writing seems to be a compromise between more spaced-out ideas and heavy riffs without ever getting to grips with either. Having gone so high, it's the hardest job in the world to stay on top. Perhaps a cool appraisal of this album will spur them on to greater efforts. They have it in their power to stun us all. **MM**

"Each track is different"

AUGUST 31

The Stones' 11th album analysed.

The Rolling Stones *Goats Head Soup*

"**SILVER TRAIN**" is a fast rocker, could be described as typical Rolling Stones, and said Mick: "It's the only one like it on the album." It featured some nice slide guitar by Mick Taylor, with a powerful bassline from Bill Wyman, and chugging rhythm guitars.

"Winter" followed, a pretty song, with overtones of a Jimi Hendrix-style ballad. And here Mick sings with great emotion and power. Mick also added rhythm guitar and there is much clunking piano.

"Hide Your Love" is a Stones boogie with much handclapping and boogie piano. Who was on the piano? "Me."

"Can You Hear The Music" is another rocker, with much phrasing on the organ, and the Stones sounding a bit like The Band in a Dylanish groove. Here Charlie Watts excelled himself with that flat, laid-back sound. Flute makes a surprise appearance – highly dramatic.

"Dancing With Mr D" is a highly evil rocker and my favourite track on the album. Loosely termed a boogie rocker with lots of noise and aggro. "Dance!" yells Mick in a kind of demoniac exhortation.

"100 Years" has Mick singing solo, once again in Dylanish mood (and here I am open to correction), with saucy tempo changes of a kind we are not accustomed to hearing from the Stones. Again the lead guitar shows signs of a Hendrix influence, and as the piece returns to its original tempo, takes on a country-soul-blues mood that cues in a noisy, raucous climax.

"Coming Down Again" has Nicky Hopkins on piano, and is a very funky, slow blues.

"Heartbreaker" has a hook line that as far as I can recall without having a copy of the album at my elbow went something like this: "Doo, doo, doo, doo, doo", to which my response was "yeah," and "rock on". The brass helped a lot here.

"Angie" is the single, with another chance for Jagger to shine as a vocalist of some stature, a fact which sometimes gets lost amid the general ballyhoo. Charlie clips beats off his hi-hat, and there is more good piano beating. Who was Angie? Mick affected deafness.

"Each track is different," he said by way of explanation, "and there was not a lot of overdubbing. The flute and stuff was added afterwards."

One of the tracks Mick didn't play me was the controversial "Starfucker", with its lyrics which, if included on the album, would guarantee it being banned on most radio stations. "Starfucker" has such lines as: "If ever I get back to fun city, girl, I'm gonna make you scream all night/Honey, honey, call me on the telephone/I know you're moving out to Hollywood with your can of tasty foam". It sounds damn rude to me. What always amazes me about the Stones is that they seem such nice lads in conversation, and yet all hell breaks loose around them – enough to keep papers in endless headlines. **MM**

◀ Gram Parsons wearing a Gram Parsons and the Fallen Angels T-shirt at a party in the park in Los Angeles, June 1973

"I don't know what country rock is"

**"Contemporary country artist" GRAM PARSONS
on the Stones, The Flying Burrito Brothers and why
he had to leave The Byrds.**

NOWADAYS IT'S THE done thing for your heavy friends to drop by the studio and lay down some choice licks on your album for kicks and maybe expenses. And when those friends are pianist Glen D Hardin, drummer Ronnie Tutt and that much-emulated guitar hero James Burton – the mainstays of paunchy Presley's back-up band – then you're really well in. Well, they were all there when Gram Parsons decided to cut his long overdue solo album.

"Country music is sincere in the same way as R&B and BB King"

And Lord knows, it's not that these cats need the money.

"They can command any fee they want," says Parsons. "The fact is, they were really keen to do the album, and beyond that, a lotta times they came along for free."

What Parsons doesn't say, but you can read between the lines, is that these musicians needed an alternative to churning out "Lord, You Gave Me A Mountain", "My Way" and hurried facsimiles of the Hillbilly Cats past glories amidst the Las Vegas facade. "Actually... Glen, Ronnie and James are pals from a long way back," drawls the mellow country gentleman, "so I guess it was relatively easy for me to get them down to my sessions."

Without any trace of egotism, Parsons continues: "You gotta understand that cutting this album was entirely different from playing on some plastic group's record. Now that may not sound like a lot to you, but for these guys it was incredible."

And so are some of the recorded results. It's certainly true that Gram Parsons has garnered a fine reputation since the mid-'60s, when he hauled his patched-denim ass out of the East and settled in LA to re-pioneer the musical heritage of the Old West. Parsons was the man who instigated the much-abused cosmic-cowboy movement with The International Submarine Band, got The Byrds to record their *Sweetheart Of The Rodeo* masterpiece, and helped form the sun-kissed Flying Burrito Brothers.

So even LA's hordes of paranoid poseurs reacted with almost unprecedented enthusiasm to the news that Gram Parsons was finally taking a band out on the one-night ulcer trail. Even the jaded ladies of the canyons were far more interested in getting into the group than actually getting into the group. And there's a subtle difference.

There he was going out on the road, resplendent in his Mr Nudie "dude ranch Wild West" suit, a dashing, elegant figure. But even a good ole kicker like Gram Parsons has to contend with avoiding images such as being called a country rocker.

As laid-back as a field of corn having been thoroughly worked over by a bulldozer, Parsons reclines in the back of his Greyhound touring bus, parked out front of his rustic Coldwater Canyon ranch-style house, and softly mumbles: "Man, I still don't know what country rock is!"

He gazes at this beer can, takes a throat full, and gurgles: "I would say I'm a contemporary country music artist with an electric rock'n'roll band."

Again he pauses, nods and concludes: "Yep... I guess that's exactly what I am."

Though to a large extent responsible for the spate of cosmic-cowboy bands that have sprung up almost as regularly as spaghetti Westerns, Parsons' opinion is less than favourable towards such outfits.

"Sure, they're fun to watch," he concedes, "but in no ways are they country bands. Most of them are just San Francisco drinking bands as opposed to the regular San Francisco acid bands. The only guy among that lot who has any taste is Jerry Garcia, but apart from what he does, most of the music that these bands call country rock just doesn't turn me on."

Although country music is the largest single market in America, there's still this mis-conception held by the heavy-metal kids that country folk are nothing but rednecks, beer drinkers and blue-rinsed blonde honky-tonk queens. And country types reckon their detractors are just decadent, long-haired hippies. In short: the Easy Rider is still in search of America. To try to rectify these injustices, Gram Parsons joined The Byrds and persuaded Roger McGuinn to record *Sweetheart Of The Rodeo*.

"When I first joined The Byrds I was quite pleased with the result, simply because it had been so damn hard for me to get a real country thing going," Parsons recollects. "But the more I played with The Byrds, the more I wished I could get them to do real country songs like 'That's All It Took' instead of some of their more familiar songs, which I felt were a waste of time. At this point, we were working to really big audiences but weren't getting the response we could have gotten had we pursued the direction of the *Rodeo* album."

Though there were no major clashes over musical policy, Parsons was to split from The Byrds on a matter of principle – he refused to perform before segregated audiences in South Africa.

He tells me: "I was raised in the South by some wonderful black people and what common sense I have I owe to them. Listen, man," and for once his voice rises above its mellow monotone, "I couldn't play before segregated audience. That's something no person should ever do."

The subject gets his adrenalin working overtime, and he cites a number of cases illustrating the evils of apartheid. He spits: "I think the South African government are nothing but a bunch of skunks and really behind the rest of the civilised world."

Calming himself, he takes a retrospective look at his days as a Flying Burrito Brother.

"I loved the Burritos," he drawls, "but I got tired of it all after a while. Again, it was a question of trying to get the right kind of people to form a real country band. I can remember some really inspired moments when we recorded *Gilded Palace Of Sin*, but soon after that everything just bored me. If you really wanna know, I was going to leave when Chris Etheridge left, but I stayed on to front the band until they found a suitable replacement. The trouble was they took so long that finally I had to wish them all the best and quit."

This was to bring Parsons back to Britain and to re-establish his friendship with Mick Jagger and Keith Richards, who had dedicated "Wild Horses" to him. It was to be a fruitful collaboration, and it could be that his presence influenced the more country-esque cuts on *Exile On Main St.*

Parsons says: "I think it was a logical step for the Stones to get into country music, because they've always been well into the old blues since they first began. Whether it was subconscious or not, they were trying to get into an old country-blues type thing, which is part of the Rolling Stones sound.

"I suppose it was a coincidence that I happened to come along with The Byrds, and Mick and Keith liked a few of my songs, coupled to the fact that we gotta lotta kicks outta just sitting around playing together.

"By this time, I'd had it with LA, the Burritos and the rush. So I had to do a solo album, but at that time there was just no way to do it. I couldn't get the right musicians or a record company. So I called Keith and said that I wanted to come over to London and hang out, play some country music, because he wanted to produce me.

"Unfortunately, for a number of reasons, including Keith's prior commitments and the lack of suitable musicians in Britain, all I did was sing and pick with the Stones and sing on 'Lovin' Cup' and 'Sweet Virginia'."

Returning to LA, Parsons once again set about getting together his band The Fallen Angels. And his prize acquisition was singer Emmylou Harris.

"She's so important to this band," he insists. "You see, there aren't many country tenor singers around except for those straight session Nashville cats."

Parsons is confident that The Fallen Angels will succeed where others failed to establish a common denominator for both rock and country music fans.

"At the moment I'm still having trouble in figuring a lot of country folk out," he began, curiously. "I've found out that they're not prejudiced just as long as you come to their city and spend your money in their recording studios. I can remember when they were prejudiced no matter what."

Parsons believes his Fallen Angels will help people who've only listened to the likes of Doc Watson and Flatt & Scruggs to enjoy a more contemporary approach, while rock fans will then become exposed to artists like Waylon Jennings, Merle Haggard, George Jones and Tammy Wynette.

He sums up: "Today, people wanna hear about the dealer on the street, 'Superfly', and anything that goes against the accepted establishment, and because of this I think they wanna hear country music.

"Country music isn't bubblegum and it isn't geared to sell like bubblegum. It's sincere in the same way as R&B and BB King. Now, if that can appeal to younger people, I see no reason why country music can't have the same appeal." ***NME***

Collapsed in a motel

SEPTEMBER 19

RIP, Gram Parsons.

GRAM PARSONS, EX-MEMBER of The Byrds and co-founder of the Flying Burritos died in California last Wednesday (19) aged 27. He collapsed in a motel and was rushed to hospital in Yucca Valley but was found to be dead on arrival. An initial post-mortem failed to reveal the cause of death and further tests were being made. ***NME***

"It's a fight to keep your identity"

They're calling BRUCE SPRINGSTEEN the new Bob Dylan. As he explains, John Hammond connection or not, he's just trying to be himself. "I sit at home and write music," he says. "Nobody comes down and hypes me."

POOR BRUCE, HE SEEMS so lost lying here on the floor in his manager's office, a vague smile playing around his face as he picks slowly over his words. Bemusement chases amusement across the whole length of him, from the itchy scrub of beard that he's constantly fingering, along past the soiled shirt to the denim-scruff of his legs: a whole mind and body trying to come to terms with what's happening around it.

He wasn't like this last month when Bruce Springsteen and his band played at Max's in New York. They say Mrs Ted Kennedy

▶ Bruce Springsteen posing for a portrait at the Jersey Shore in his native New Jersey, August 1973

▶ Bruce Springsteen and the E Street Band. Left to right: Garry Tallent, Dave Sancious, Vini Lopez, Bruce Springsteen, Danny Federici, and Clarence Clemons). August 29, 1973

turned up to see him, to catch his playing on guitar and piano, his dramatic, intense presence, with the words rolling and spitting out… and those songs, stuffed and trussed with images that he slit open and spilled out. What was there to say afterwards?

"Interesting", heads nodded, "very interesting", but there was much puzzlement. He was hard to sum up. The band, particularly Clarence Clemons on sax, drove ferociously in the most relentless style, and he sounded at times like Van Morrison. Yet there remained this feeling of the poseur, not detrimental, but that an attitude was being struck; he was challenging but distant, and this was somehow unsettling. Later, one realised, Bruce Springsteen was truly a lone spirit.

He was born in Freehold, New Jersey, and since his schooldays he never did anything apart from play music: his only regular job was during summer vacation in high school, and that was as a gardener and odd-job man, tarring roofs and painting houses; he took the job to buy a guitar.

There was a college, of course – Ocean County Community, NJ, "studying draft evasion" – but it was unhappy. The students didn't like him: the psychiatrist there told him so. He recalls this, and the flash of amusement grows wider.

"I think it was my appearance. He thought I was disturbed, else I wouldn't have looked the way I did… which is pretty much the way I do now. But you gotta dig where it was at in '68; it wasn't cool to look like them. It was traumatic, and that's when I left. It seems funny now, but it was hard then."

And he throws his head back and laughs out loud. After that it was only music; the army didn't take him at his physical. Then it was a succession of bands, including a New Jersey group called Steel Mill, which lasted two years. When he was 18 he played at the Fillmore West and then did an audition tape for Fillmore Records, but there was little recognised success. Until, last May, he went to another audition: at Columbia Records, and before John Hammond.

Twelve years ago, Hammond signed Dylan, maybe the most momentous deal in the history of Columbia, and now in walks this kid, 22 years old with his curly hair rough and thick on top, just like it was, and the same look, not hippy but beatnik, and he's singing this composition, his own, called "It's Hard To Be A Saint In The City", and that, more than anything else, must have felt familiar.

So Springsteen was signed, and although it was undoubtedly done on his own merits, because who needs a facsimile, the publicity machine went to work, it gathered momentum as writers took heed and – suddenly! – here was a singer-songwriter making contemporaneous the Dylan of '65. Poor Bruce.

▲ Another shot of Springsteen enjoying time out in his old stomping ground of the Jersey Shore in August 1973

So Springsteen sits and ponders on the floor of this office: ramblings in mid-afternoon New York. And it's awful to admit, but the facial resemblance is striking, even down to the sensuous nose of seven or eight years ago. Dylan's shadow falls long across singers and writers of those years.

"Under a shadow? Sure I think I am. What happens is, once you start creating somethin', people magnify different aspects for different reasons. Record companies might do it to sell records. Every year somethin' comes along."

Some people have got him wrong, he says; his first album, *Greetings From Asbury Park, NJ* (which is where he now lives), doesn't give a true picture of his artistic position: "The things on the record are pretty much what I did when I began writing; I had been playing in a band for nine years! I was essentially a guitar player! But these songs came out and I didn't have a band, so... they figured I was a singer-songwriter, and I figured I'd give it a try.

"It was almost produced to lean towards that – more towards the lyrics than the music, which was just 'bam, bam, bam'. Originally they just wanted me and a guitar. I said 'forget it'. That's why I want to do more music on my next record. On the records a lot of emphasis was put on what was being said, which was not the point, but people listened and interpreted what it was.

"You see, it depends how seriously you take yourself. It's really hard for me to talk about the words, 'cos I have no particular things to say. I mean, I never read poetry 'cos I don't like to read too much; I never read anything to the degree of remembering. Y'know, as soon as someone says 'this guy is the next Bob Dylan', you're dead, and I can't believe they don't know that.

"Of course there are similarities! First thing I heard was on AM, 'Like A Rolling Stone', and I grew up with that. But the public always has this huge mouth, open wide and going, 'More, more!' Even if someone was dropping dead they'd still shout 'more!' They're brought up to do that, but it's a fight to keep your identity against people who want to cloud it over. Columbia, they didn't want that album cover [it's a picture postcard view of Asbury] and I had to fight that, and one of the reasons I wanted it was that that's me! That's where I'm from!"

He stretches flat, laughs from his belly, and then hoiks himself on to his elbows. The fingers are in the beard; then they rub through his hair. There's a lot of US Marine insignia on the wall that becomes unaccountably noticeable. He looks absent and amused again.

"Despite all the hype," he begins, "I'm remaining pretty obscure, which just goes to show – oh, but we do get a good response from the audience." Silence.

"It's all done by people who mean well, I guess, who actually feel it's the right thing to do. The one straight guy is John [Hammond]. He looks at stuff and says it's either terrible or good."

Silence again. "The situation gets overwhelming. Really, I can't be bothered with what's goin' on here, at Columbia, and I don't much care. I sit at home and write music. Nobody comes down and hypes me."

Shadow lifts, ever so slightly. **MM**

Dark Side of the Sleeve

MARCH 24

I have just bought Pink Floyd's new album *Dark Side Of The Moon*. I was astonished at the price – £2.50 for less than 45 minutes of music. This is ridiculous. Packed with the album, in a double sleeve incidentally, were two useless posters and two equally useless stickers. Without these and the double sleeve, I reckon that the album could have retailed at around £2.10 and everyone would have been happy.

Why should we pay for this trash when after all we want to listen to the music and not look at the sleeve? Record companies should instil a feeling of goodwill rather than an "I've been conned", as I have.
GP KELSEY, Brough, Yorks. **NME**

"I have been told to make no comment"

JUNE 2

David Bowie cancels an enormous show at Earls Court.

DAVID BOWIE'S PROJECTED RETURN concert at London's Earls Court stadium on June 30 – which was to have been the final date in his current massive tour schedule – has been cancelled. The decision to scrap this show was taken by his manager, Tony Defries, who said: "Neither David nor myself will make any further comment on the matter."

The 18,000-capacity arena was the starting point for the Bowie tour on May 12, and his concert on that date was subjected to widespread criticism from sections of the audience who could neither see nor hear him. Visual and acoustic improvements were promised for his June 30 return. In the absence of any official explanation, it seems likely that the gig was cancelled in case these new standards could not be achieved.

Commented Defries: "It appears that the box office has been opened before the appointed date without my knowledge or permission, and that a very large quantity of mail has been received from prospective ticket-buyers. I will do my utmost to ensure that all of this is sorted and money returned as soon as possible."

Promoter Mel Bush told the *NME*: "I have been told to make no comment on the Bowie cancellation. But I would emphasise that my Slade concert at Earls Court the following day (July 1) is definitely still on."

Bowie's *Aladdin Sane* album is now in the charts in six different countries – Britain, the United States, Italy, Holland, Sweden and Norway. It is also on release in Germany, France, Belgium, Denmark, Switzerland and Austria – and is about to be issued in Australia, South Africa and Japan. At press time, the LP was approaching £500,000 gross in British sales alone. *NME*

▶ Bowie in full 'Ziggy Stardust' mode in a New York hotel room, 1973

"That's it. Period"

JULY 14

David Bowie is retiring from pop to pursue other activities, he tells *NME*.
"Those were the final gigs."

DAVID BOWIE'S CONCERTS at Hammersmith Odeon on Monday and Tuesday marked the end of his career as a live performer. He told *NME*'s Charles Shaar Murray this week: "Those were the final gigs. That's it. Period. I don't want to do any more gigs, and all the American dates have been cancelled. From now on, I'll be concentrating on various activities that have very little to do with rock and pop." After his hit with "Space Oddity" in 1969, Bowie retired from rock and ran an Arts Laboratory in Beckenham for 18 months, eventually returning at the insistence of Mercury – then his record company – to record *The Man Who Sold The World*. A year ago Bowie told *NME*: "I can't envisage stopping gigging for the next year at least, because I'm having such a good time doing it." This week he told Murray that he did not wish to say anything further at the moment, but added that he would reveal the full reasons for his shock decision later. **NME**

▲ Fans reaching out to touch David Bowie during the concert where he announced he was retiring Ziggy Stardust: Hammersmith Odeon, July 3, 1973

The Beatles // Bob Dylan and The Band
David Bowie // Genesis // John Lennon
Mick Jagger // Mick Taylor // Neil Young
Phil Collins // Queen // The Rolling Stones

1974

After eight years off the road, Bob Dylan is back on tour with The Band. The Stones, still rolling, lose their guitar man Mick Taylor, and prog rockers Genesis hope they've cracked the tough American circuit at last.

The Beatles are back on speaking terms, David Bowie adopts yet another musical persona for *Diamond Dogs*, and Neil Young releases his highly personal *On the Beach*. Queen, promoting their album *Sheer Heart Attack*, display a potent mix of heavy metal and glam rock on their first major tour.

"I'm scared he's gonna blow it"

After eight years away, BOB DYLAN and THE BAND return to performance. In Los Angeles, it's a triumphant, three-hour show – audience member Phil Ochs sees Dylan in opposition to prevailing trends. "Here is a real man," he says, "standing up on stage with no props."

CYNICISM AND ADRENALIN flowed swiftly round Los Angeles last week as Bob Dylan climaxed the most impactful and influential tour in popular music since The Beatles changed the world and set up a few records, more years ago than it would be polite to recall.

And even the deadliest cynic had to admit that Dylan had re-emerged from his self-imposed isolation to rapturous acclaim. Twenty-one cities and forty concerts later, and Dylan has regurgitated the entire network of rock, restating his undeniable power as the most significant contemporary composer.

With audiences whose ages range from the lower teens to the late 30s, this has been a triumphant return to the spotlight for an older, wiser man who has turned full circle.

More than being a mere dollar spinner, Dylan's USA tour has acted as a reaffirmation of some basic musical values at a time when, for many rock students, there is a vacuum – or, as Dylan would have it, "no direction home".

Eight years is a long time to be away from touring, but having attended Dylan's final three shows of the trek, last week in Los Angeles, I was astonished at the great shape he was in, physically, philosophically, and musically. On stage, more than ever before, Dylan has acquired a piercing dramatic sense, a total realisation of what each show should be, and any throwaway postures of his early days have been swapped for a scientific approach to what will build up the suspense and please his audience.

The crowds at Los Angeles' cheerless Forum last week totalled 60,000 for three concerts. He could undoubtedly have sold out a dozen shows in a town like this. Tickets priced at $9 (£4) were fetching up to $150 (about £65) outside the hall. I saw three young girls weeping because they couldn't afford black market tickets. Those paying homage stood soberly in queues, as if waiting to enter church.

The mood of the crowd seemed one of awesome anticipation at the start, then relieved joy at the end of each three-hour show. To those of us who have been on a Dylan trip for 11 years, for him to make such a successful comeback was more than we could have hoped for.

He whipped through most of his big hits with just a minimal amount of spoken words to each audience, and while some knockers moaned that he had been just going through the motions like a puppet of the past, his treatment of every song was different from all recorded versions. I found it reassuring that he was not simply repeating his show and his phrasings of eight years ago. That would have been the easy way.

The California crowds were un-freaky. "Folkies, not rockers," observed my American friend. Less dope was smoked than at the average American rock concert, which may have indicated that more people were willing to submit to a natural high.

In the car park (£1 to leave your vehicle), a young man poked his head in our car window and offered a Hare Krishna book which, he insisted, was Dylan's personal wish that everyone should read – and, more importantly, buy.

"I don't believe you," I said to him, but the point was lost. Next came Dylan T-shirts at $3. But strangely, there were no programmes.

▲ Bob Dylan with The Band in 1974 (left to right)
Robbie Robertson, Levon Helm, Dylan

▶ Bob Dylan performing at The Boston Gardens, January 14, 1974

Dylan came on stage immediately at the start of the shows, to standing ovations. He raced into a speedy "Most Likely You'll Go Your Way And I'll Go Mine" and we were off. The song was a perfect opener with heavy symbolism in the words: "Time will tell just who has fell, and who's been left behind".

Bob has a wiry presence, legs astride the mic, yet not in the guise of your average phallic-guitar swinger. His microphone technique, especially during the acoustic set, is now extremely polished and he veers to it and from it at precisely the right moments for emphasis.

And the sound! In this revolting construction of a basketball stadium, the effects are perfect – a great achievement for the technical crew, working against terrible acoustic prospects.

The Band rocks behind Dylan, stunningly good musicians whose sound texture and empathy is perfectly attuned to Bob's every move.

"Lay Lady Lay" is next, the words slurred into an even more countryish flavour, and when he goes into "It Takes A Lot To Laugh, It Takes A Train To Cry", the words are often incomprehensible. He sings most songs "up" at the end of each line now, giving them a new urgency but tending to expect us to know what the words are.

The Band were in mighty form by this time, with the organ of Garth Hudson, never obtrusive, setting up a wall of sound across each song. All The Band stood out, but on the three shows I saw, Hudson shone. On "Rainy Day Women", with Dylan and the crowd really hammering across "Everybody must get stoned", Levon Helm's drumming was stupendous.

By now, Dylan was more aggressive than when he first stepped on stage. "It Ain't Me Babe" followed, with completely fresh intonation and excellent vocal back-up from Robbie Robertson and Rick Danko. Now, after a drink from a can, Dylan switched to the piano for a stabbing version at one of his finest finger-pointing songs, "Ballad Of A Thin Man".

Applause for this was so heavy that Dylan actually bowed as he made an exit to allow The Band to do their own set.

This proved magical; they make no concessions to appearance but are so tight that one day they could snap. Vocally and instrumentally, they give out an elegant, irresistible sound, perfectly rehearsed and all their own with its subtle infusion of country music. And the songs are fine.

"I Shall Be Released", a slow dirge with a great vocal performance, was followed by the return of Dylan for "All Along The Watchtower", with its splendid imagery lost at such a racing tempo; "Hollis Brown", its raunchy treatment contrasting starkly with the simplicity of the original recording; and then "Knockin' On Heaven's Door" – sung by Dylan as "do-wer" – with The Band doing good back-up vocals.

Dylan's first spoken words came next: "Thank you, we'll be right back." After the interval his acoustic set proved a beauty, but slightly too short. He came out with "She Belongs To Me", sounding fragile, and the biggest roar of the night so far came when he blew harmonica.

It's odd: you might have expected Dylan, conscious of the passage of time, to have renounced all these golden oldies as his creations of yesteryear and not relevant today. But he was instilling them all with an unequalled energy and urgency, and had chosen the list of songs to be performed with painstaking care, according to his friends.

There was, after "Like A Rolling Stone", an unusual sight. In a rare acknowledgement of the audience, Bob turned to the people sitting

behind the stage and nodded his appreciation of their applause – and perhaps at their patience for looking at his back for so long.

Now all the goodies came pouring out with vigour as Dylan knew the marathon performances of his life were nearly over and that he'd won: "Love Minus Zero (No Limit)", "Don't Think Twice, It's All Right", with real honky harmonica, better than ever; "Just Like A Woman", with the old melody barely recognisable, the words moulded into an altogether more forceful message, with the accent on "woman". Now he went speedily into "It's All Right, Ma, I'm Only Bleeding", with the spine-chilling topicality of that knife-edged line: "Even the President of the United States sometimes must have to stand naked".

The Band returned with marvellous songs "Rag Mama Rag", "This Wheel's On Fire", "The Shape I'm In", "The Weight" – as solid as rock. The Band's whole feel is like a blood brother to Dylan's music.

"Forever Young", from the warm and fresh album *Planet Waves*, opened Dylan's final set.

Much of the stuff on the new album is openly personal, the first time I can recall Dylan baring his soul in public. Many artists would be slayed for being maudlin, but somehow he stops just short of it, and "Forever Young" is a simple statement of hope, a song from a father to his five children, a loving piece of paternal poetry.

After that came a thick, heavy and driving sound: "Highway 61 Revisited", and what a great, jumping track it was. Then, like a clarion call from all our yesterdays, "Like A Rolling Stone".

Hudson's swirling organ filled the auditorium. A touch of genius from the head of Bill Graham came next – a revolving ball of light which spun round the entire Forum and made it like fairyland. And

"He instilled all those golden oldies
with energy and urgency"

◀ Bob Dylan and the Band at New
York's Madison Square Garden, 1974

on the February 14 shows, a giant "Happy Valentine's Day" card lowered into the back of the hall. The atmosphere was vibrant as Dylan and The Band roared through verse after verse of that mean old song so loaded with innuendo.

We demanded an encore with the traditional American routine of everyone lighting a match or cigarette lighter, and he came back, fittingly, with the song with which he had begun, "Most Likely You'll Go Your Way And I'll Go Mine". It really swung. Dylan had returned to the stage for this with shades – a neat piece of theatre.

Then he made a mistake, pressing on with an abysmal "Blowin' In The Wind". He reduced the song to muzak, at a dreary singalong tempo, and although the crowd duly sang along with it, any meaning or melody the song once had was lost. But that was only one dud moment in a majestic performance.

On the final show in Los Angeles, Dylan – always a man of few words – preceded his encore with: "We'd like to introduce the man who's put this tour together. Without him there would have been no tour. Mr Bill Graham." On stage with a broad smile came Bill Graham, and at the end of this tour, which had gone without any big hitch, his release of tension was easy to see.

So was the release of the road crew, who in the time-honoured tradition then soaked Bill Graham with buckets of water. After the encore, Dylan held his guitar to the sky in a gesture of triumph, shouted "Goodnight", and it was all over now, baby blue.

Millions of words have been written and broadcast about this event, but few more pertinent than those I gathered from an early Dylanologist and friend of Bob's during his earliest days in Greenwich Village, singer Phil Ochs. Phil saw the shows in Philadelphia, New York and Los Angeles, and told me:

"The net effect of this tour is very healthy for the state of the country and the state of music and the development of new songwriters. In my opinion, popular music has become very degenerate from 1967 on. Look at this possibility: a 13-year-old kid who's listening to today's new stuff, or maybe even playing in a rock group, is experiencing Alice Cooper, David Bowie, Mick Jagger or Lou Reed. These people he has to regard as giants!

"But to me, Alice Cooper is a reflection of a sick society. So young kids think, perhaps, that making music has to go hand in hand with a stupid stage show. This is ridiculous, and that's what Dylan's concerts have proved.

"The social value of Dylan's tour is that here is a real man, standing up on stage with no props, and making some fine music. The man whom I, and many others, consider to be the greatest song lyricist of all time, going through his paces.

"I hope and believe," said Ochs, "that this will have a healthy and sobering effect on the state of music, and cut out the madness."

And that's a passionate piece of intelligence. Emotional attachment to Dylan aside, critical evaluations are hardly necessary in assessing the musical worth of the 1974 American tour.

It doesn't matter that his guitar was occasionally out of tune, or that his voice showed signs of overwork, or that some people were enjoying sneering at the amount of money the tour will gross, or whether he did it for personal kicks or even to simply feed his ego.

What matters only is that he did it. And the vibes have been great. At a crucial time in the evolvement of music, the tour will hopefully act as a catalyst for a saner world of music.

And at the very least, the Dylan tour has made a lot of old men very happy. *MM*

▲ Dylan playing a benefit concert for ousted Chileans at the Felt Forum in New York, September 5, 1974

"Nobody would mind"

JANUARY 12

The Beatles are back on speaking terms.

▲ Paul and Linda McCartney at the 46th
Academy Awards, Los Angeles, April 1, 1974

THE BEATLES BACK together again? It could happen, according to Paul McCartney. He commented in New York that the financial dispute between him and the other three Beatles will be decided this month. The three-year legal entanglement has effectively stopped him working with the other three, although he recently contributed to the Ringo album.

"We have broken up as a band, but I'd like to see us work together on a loose basis – and I think we will," he said. This confirms rumours that relations between all four have improved greatly over the past few months. John Lennon told *MM* in Los Angeles: "Nobody would mind doing some work together again." **MM**

David Bowie *Diamond Dogs*

MAY 24

A NEW ALBUM release by David Bowie is today looked on with as much awe as a release by The Beatles in the '60s. Later this month it will be with us, and by June it's guaranteed the album will have sold by the thousand regardless of musical merit.

Bowie's new album really is excellent. It's a departure in that the Spiders are no longer with him, and it's also a departure in that the whole production of the songs is far more lavish than anything he's previously attempted. For most of the tracks he's adopted a "wall of sound" technique, borrowed not a little from Phil Spector, but the richness of it all enhances his voice no end. He is accompanied by one old Spider, Mike Garson, on keyboards, and has also recruited Herbie Flowers, of Blue Mink and session fame, to play bass, and a couple of drummers in Tony Newman and Aynsley Dunbar. Alan Parker plays guitar on one track only, while David is credited with acoustic and electric guitar throughout as well as various reed instruments, Moog and Mellotron.

The theme of the album is the aftermath of a nuclear holocaust, and the scene is set in the opening track, which is a recitation by Bowie over some eerie horror-movie soundtrack. The track's called "Future Legend", but any thoughts that the entire album is one of the recitations on doom through science fiction are quickly dispelled as the piece blends into the title track, a chunky rocker in the Stones tradition.

"Diamond Dogs" reflects the tone of the record, in fact. Many of the following numbers are heavy, bouncy pieces. They're commercially orientated and reminded me of the Stones' work on *Exile On Main St*. The "hot tramp" of "Rebel Rebel", for example, seems synonymous with Mick Jagger's "Bitch" and "Brown Sugar". They bite hard and have a ring of decadence that's never out of place in a good rock song.

On the "Dogs" track, David plays reeds, pushing out the riff in King Curtis style, rasping over the guitar lines. It's a long song – almost six minutes – that's left deliberately unfinished. The first side contains another two rockers in similar vein, "Candidate" and "Rebel Rebel". The latter has been taken off the album as a single and needs little explanation. "Candidate" is slotted in-between two cuts of the same song, a slower number called "Sweet Thing", which opens with Bowie singing in a deep bass voice over another space-fiction type introduction. The bass voice gives way to a more recognisable Bowie vocal sound that's eventually caught up in a sea of voices. A soprano sax solo leads into "Candidate" and back into a reprise of the first song. "Rebel" closes the first side – an ever-so-slightly different version from the original.

In general the second side is mellower than the first. The opener, "Rock And Roll With Me", is the best track of the lot. Despite its title, it's not an out-and-out rocker, more of a song in "Changes" vein, in a heavy, slow time signature that invites an audience to sing along. "We Are The Dead" was a disappointment, perhaps because it is over-long and didn't seem to say a great deal. Opening with a jerky rhythm backing, it's almost exclusively David singing over a Clavinet or electric piano. Somewhat anonymous.

Bowie has been playing "1984" live for over a year now. Opening with some Ringo Starr packing-case drum work, it's another that builds into a wall of sound that captures the drama of the hooklines at the end of each chorus. "Big Brother" is another huge production number with a trumpet fanfare and a large choir backing up Bowie's deep vocals.

It's almost an operatic piece, and at times Bowie's voice seems to be joined in the mix with various girls' voices. The trumpet plays a marching time signature that leads into the closing music, a chant that's deliberately repetitive. Title is the "Chant Of The Ever Circling Skeletal Family", and it's really a tape loop going round and round again and again. The backing gradually disappears until the fade-out.

The overall effect from the album is that Bowie is more concerned with good production than ever before – and that he's consciously writing songs suitable for his upcoming stage show.

At least half the tracks on this set are bound to be firm stage favourites, especially if he can recreate the recorded sound. David has produced another really good record. **MM**

▶ David Bowie, photographed in 1974 in New York City

"We had an underground mystique"

With remarks from "the Geesin report" in mind, GENESIS embark on a landmark year. In spite of setbacks (cancelled tour, stolen equipment, faulty explosions), PHIL COLLINS is confident.

WELL – HAVE GENESIS finally cracked America? Are they now in the Moody Blues/Jethro Tull bracket? "It's still early days," says their ebullient drummer Phil Collins. But a certain bounce to his gait, and a swift hand at cracking open cans of powerful foreign lager, would indicate that all is well with the lads who just scored a home run with "I Know What I Like".

While Genesis have been romping around the concert halls of America, they have been keeping up appearances at home with their first big hit single, a cut from *Selling England By The Pound*, and it has certainly given this most unusual of groups a cheering boost. Phil was sporting a drastically trimmed hairstyle when he appeared at the Soho headquarters of his record company this week. And a commando jacket gave the impression of a man who will brook no nonsense and is going places, armed to the teeth.

Except that Phil's armament consists of tough tom-toms and sniping snare drums. And he is planning to add more to the battery of percussion effects that made "What I Like", such a success.

"It's strange. We were in Boston when we heard it was a hit. We only released the single to help people get into the album, and it certainly seems to be having an effect. Even *Nursery Cryme*, one of our oldest albums, is starting to move again. The single hasn't been a hit in the States yet, but it is being re-released.

"The band is going to take two months off for writing now and we're all going to live in a house in Surrey to work. They're going to bring the new Island mobile studio down to us to try and capture more of the excitement and feeling we put into our playing. Whenever I tape a rehearsal it always seems to have more feeling than when the final LP comes out after it's been mixed and remixed in the studio."

It seemed as if Genesis weren't getting much time off from work?

"Not really. We had our guitars stolen in America and that put us back on schedule. Peter has moved house from London to Bath and his wife is expecting a baby, so naturally he wants to spend some time at home. I've inherited a family, too, so things are pretty good."

What happened about the guitars?

"Oh, we had six pinched, but two were returned. What puzzles me is that the guitars returned were virtually un-sellable. There was a double-necked 12-string bass and a special 12-string acoustic guitar. No dealer would accept them because they are so rare. After this next LP we've got a European tour, and then a short British tour, playing two or three nights at different places, and ending up at Wembley on November 4.

"Then we go back to the States. The plan is for a month on the East Coast and Midwest."

Last time we spoke, Phil had been talking about the possibility of a solo LP, as apart from his drumming talents he is also a fine singer.

"At the beginning of next year we'll get our own things together – maybe the solo albums. The band is reaching a stage where it can afford to do solo LPs. The concerts were very well received and attended in America. We played to 4,000 a night and most of them were sold out.

▶ Genesis in 1974 with (left to right) Mike Rutherford, Tony Banks, Peter Gabriel and Phil Collins

◄ January 15, 1974: Genesis at London's Drury Lane Theatre, with Peter Gabriel suspended on a wire, with Mike Rutherford on guitar, and Phil Collins behind the drums

"In America we were playing our own concerts this time, and not supporting anybody, which meant that at least 60 per cent of the audience came to hear our music.

"The rest were either curious, or had come to see something that we're not. We are very vulnerable as an act. We're so open to heckling, when Peter tells his stories or there is a very quiet section of music. But there was surprisingly little heckling.

"One night Peter was moving from microphone to microphone to speak to the audience, and every one 'died'. We just didn't realise what was happening and the audience began to heckle.

"Peter started shouting back, but of course, the kids were just complaining that they couldn't hear us. Terrible!

"One of the bad spots was the Winterland in San Francisco, which is a boogie hall. People have to stand up to see the band – no seats. So anybody who has to stand up for two hours to see a band is bound to get irritable. There were people just wandering around, they probably didn't even know a band was on.

"Overall we were very satisfied with the tour and it's given us a lot more confidence. The money has gone up a bit – but it's still early days. No, we didn't do any TV. We had a disastrous show in France once and we vowed never to do TV again. We had to play 'Supper's Ready' five times before they could get it right, and the piece lasts 25 minutes each time. They had some good effects and were really trying, but in the end we walked off and said, 'We're getting the plane home!' By the fifth time you've played it, there's no feeling left and it just drives you mad when they keep calling out 'STOP!'

"We tried to make a film of the act at Shepperton Studios, but for some reason it just doesn't come across. When we saw the film, we couldn't say anything to each other. It wasn't right. They were going to use a bit for *Top of the Pops*, but we'd sooner have Pan's People dancing."

Phil shook his head when it came to discussing plans for the next Genesis album: "I can't think in terms of what it will sound like. It's daunting. I'd like it to be freer, even more so than the last one.

"The stage act will be the next LP, and how that will be presented, no one knows. I'd like to see it veer away from headdresses and costume changes, and for Peter to use his hands more in mime, just in the black suit. But we haven't talked about it.

"The last LP related to England, but we only realised that halfway through making it. The theme just seemed to emerge. It helped us a lot in the States, and anything English seems to be a help. For instance, the waitress in the cafe won't spit in your eye, and you get double helpings instead." **MM**

▲ Steve Hackett playing with Genesis at the Academy of Music in New York City, on May 4, 1974

"I'm Ed Sullivan"

MARCH 12

John Lennon is thrown out of an LA nightclub.
"He was disrupting the act by heckling," says one witness.

HEY, WHAT'S HAPPENIN' to Johnny Lennon? The stories going round about him these days recall his hard-case period pre- and early Beatles. The latest one took place yet again at the Troubadour club in Los Angeles, where Lennon heckled and hissed all the way through the return of the Smothers Brothers. A few weeks back he showed up there with a Kotex on his head.

Crazy John, accompanied by Harry Nilsson and Yoko Ono's former assistant May Pang, apparently shouted out obscenities and shouted out more than once, "I'm John Lennon." After this continued for several minutes, Smothers Brothers manager Ken Fritz asked Lennon to leave, whereupon Lennon purportedly punched Fritz and missed. Fritz swung back but then Lennon threw a glass, missing the manager but copping a waitress. He also managed to upset several tables on his way out the door. By 12.30am Johnny had been escorted by Nilsson from the club to his car – where he told the attendant, "I'm Ed Sullivan" – but not before allegedly hitting a woman who was trying to take his picture.

The woman, a 51-year-old Hollywood matron, filed suit in the West Hollywood Sherriff's Department, charging assault. Another photographer said: "He was yelling, 'They're all a bunch of phonies...'" Fritz commented: "He was disrupting the act by heckling, so I went over to ask him to be quiet." No one seems to know the cause of the ruckus or who the phonies were in an audience that included Paul Newman, Joanne Woodward, Flip Wilson, Helen Reddy, Linda Lovelace, Peter Lawford and Lily Tomlin.

No one is saying much about the split between John and Yoko, who have been separated now for five months. Yoko is still in New York and neither of them is discussing divorce for publication. For those of us with long memories, however, it's just like old times. **MM**

▲ John Lennon poses for a portrait on October 25, 1974 in New York City

▶ Mick Jagger on stage with the Rolling Stones at the Winterland Ballroom in San Francisco, in 1974

"I can handle all the angles"

A catch-up with MICK JAGGER, soon to offer new LP *It's Only Rock 'n Roll*. "The title is self-explanatory," he says.

"SORRY I'M LATE." "It's all right Mick." "No – it's not all right."
Mr Jagger, much forehead exposed by a somewhat drastic haircut, paced into his suite at London's Ritz Hotel, looking just a shade tired. He'd been up all night at mixing sessions for his forthcoming long-player, but this wasn't going to stop him discharging his duties as our most esteemed and celebrated statesman of rock.

It's extraordinary to think how long Mick Jagger has been pitting his talent and wits against the demanding, all-devouring public. Eleven years have passed since Mick and the Rolling Stones first emerged with "Come On", the hit that launched an era, and set a lifestyle and pattern for all that was to follow.

And yet still Mick leads the good fight in the cause of outrage and rock'n'roll. But there are changes. The aggressive glint to his probing gaze, the insolent curve to his mouth and businesslike bustle involved in entering or leaving a room are still there. But occasionally the resolution slips, and you glimpse a softer, more vulnerable Jagger beneath the flippancy and cynicism.

He impressed with his desire to communicate and extend courtesy, when he of all rock stars has the most excuse for being impatient with the askers of questions. For Mick has not always been used fairly by the media, and "used" is the operative word when it comes to some of the books that have been written about him in recent times.

In recent weeks he has spent some time in the States, where he kept up his habit of attending the top concerts, and keeping well in touch with events. Eric Clapton and David Bowie's show were among his engagements, but somehow he managed to miss his brother Chris Jagger's American debut. "Chris did some shows at the Bottom Line in New York, and I heard that his band was really good. You know he did a few gigs in England to warm up, under another name. He's getting into it now, and you've got to remember it's the first shows he's ever done. But somehow I missed him in the States. I can help him in some ways, and he's asked me for bits of advice, but he's got to do it on his own.

"I went to see Eric Clapton and David Bowie in New York, and they seem to attract the same people to each show. They have very Catholic tastes in America. Eric was playing very well – really nice. I was sitting on the edge of the stage. I saw the Bowie concert from the hall and he was very nervous, but everyone gets nervous in New York."

We hadn't seen Bowie in Britain with his new show and it didn't seem likely the Stones were going on tour for a while either. Was it now a case of bands gearing their acts for America first, while Britain came second?

"With a show like Bowie's you can mount it much more easily in America, and obviously it costs money to put on. What can you do in Britain, apart from the few big gigs and outside events which are at risk through the weather?"

There had been wild rumours of the Stones playing at Charlton. "Wild rumours! We won't be doing anything until Christmas, or failing that, early next year. And the reason is – we just didn't want to play gigs this year. I don't know why. I just felt it was worth waiting until we get a new show together. I don't know how the others felt but I wanted to wait until we had new material. We

▲ A great close-up of Jagger in action, another shot from San Francisco's Winterland Ballroom, 1974

"We are most sorry he is going"

DECEMBER 12

Mick Taylor announces his departure from the Stones.

MICK TAYLOR HAS left the Rolling Stones, the band he joined in 1969 as replacement for Brian Jones, and has joined a new outfit currently being formed by Jack Bruce. The Stones, at present recording as a four-piece in Munich, will engage a new guitarist in time for a major tour of America in May.

News of Taylor's departure broke when it became apparent that he was not working with the band in Munich. Reports from Germany last week suggested that he had been sacked, but Jagger quickly squashed these rumours in a statement saying: "After five years, Mick wishes a change of scene and wants the opportunity to try out new ventures, new endeavours. While we are all most sorry that he is going, we wish him great success and much happiness."

It was widely believed that Taylor had become restless due to the Stones' lengthy periods of inactivity, but on Monday of this week Taylor put out a statement saying: "The last five years with the Stones have been very exciting, and proved to be a most inspiring period. [...] I have nothing but admiration for the group, but I feel now is the time to move on and do something new."

The "something new" to which he referred proved to be membership of the new Jack Bruce band. Also in the lineup are noted US composer and keyboard player Carla Bley, who has worked with Bruce on many occasions, notably on the *Escalator Over The Hill* album – and pianist Max Middleton, who was most recently in Jeff Beck's group. A drummer has still to be signed, but in the meantime the four confirmed members are working out ideas in a London recording studio.

The Rolling Stones are to undertake an extensive US concert tour in May, and *NME* understands that selected concerts in Europe are also in the pipeline for next year.

The Stones' 1975 tour will be a "new-concept show", said Mick Jagger this week. "We shall be playing very few old numbers and the act will mainly be a showcase for new material."

Meanwhile, the Stones continue their recording sessions in Munich as a four-piece. No stand-in musician has been brought in to replace Mick Taylor, and Jagger and Keith Richards are playing all the guitar parts between them.

An attempt was made to secure the services of Ron Wood, but he was involved in the Faces' British tour. *NME*

"There's still a lot of energy in the music business"

didn't play America last year and there are two LPs we've not played songs from.

"But if we'd gone out two months ago and played gigs in England, we wouldn't have new numbers, which I need to keep me at it. If we wait for the new LP then I'll feel happy. We weren't even offered Charlton. Maybe we were, and I didn't hear about it. I want to do a new show – change the whole look of it. I want to do something – I dunno – different!

"Most bands want to just play – fine – but I want to put on a new show and of course we can't just do England. I'd rather wait until the show is together and play everywhere. It keeps me interested in being on the road and it takes a lot of energy, time and thought. So rather than just play England, I'd rather take it around, and then when we got to England it would be better anyway. It's economics, too. It costs a lot of bread, and we don't want to charge a fortune for tickets. £2.50 is enough."

What will the new show be like?

"Wait and see. Can't tell you!" Mick smiled like a mischievous boy, but doubtless there will be an extravaganza, perhaps like the foaming soapsuds that engulfed them on the Stones' recent videotape of "Only Rock 'n Roll (But I Like It)".

"Oh, that was detergent. Most unpleasant and it took such a long time to do. We couldn't have the lights and cameras inside the tent in case we all got electrocuted and we had to be insured for quite a lot of money just to shoot the scene. We did the film for promotion. There are a lot of young people who might not have heard of us. They might never have heard the band."

Mick looked quite serious, and although incredible, it did seem possible there might be a budding pop fan, with satchel and lollipop, going about her business in Cheam, oblivious to the activities of Michael and his Stones, Rolling. And talking of activities, what did he think of Bill Wyman's sudden lurch towards stardom? "Great –

▲ March 12, 1974: John Lennon and Mick Jagger at the American Film Institute Salute to James Cagney, at the Century Plaza Hotel, Los Angeles

▶ Jagger arriving at the tribute to James Cagney at the Century Plaza Hotel, Hollywood, March 12, 1974

Stones: Gathering Moss

DECEMBER 7

I have recently heard the Rolling Stones' new single release, and it has finally convinced me that they are the paper tigers of the '70s. Gone are the days of "Jumping Jack Flash", "I Can't Get No Satisfaction" and even the more recent "Angie"; the moss is gathering as the Stones stop rolling.

Has the creative talent of the Jagger-Richards combo dried up at last, as seen from the last two offerings: "It's Only Rock 'n Roll But I Like It" and the new "Ain't Too Proud To Beg"? They seem to have exhausted their Buddy Holly/Chuck Berry repertoire which contributed to part of their success in the '60s.

Are we to see the influences of different writers in an attempt to halt their waning popularity, as they are obviously no longer able to produce the old magic?

Mick Jagger is now a spent force as far as musical creativity is concerned, as can be seen when the recent records are compared with the earlier golden discs. Are the Stones relying on their name as former kings of rock'n'roll to try and pull them through the void into which they have sunk? The Stone Age is gone.
DAVID JONES, Water Lane, Cobham, Surrey **MM**

---

he's got it off his chest at last. No one was stopping him. Mick [Taylor] wants to do one and I'd like to do one. I've never actually started one, but we could all do bits of recording in-between working with the Stones. And not everything we record with the Stones comes out. Maybe now we'll have time to think and do what we want.

"Mick is producing somebody at the moment – a solo singer called Robin Miller – and Mick will be playing on his single, and maybe I'll do something when we've finished the Stones LP. It's finished really, and it'll be out the first week in September. We're choosing which songs to use. It'll be called *It's Only Rock 'n Roll*, and the title is self-explanatory.

"The album is a very mixed bag – there's even a bossa nova, a couple of slow ones, some ballads, a Caribbean tune… Well, you'll hear it. It's a lot different from the last one, anyway. We're aware of what's going on in the rest of rock, sure, but it's not a race."

How did Mick feel about artists who stage comebacks in rock? "It's great to see Eric back again, and the new Georgie Fame LP is good. It's hard, really. You should never get out of it. You should always stay in there. That's what I aim to do. There's never been a long period when we haven't made records. We've not missed a year since we started in 1963."

But hadn't Mick ever felt sickened by the whole rock business, and wanted to quit? "No, no. I can handle all the angles. Some people are pressurised, but I don't feel like that. If you get the feeling you can't take it any more, then you should get out. I don't feel any pressures and I'm going to stay."

But why keep at it, after all this time? "It's still exciting and there's a lot of energy in the music business. And there's a lot of music going on. That's why I want to stay in it. I'm not on the road all the time, and I just take life as it comes. I never look at the future, because no one can see it – so it's pointless. I have to think for now, and I'm in control of that.

"If the Rolling Stones put out a single, it doesn't necessarily mean it will be a hit. We've got to be prepared for failures. We could be failures in some places and not in others. You can make movies that are not particularly successful, but they can be enjoyable, and it's all experience.

"It's funny with films. Even the biggest actor can die and the film can lose money, but he'll just go on to the next picture. No you can't talk about my film career – it was not a career, just an interlude. But they were great to do. Performance was not promoted, because the company didn't like the film. I've never talked to James Fox [Mick's co-star] about it, but he's never done a film since. I never saw the film myself."

If Mick was not willing to be drawn on movies, he spoke out vigorously about the books that have purported to tell his life story. He was cool, but not unemotional.

"They were mostly fictional, written by people that had never met me, and wrote them based on rumours or their imagination. J Marks' book you've got to read. It's pretty bad. I never met the guy and yet he's written some complete rubbish that's just a figment of his imagination. It's just people wanting to make a bit of bread and I don't want to see another book about me again. The less the better. But I can't do anything about them, because they are very careful not to libel you.

"I don't want to get involved in the legalities, because what do you get out of it? Just for an example, Anthony Scaduto wrote about me and Brian Jones having a sword fight, which he's glamourised and just didn't happen. It sounds very romantic, me and Brian jumping about, fighting with swords, but it didn't occur. I've got no time for that kind of biography. It's not very nice – in fact it's quite vicious.

"It's all pretty sick, really, pretty bad. I expect he'll be writing a book on John Lennon next." **MM**

▶ The Stones in full sailor uniforms during the video for "It's Only Rock 'n' Roll (But I Like It)", directed by Michael Lindsey-Hogg, June 1974

Stones: In F   , Still Rolling

I am
Dec
so, bu
single
which
force ir

Gone
uninspi.
and raw
its best.

Tracks
show tha

know is still there, both as musicians and people. "Till The Next Goodbye" far surpasses "Angie" in its role as a rock love song. It is loose, spontaneous and warm where "Angie" was cold, calculated and colourless, and it deserves to succeed.

"Time Waits For No-One", with its superbly balanced guitar work, shows an insight and maturity that is surprising in its beauty – could you imagine the Stones writing this in 1966?

The Stones are progressing and no amount of "waning popularity" (their album at No 18 in the British charts, and No 2 in the States) on the part of Mr Jones, or anybody else for that matter, will stop it.

A ROSLING, Newark Road, Lincoln **MM**

Addictively Dangerous

JULY 16

One half of Neil Young plays the hits with CSNY.
Meanwhile, his own new album embraces the "psychotic surreal".

Neil Young *On The Beach*

RIGHT NOW, NEIL YOUNG is in kind of an invidious position. *On The Beach* is his equivalent of Lennon's *Plastic Ono Band* album in terms of being a reaction to and rejection of his earlier work, but whereas Lennon's change was both gradual (starting, really, from *Help!*) and included in its course pieces like "Lucy In The Sky With Diamonds", Young has made his artistic stock-in-trade the investigation of personal pain from the very beginning.

And that's the catch, really. In our July 20 issue, Steve Clarke attacked *On The Beach* as too negative too self-pitying: "It's a downer in that depression is the mood which most of the album evokes." Steve's a devotee of Neil Young. Probably knows the man's work in twice the careful detail that I do. I'm not a Young devotee. I could never totally accept his employment of self-pity as a creative focus. Sometimes I felt it a shade dishonest or manufactured (e.g. "Tell Me Why"); other times the whole thing got just a little too deliciously lush (e.g. "When You Dance I Can Really Love"), like Leonard Cohen. A sugared pill just the correct distance into commerciality to be still believable. And that could be the main reason why the majority of Neil Young fans won't get into *On The Beach*. The pill is no longer sugared – either by sweet melody or by garlands of posies. Young has, quite simply, welched on the deal. Which, in turn, suggests he's Woken Up.

On The Beach isn't, as previously interpreted, the fag-end of Neil Young's romance with rejection, but actually a quite positive piece of work in the Merciless Realism bracket of Lennon's primal period. How else to account for the reportedly totally revived Young now touring the States with CSNY, I don't know – but it's now up to me to provide the documentary evidence from the album itself. An album that seems clearly to be Neil Young's best so far.

Steve, in his original review, suggested that *On The Beach* was the result of Young's supposed disenchantment with studio recording. He'd done *Time Fades Away* "live" and *Journey Through The Past* was a rag-bag of "live" cuts and studio outtakes; *On The Beach* was his first serious studio effort since *Harvest* in 1972. The supposition is that Young was postponing the inevitable because he knew he couldn't cut it any more. The "postponement" guess is probably fairly accurate and it supports both cases. If he had no faith in himself any

more, he'd hold off – and if he didn't quite know what he was about to say, he'd hold off just the same.

It's still supposition, though. On the other hand, if we've "supposed" so far, we might as well keep on supposing. Suppose Neil Young was getting towards his wits' end, what with all that's expected of him, and fatigue and drugs and directionlessness-made-a-virtue and all. Suppose it was time to make a new album and he had the material ready, just like he had six times before, but somehow didn't believe in it any more – didn't believe himself, didn't believe his audience were picking out what he regarded as important in his songs. He's stymied and he's going down fast. Then something happens that Opens His Eyes. Someone says something to him, something happens – whatever. He suddenly realises where he is and what he's doing. Perspective. Reality. He writes a new bunch of songs fast. Out comes *On The Beach*. The precise nature of the occurrence which changed Young's head, will be looked at later. For now, let's keep that supposition in mind and begin looking at the album.

"Walk On" walks the album on. Gently rocking, very "live" sound, but very clear too. At once we get perspective: "I remember the good old days...". And straight after we get the reality available from that vantage point: "Sooner or later it all gets real/Walk on".

Say the person he's talking to here is his current lady, Carrie Snodgress, and the "them" in question is Young's audience. Ze pieces begin to fit together, *nein*? A lyrical bitterness about "the man" (and you can take it straight as Big Business or bend it towards the Drug Connection) is reiterated constantly, from his showbiz/high society aspect in "For The Turnstiles" ("Singing songs for pimps with tailors/ Who charge 10 dollars at the door") to industrialist magnates in "Revolution Blues". It's hard to say whether "Revolution Blues" is meant to be seen from Young's point of view or from that of a persona. Manifestly he doesn't live "in a trailer at the edge of town" or possess "25 rifles just to keep the population down". Manson's lot, maybe – or, more relevantly, the SLA. But not our Neil.

On the other hand, he evidently identifies strongly with that outlaw-avenger attitude, even if he's laughing about it while he's pulling triggers in his head. The mode is prime '65 Dylan. Militant psychotic-surreal. **NME**

▶ Neil Young performing live on stage at Wembley
Stadium, London, on September 14, 1974

"For The Turnstiles" is about how everybody gets nailed by the business of fame sooner or later, underlined in an extraordinary closing verse in which Young sees all the baseball stars "left to die on their diamonds" (batting bases) while "In the stands the home crowd scatters/For the turnstiles".

On side two we get to the real meat: the tale of Young's personal experience in the last few years and the story on which this whole interpretation hangs. In successive verses, Young finds himself alone at a microphone after a radio interview and interjects the image of

"The pill is no longer sugared by sweet melody or garlands of posies" being "out here on the beach" where "the seagulls are still out of reach"; he resolves to get out of town, head for the sticks with his bus and his friends, and follow the road, although he doesn't know where it ends – the song closing with a repeat of the solitary line "The world turning/I hope it don't turn away" and a beautiful guitar solo over a slow fade.

"Motion Pictures", dedicated to his girlfriend, Carrie, star of *Diary of a Mad Housewife*, is the work of a man who had a shrewd suspicion that The Business was doing him in, and only just found out how. It covers this ground with the impressive economy which characterises the whole album: "All those headlines, they just bore me now/I'm deep inside myself, but I'll get out somehow/I'll bring a smile to your eyes". Which has in turn been arrived at via a verse that represents the young policy statement for the past: "Well, all those people, they think they've got it made/But I wouldn't buy, sell, borrow, or trade/Anything I have to be like one of them/I'd rather start all over again". Note the echo of the last line of "Stage Fright" and the deadly seriousness of the proposition.

All the loose strands are woven together in the final track, "Ambulance Blues" – a beautiful song, possibly Young's best ever. Young picks an aged acoustic and blows smeary harp, Ben Keith slaps a bass that keeps getting its shoes caught in the mud, Ralph Molina pats hand-drums almost inaudibly, Joe Yankee chinks an "electric tambourine", and Rusty Kershaw's violin sounds like the hillbilly cousin of Robin Williamson's creaking gimbri. It's raining. Obsessively so.

The lyrics open with a direct reference to the perspective outlined at the beginning of the album: "Back in the old folkie days, the air was magic when we played…"

The verse again, and a crucial one: "I guess I'll call it sickness gone/It's hard to say the meaning of this song/An ambulance can only go so fast/It's easy to get buried in the past/When you try to make a good thing last". Which supports the case for the Traumatic Change Theory quite admirably. Now it's just a case of: (a) What caused the change?; and (b) What does the change involve? While we're mulling what this character means, Young blows some more, now rather deflated, harp. Only it isn't a breather. It's a Dramatic Pause. Young slams back with the rebuttal and a clear statement of where he's at now: "I never knew a man could tell so many lies/He had a different story for every set of eyes/How could he remember who he's talking to/'Cos I know it ain't me and I hope it isn't you…"

That certainly doesn't sound like the work of a depressed, negative man to me. It sounds extremely positive, actually – and note that "Ambulance Blues" is the only track thus listed which isn't any kind of blues at all. There's scattered evidence for a Dylan experience in many tracks from *On The Beach*, but the more important thing is that, though Dylan and Young may have taken a parallel path recently, Young now sounds actively dangerous, whereas Dylan's just singing his own peculiar gospel. **NME**

◀ Neil Young backstage at Oakland Stadium, California, on July 14, during the Crosby, Stills, Nash & Young 1974 US Tour

Merseybleat

JANUARY 19

I must let the people of Britain know what a musical desert Liverpool has turned out to be; it's so bad now that it wouldn't surprise me if The Beatles said they hailed from Manchester.

Firstly, with the rise in "pub rock" around Britain now, Liverpool has tried to join in, with disastrous results.

Nearly everyone has turned out to be the "cheap and nasty" type, banging out tuneless "self-composed" drivel.

If it's a number we're all supposed to know, we are treated to an unrecognisable din churned up out of distorted chords, pneumatic drumming and flat, nasal gruntings (if it is, of course, possible to grunt flat).

The standards of the groups in Liverpool are laughable, if not hilarious. The Cavern is the musicians' graveyard, and has been for the past five years.

The audiences are nothing but lethargic zombies – "wind me up, let me go".

Any good group that does "make it", if they value their sanity, will never come back to Liverpool.

JOHN HERDMAN, Lessups Road, Liverpool **MM**

FEBRUARY 2

I don't know where John Herdman (Mailbag, January 19) has been all these years.

Far from "joining in" the current boom, there has been pub rock in Liverpool since the Liverpool Scene first used O'Connor Tavern for weekly sessions back in '67.

Since then scenes have developed in the Masonic Arms, featuring the best in local soul music most nights, the Sportsman – where Supercharge are the main favourites with an enthusiastic crowd – and several others around the city.

O'Connors itself continues to flourish – in the last year it's featured local bands most weeks, plus guests from out of town of the calibre of Victor Brox, Pete Brown and Lol Coxhill.

Nobody pretends that the scene – in terms of venues or groups – is as healthy as it was in the heady days of the early '60s, but attitudes such as those displayed by Mr Herdman can only do a disservice to local live music, which needs all the support and encouragement it can get.

MIKE EVANS, Huskisson Street, Liverpool **MM**

A Curious Mix

NOVEMBER 1 · **LIVERPOOL EMPIRE**

Queen's combination of heavy rock and glamour sparks scenes of tumult in Liverpool.

THE GIG: AN atmosphere approaching bedlam is prevalent inside the Empire, long before Queen emit a hint of activity behind the sombre barrier of the safety curtain. Hustler have come and gone, and now the audience are hungry for action. Bad reviews? Supermarket rock? Thousands of Queen's Liverpool supporters look suspiciously as if they couldn't care neither jot nor tittle. They whistle and chant and clap with all the precision of the football terraces.

The ancient cry of "Wally!" still heard in northern territories echoes around the faded gilt decor. Jack Nelson is intrigued by the cry, wonders if Wally are a local group and wants to sign them, until informed Bob Harris already has a stake in the real thing. Mersey accents boom over the PA: "We do apologise for the technical hitch – it's to do with the PA system and we are assured the show will start in two, three or four minutes."

More whistles, as tough-looking lads in white trousers and combat jackets with ELP and Jethro Tull emblazoned on the back pass beer bottles and conduct the audience with cheeky gestures. It's all in fun and the only mild aggro comes when the Queen's entourage from London try to claim their seats near the front. "Fuck off!" directs one youth as PR Tony Brainsby pleads for his seat. "All these seats are taken, up to that gentleman there," says Tony, pointing at me.

Ribald laughter from the watching stalls, and repeated cries of, "Ooh – gentleman!" Grousing, the seat pirates eventually relinquish their hold, with dark mutterings of, "Alright, but we'll see you outside."

The battle was in vain, for as the party took their seats, the safely curtain went up, and the audience rushed forward. Instantly the house lights went up again and the curtain jerked uncertainly down. A nervous man with face ashen of hue appeared at the side of the stage clad in incongruous evening dress, as if he were the master of ceremonies and this was old-tyme music hall.

"There is no way we are going to start..." he began. "All you have to do is enjoy the show..." But there was a way. Somebody turned a blinding spotlight on the managerial figure, and he retired defeated, as the curtain halted in mid-descent and began a jerky upward movement. Within seconds most of the audience were standing up to gaze desperately at the darkened empty stage, and there they were – shadowy figures bounding towards the waiting instruments. The lights blazed, and there was evil Fred, clad all in white, the archetypal demon rock singer, pouting and snarling: "Queen is back. What do you think of that?" A tumultuous roar indicated that the mob were well disposed to the idea.

It was difficult to assess the early part of the band's performance because the fans, with that wonderful selfishness of clamorous youth, decided to stand on their seats, their bodies screening both sight and sound. As a guest, I was not too worried on my account, but felt sorry for the kids at the back who had paid their cash.

Retiring to the back of the theatre, and giving up the hard-won seats, we watched the scenes of tumult, including a boy on crutches, perhaps unable to see, but desperately waving his steel supports in supplication. The band's strategy and appeal began to take shape as they tore through such dramatic pieces as "Now I'm Here", "Ogre Battle", "Father To Son" and "White Queen" from the second album.

Roger's drums are the band's workhorse, punching home the arrangements, and mixing a sophisticated technique with violent attack. Roger says his favourite drummer is John Bonham. Brian is a fervent, emotional guitarist, who is like a Ronno figure to Freddie, and is obviously a gifted musician. The onstage attention is judiciously divided between them, and when May takes a solo on his homemade guitar, Mercury leaves the stage, only to return in a stunning new costume.

Into a medley now, and apart from their slickness and Freddie's dynamic presence, the extra power of almost choral vocal harmonies is appreciated, something that few bands with a central lead singer can achieve. The camper aspects of Queen are displayed in "Leroy Brown", a gay, Dixieland tune that Freddie insists is inspired by The Pointer Sisters. Then their first hit, "Seven Seas Of Rhye", and a lunatic tempo on "Stone Cold Crazy", "Liar" and the finale from "Lap Of The Gods".

Dry ice began to envelop the stage, and as red light glowed through the fog, group and audience took on an eerie aspect, like a scene from some Wagnerian forest, as arms waved like young saplings in a night breeze. Then an explosion of white light, and two red flares burn over a deserted stage. Queen have gone, signalling a desperate roar of "MORE!" After some three minutes, the band responded to the insistent demand "We want Queen", Wally having been long forgotten. Into "Big Spender", with its slow, measured pace, and finally "Modern Times Rock'n'Roll", an apt anthem for a group of our times.

The band are still developing, and their mixture of heavy rock and glamorous display might seem curious. But as Queen makes its royal tour of the land, the effect on their subject is to inspire unmitigated loyalty. And amidst predictions of gloom for the British rock scene, it is a healthy and encouraging spectacle. *NME*

The 101ers // Brian May // Eagles // Faces
Fleetwood Mac // Joe Strummer // Joe Walsh
John Lennon // Led Zeppelin // Patti Smith
Pink Floyd // Queen // The Rolling Stones
Ronnie Wood // Tim Buckley

1975

Queen guitarist Brian May talks technical, and riots beset Zeppelin's latest US tour. John Lennon goes back to his roots with his *Rock 'n' Roll* album, while winning his fight to stay in the USA. In a move towards the mainstream, Fleetwood Mac recruit singer Stevie Nicks; and Ronnie Wood, still with the Faces, goes on "permanent loan" to the Rolling Stones.

And despite the prog-rock posturing of bands like Pink Floyd, there's a breath of fresh air on either side of the Atlantic: in London, Joe Strummer with his proto-punks the 101ers, and in New York the new wave poetess-singer Patti Smith.

"The next step was experimentation"

How QUEEN's BRIAN MAY made a guitar from an old fireplace. "You can measure the tension of strings with spring balances," he explains. "It's pretty straightforward."

QUEEN, WITH THEIR glam image and legion of young admirers, would hardly be the first band to spring to mind, for most people, as arbiters of musicianship. And yet, they're all competent instrumentalists – even Freddie Mercury, darling of the pin-up brigade and arch poseur, can play a mean piano. And he's no novice when it comes to writing, either.

Lead guitarist Brian May, as well as being a good musician, also has another reason for respect – he built his own guitar. Brian's guitar took him two years to build, mainly in his spare time, and he used an averagely well-equipped workshop to fashion it.

"At the time the only guitar I had was a little old acoustic with a pickup which I had made myself stuck on. That was about 10 years ago," he said.

"That was the only electric guitar I had; it was the only one at all, come to think of it, and obviously there's only so far you can get with something like that. You haven't got enough frets, the sound wasn't very hot and that sort of thing. At the time I couldn't afford one of the high-priced guitars.

"A Stratocaster was my ambition in those days but I couldn't afford one. And I didn't really like the cheaper one; I didn't feel they were what I wanted at all, so I decided to make one. I was interested in making things anyway.

"I was lucky to have a father who was interested as well and I'd always had woodworking and metal-working tools around, so basically we just sat down and made lots of designs. We drew lots and lots of pictures, thought about the stresses and strains, tremolo-design, truss rod design, how the strings ought to be anchored down

to what shape the body should be, the curve of the fingerboard – all that sort of thing.

"We drew lots of little drawings and gradually worked our way up to gigantic blueprints, all the time thinking about the kind of thing I would want to play.

"The next step was a lot of experimentation. I wanted a good tremolo which was sensitive and yet could change the pitch of the strings and yet come back to exactly the right position – a lot of them don't.

"So I did a lot of experimentation with tremolos, tried two or three different designs, some with pivots, some with hinges and different sorts of things all on a piece of wood with the tremolo attached and some strings just to see what would happen,

"You have to design something which is going to stand the strain, which is quite considerable. The system I eventually ended up with was a plate to which the strings are attached, pivoting on a knife edge, which is attached to the guitar, and the tension of the strings is balanced by some motorbike valve springs on the other side. That was the second step really, and then I went on to things like truss rods which would stand the strain. You have to find something which is strong enough to counteract the bending effect of the strings on the neck. At the same time you don't want it to be too heavy. It's a question of simply finding the right material.

▶ During the early days of Queen, Brian May and Freddie Mercury on stage in November 1975

"You can look up breaking points of metal and stresses in books. All the information is there if you just know where to look for it. You can measure the tension of strings with spring balances, which are quite cheap. So it's pretty straightforward.

"The next thing was to bend the wood. I was lucky in that as well because there happened to be some wood kicking around in some of my friend's houses. Particularly the neck – the mahogany came from a 100-year-old fireplace which had been ripped out of a house someone was knocking down nearby. It's a beautiful piece of wood, really well seasoned.

"I used mahogany simply because it was handy at the time but it's a lovely material to work with and I think I would have used mahogany or oak anyway.

"Shaping it? It was just a plank of wood when I got it, so I drew projections of the shape I wanted on all four sides and then I just started hacking away. First of all I cut in the planes and that left me with an angular sort of thing and then it was just a question of rounding it off. A lot of it was done with a penknife. I just worked away and kept trying the templates I'd made until it fitted. When it was roughly the right shape I attacked it with sandpaper for the final shaping, and then finer and finer grains of sandpaper to get a good finish.

"Then of course there's the polishing, which I did with plastic-coating stuff. You just pour it on in quite thick layers, let it dry and then start sanding again! Finer and finer grains until you get down to something like metal polish for the final shaping and polishing.

"And that's the woodworking side. The same sort of thing goes for the body. The way I designed that was that the strain was taken by a solid piece of oak – that's what the neck is screwed to – and the rest of the body, which takes no strain at all, is just glued to that.

"At that stage you do all the hollowing out and you have to decide what you want in the way of electronics. There are quite a few hollow pockets in this one which help the sound."

What about the electronics, the pickups and so forth?

"I started off making my own pickups, just getting some magnets and winding wire around them; that's all it is really, and they were very good. They made an excellent sound, but because I hadn't

▲ Freddie Mercury and Brian May performing at the Hammersmith Odeon, London, November 29, 1975

▶ April 22, 1975. Queen in Kyoto, Japan; left to right, Brian May, John Deacon, Freddie Mercury, Roger Taylor

"I made my own pickups, getting some magnets and winding wire around them"

designed them properly, when you pushed the string across the fingerboard the field wasn't uniform enough to take it.

"I bought some Rose pickups and they were so different in sound to my own that I decided to put new coils in them. I kept the magnets and that's what I ended up with.

"The sound of the pickup is only the start; it's a question of how you combine the different pickups – I've got three – on the guitar. There are practically no electronics in the guitar at all. If you combine two of them and just have the two sounds you get a normal blend of the two. If you reverse the phase you're in the situation where one is cancelling out the other to a certain extent, and what gets cancelled out is the thing they've got in common – the fundamental.

"By using different combinations you can bring out different harmonics from different parts of the string. You can vary the sound a lot.

"By the switches I've got you can get every combination from the pickups I've got. I've got six push buttons on the guitar – one phase reversal for each pickup and one cut-out for each."

Brian estimates his guitar cost about £8 to build but says he was fortunate to have a reasonably well-equipped workshop at his disposal. So it looks like a good deal to put some time away and set about building your own guitar, but Brian stresses one thing: "If you are going to build a guitar you've got to remember that it doesn't happen overnight. You've got to have patience so that when something goes wrong you can go away, think about it and come back again in a constructive frame of mind." *MM*

1975

ALBUM REVIEW

In a Completely Different Vein

FEBRUARY 24

More variety and more vinyl from Zep.

Led Zeppelin *Physical Graffiti*

NO OTHER TOP BAND in the world gets as much stick as Led Zeppelin. Every time they bring out an album there's six months of carping because it's not full of remakes of "Whole Lotta Love"; followed by another six months of moaning because they haven't played any live dates; finishing up with six months of complaints about the time it's taken them to make the new one.

Not this time, though, I suspect. By allowing themselves the luxury of a double album, they've managed to cram in a bit of everything and in enough quantity to keep that vocal minority of moaners at bay.

For once they will have to admit that the wait since *Houses Of The Holy* has been worthwhile; some may even be moved enough to recognise *Physical Graffiti* for what it is: a superbly performed mixture of styles and influences that encompasses not only all aspects of Led Zep's recording career so far, but also much of rock as a whole.

This is not just a collection of great tracks, but a perfectly balanced selection of music that weighs heavy rock with acoustic, ballad with out-and-out rocker, in such a way that you can play the album non-stop day and night without ever needing to pause for a bit of peace. And for one of the world's heaviest bands, that's some achievement.

Physical Graffiti has not just been "worth the wait"; it had to take a long time to produce music of this calibre. Unlike so many bands today, who hurl out albums like they were Frisbees in Hyde Park, Led Zep can be bothered to take the time and trouble to make this one even better than the last one.

They are, if you like, one of the few "progressive" bands left – you remember them, the groups who were always going to move forward and keep exploring new avenues. Zeppelin have, and still are, doing just that. They established their base with heavy blues-rock on *Led Zeppelin I*, and have constantly sought to build on that, investigating new fields, from the folky "Battle Of Evermore" to the reggae-influenced "D'Yer Maker". Now they've taken electronic space rock

◀ Jimmy Page, with drummer John "Bonzo" Bonham in the background, 1975

▲ Led Zeppelin in full flight at a Madison Square Garden gig during a 1975 tour

"It's a superbly performed mixture of styles and influences"

for "In The Light", one of the two most immediately striking cuts on *Physical Graffiti*.

It opens with eerie keyboards that sound like they belong to Pink Floyd's "Set The Controls For The Heart Of The Sun", before moving on to more familiar Zeppelin riffing. What marks it as the work of true craftsmen, though, is the linking: those space sounds are not just a frill tagged on for the hell of it, but properly joined to the core of the song, first led in by Robert Plant's voice, then led out for a reprise in the middle by Jimmy Page's acoustic guitar.

"Kashmir" hits you just as immediately. It's in a completely different vein: heavily orchestrated, with a chopping string riff which builds up to a crescendo at the end of each verse. The nearest equivalent is the work of the classical composer Moondog, who uses the same richly descriptive style.

So effectively is it used though on "Kashmir" that it actually sounds like you're travelling on a caravanserai through the East.

But the band's strength does not always rest on the new. They take that old, old theme of the blues on "In My Time Of Dying" and come up with a fresh approach, by constantly changing the pace, veering from the breakneck to the dead slow. Plant holds a note here, John Bonham continues a drum pattern there, and it joins together as tight as a clam.

And if it's heavy rock you want, Zeppelin can dive a number along like no other band on Earth. Listen to them roar through "Custard Pie" and "Night Flight" and "Sick Again", always giving that little bit extra that's the sign of class – a bubbling keyboard here, a nifty riff there, an intricate pattern elsewhere.

They can be wistful ("Down By The Seaside", fun ("Boogie With Stu") acoustic ("Bron-Yr-Aur"), melodic ("The Rover") – just about anything in fact. They can take as long as they like with the next album: *Physical Graffiti* will last 18 months or 18 years. And then some. *MM*

Windows were broken

JANUARY 6

Led Zeppelin shows in doubt as fans riot while queuing for tickets in New York and Boston.

THOUSANDS OF LED ZEPPELIN fans rioted at the weekend when tickets were put on sale for the band's three shows at Madison Square Garden on February 3, 7 and 12. (The dates are so spaced because of sports fixtures taking place at the Garden on the intervening nights.)

Tickets were due to go on sale on Monday morning, but fans began congregating outside the Garden on the Friday evening despite freezing weather. So many fans had gathered by the Saturday evening that the Garden management decided to begin selling tickets late Saturday night. More than 50,000 tickets were sold until Sunday afternoon, when the crowd swelled to such mammoth proportions that box-office windows were broken and seat sales suspended.

The remaining 10,000 tickets were placed on sale via Ticketron outlets spread across the city, and they soon sold out on Monday morning. The plan was to disperse the crowds to various selling points instead of congregating them at one outlet.

Another 40,000 or so tickets were sold for Zeppelin's Nassau Coliseum concerts, making a total of about 100,000 tickets sold in the New York area alone. At Boston, where Zeppelin are appearing at Boston Gardens, similar scenes occurred and the City Fathers – the local government authority – are considering cancelling the concert. Boston has recently been the scene of racial disturbances prompted by school-bussing arrangements, and the City Fathers may be unwilling to allow a large crowd to gather, whether it be for a rock concert or political meeting. **MM**

◀ Robert Plant, Madison Square Garden, New York City, 1975

▶ Jimmy Page with a backdrop of laser beams, Madison Square Garden, NYC

Keep 'Er Dancing

FEBRUARY 17

Lennon's long-awaited new LP is "the best since *Plastic Ono Band*".

John Lennon *Rock 'n' Roll*

"RE-LIVED BY JL" it says on the sleeve – and that's where *Rock'n'Roll* scores over last year's spate of retrospective enterprises. Possessing no equivalent of Lennon's crazily alienated youth to obsess them, Bowie, The Band, Ferry et al could only look back in warm nostalgia and attempt, with artistry, to recreate.

By comparison, Lennon is fixated. His focus on his early teen years has the brilliant gleam of genuine obsession. He relives – and that's what prevents *Rock'n'Roll* from being charged with the archness, the indulgence, the ambiguity and the decadence that surrounded the attempts of Ferry and Bowie. Lennon isn't into perspectives. *Rock'n'Roll* is what it claims to be and no more.

And no more? Let's get this thing the right way up; this album is fine – the best sustained effort on John Beatle's part since *Plastic Ono Band*. (Although the parallel ends abruptly there; *Rock'n'Roll*'s twin principles are strength and hilarity... it's an "up" record... party time, kids.)

The quickest way to become convinced is to hammer into your local disc vendor's den and demand to hear Chuck Berry's "You Can't Catch Me" followed by Larry Williams' "Bony Moronie".

Both have gigantic sounds – lots of snare, riffing saxes, chunking 12-bar guitars, and echo unlimited – care of Phil Spector (who produced and co-arranged four of the best tracks in late '73 before his car accident).

"You Can't Catch Me" is a powerhouse rock-out that'd make a great single with its "Come Together" references and all; "Bony Moronie" is tackled at a markedly slow pace which allows the breaks to become yawning gaps in a mountain range of sound, with Lennon left suddenly alone in them, savouring lines like "Rock'n'roll by the light of the silvery moon" and "Making love underneath the apple tree".

Both tracks are genuine rock'n'roll relived; Lennon simply accentuates the beauties that were always there. Anyone else would have felt obliged to comment. The general scheme of the album is down to fast continuity (keep 'em dancing); the overall mood concerns Lennon's attitude to his own enthusiasm (a song

in his heart, a smile on his face). Witness the introduction of Lloyd Price's "Just Because" with John reminiscing over a swarm of mandolins: "Ah, remember this? I must've been 13 when this came out. Or was it 14?"

I'm utterly disarmed and expect you'll be also. Other points to watch include: (1) an extraordinary squealing guitar solo on "Stand By Me" (which I trust is by Lennon, although the sleeve provides no personnel); (2) "Do You Want To Dance" performed at a drunken lope; and (3) a rampaging "Peggy Sue" screeching to a halt for Lennon to do his "Look out!" bit before a manic rhythm guitar charges in to take the central break.

Personally I'd have preferred a punchier version of "Sweet Little Sixteen" and don't really care either way about "Bring It On Home To Me", "Be-Bop-A-Lula" and "Ya Ya", but what's left ("Rip It Up/Ready Teddy", "Slippin' And Slidin'" and "Ain't That A Shame") is, in the words of the ad man, sheer enjoyment.

One comes away from this album with the hope that these old forms are still viable; their simple strengths are very much what's needed today. If Lou Reed's oldies album hits it off (and he must have a hell of a story to tell), we might witness a complete change of direction in the next year or so. Meanwhile we leave Mr Lennon wishing his listeners well from the final grooves of his latest fave album: "Everybody here says Hi. Goodbye." **NME**

> ## "His focus on his early teen years has the gleam of genuine obsession"

> ▶ John Lennon in 1975, in the kitchen of his apartment at the Dakota building, West 72nd Street, New York City

NEWS

Not sufficient reason for deportation

OCTOBER 7

John Lennon wins his fight to stay in the USA.

JOHN LENNON has won his fight against deportation from the United States. The victory came last week when the US Court of Appeal decided Lennon's British drug conviction was not sufficient reason for the American Immigration Department's deportation order against him.

The decision came on the eve of the birth of Sean Ono Lennon, John and Yoko's first child. The Court's judgement marks the climax to a three-year struggle by Lennon to stay in the States. He entered America on August 31, 1971, originally intending to stay for a few weeks to attend a court hearing concerning the custody of Kyoko, Yoko Ono's daughter by her first marriage to film director Tony Cox.

Early the following year Lennon retained lawyer Leon Wildes

when it became necessary for him to apply for an extension to his American visa. Since that time there have been numerous attempts by the government to have Lennon deported, but constant appeals have enabled him to remain in the US.

He has not been able to leave America, however, for fear that the immigration authorities would bar him from entry if he attempted to return.

The whole case was further complicated by two actions filed against the American government by Wildes. The first and most important of the actions claimed the Immigration Department pre-judged Lennon's case without giving him a fair opportunity to state his reasons for wishing to remain in the US. *MM*

◄ John Lennon and David Bowie attending the 17th Annual Grammy Awards at the Uris Theatre in New York, February 28, 1975

"The cat's knackers"

Introducing THE 101ERS, and their frontman JOE STRUMMER. "It's all about energy," he says. "We play until they throw us off…"

IT WAS SOMETIME back in February that I first saw the 101ers. They had a residency in the Charlie Pigdog Club in West London. It was the kind of place which held extraordinary promises of violence. You walked in, took one look around, and wished you were the hell out of there.

The general feeling was that something was going to happen, and whatever that something was, it was inevitably going to involve you. After 10 minutes glancing into secluded corners, half-expecting to see someone having their face decorated with a razor, the paranoia count was soaring.

The gig that particular evening ended in a near massacre. As the 101ers screamed their way through a 20-minute interpretation of "Gloria", which sounded like the perfect soundtrack for the last days of the Third Reich, opposing factions of (I believe) Irish and gypsies attempted to carve each other out. Bottles were smashed over defenceless heads, blades flashed and howling dogs tore at one another's throats, splattering the walls with blood… No one, I was convinced, is going to crawl out of this one alive…

The band tore on, with Joe Strummer thrashing away at his guitar like there was no tomorrow, completely oblivious of the surrounding carnage. The police finally arrived, flashing blue lights, sirens, the whole works. Strummer battled on. He was finally confronted by the imposing figure of the law, stopped in mid-flight, staggered to a halt, and looked up. "Evening, officer," he said…

The 101ers no longer play at the Charlie Pigdog Club. "The builders moved in and started to wreck the fucking place," Strummer remarks caustically.

We find them now at the Elgin in Ladbroke Grove, where they have a Thursday residency, involved in a slight altercation with the manager. Jules, their newly appointed manager, and Mick Foote, their driver and unofficial publicist, are at the bar trying to placate a band called Lipstick who've turned up to play at the manager's request. The manager is under the impression that he's hired the 101ers for Monday nights, and Lipstick for Thursday. Lipstick want to play.

"Look", says Foote, "what are you doing on Monday? Nothing? Right, you play on fucking Monday then"

The argument is resolved. The 101ers will play, Lipstick can watch from the sidelines.

The band, according to Strummer (rhythm guitar and voice), was formed "in a basement early last summer. We had a couple of guitars and a few Concord speakers and we thought we were the cat's knackers… Hey, d'you want to know how I got my Telecaster? Well, I was working at the Royal Opera House carrying out the rubbish. A fucking great job. Only had to work two hours of the day. There was this hole in the basement, where I'd creep off to play guitar. Anyway, the manager found me and fired me. Gave me £120 to get out as soon as possible. So I went out and scored an AC 30."

I thought you were going to tell us about your guitar.

"Oh yeah, yeah. I was working in Hyde Park, and I met this South American chick who wanted to get married. To stay in the country, see? She paid me a hundred quid, so I quit the job, and got a Telecaster to go with the AC 30… I'll get the divorce through in about two years."

The initial lineup of the band seems to have varied from rehearsal to rehearsal, but eventually a nucleus of musicians evolved around Strummer and they played their first gig at the Telegraph on Brixton Hill on September 7 last year.

"We had this fucking mad Chilean sax player, Alvaro. He got us a gig at a political benefit for Chilean refugees. We had five days to knock something together, we could only play six numbers. Then our fucking drummer went on holiday. That's when the Snakes joined for the first time."

Snakehips Dudanski, former head boy at Salesian College and zoology student at Chelsea University, had never played drums before: "After a couple of days of frantic practising I thought I could handle it. It wasn't too difficult, I just bashed everything in sight. I

▶ Joe Strummer playing at the Red Cow pub in London with the 101ers in 1975, the year before he joined The Clash

"You want to see someone tearing their
soul apart at 36 bars a second"

still do. There's only one difficulty... playing with odd sticks. That, and having to buy them second-hand."

He is now permanently installed in the rhythm section alongside The Mole. Like Snakehips, The Mole had never even looked at a musical instrument until he was invited to join the 101ers when they were short of a bass player. For such a relatively immature musical combination, Snakehips and The Mole lock together magnetically, thrusting the 101ers along with vicious energy.

Strummer and lead guitarist, Clive WM Timperley, are the only members of the band with any substantial musical experience. Strummer once fronted a legendary outfit called Johnny & The Vultures back in 1973, an erratic but occasionally stunning formation that played a handful of gigs before sinking without trace. Timperley, affectionately referred to as Evil by Strummer, has been playing since the mid-'60s, starting with an outfit called Captain Rougely's Blues Band, which included Martin Lamble, the original drummer with Fairport Convention (unfortunately killed in a road accident in 1969). After that he worked his way through a succession of none-too-successful bands, arriving on the 101ers' doorstep in January.

He's recently precipitated a minor crisis by threatening to leave the band. He's had a lucrative offer from some "tame-brained singer-songwriter," as Strummer describes him. "He'd be a fucking fool to leave us now. But we've advertised for a new guitarist...

"We have to be careful. We want a guitarist for a beat group, we don't want any bloody acid casualties thinking they're going to join the Grateful Dead. We want someone who can whip their axe. I mean, if you go to see a rock group you want to see someone tearing their soul apart at 36 bars a second, not listen to some instrumental slush. Since '67, music has been chasing itself up a blind alley with all that shit."

As you might have gathered, the 101ers are fairly uncompromising in their attitude towards most contemporary rock music. They are about energy: pure rock'n'roll dynamics. They concentrate almost exclusively on standard rock material, but their greatest strength lies in Strummer's own compositions, like "Motor, Boys, Motor", and particularly "Steamgauge 99" and the stunning "Keys To Your Heart", and in his own ragged charisma. He's a naturally powerful performer, given to sudden explosions of passion.

"That's what it's all about. That energy. I mean, we usually have to do a two-and-a-half-hour set here. If we're on a bill with some other bands we cut it down to an hour and a half. Or play until they throw us off. Playing that long every night can kill you. Like, there's this line in 'Roll Over Beethoven'... 'Early in the morning, I'm giving you my warning/Don't you step on my blue suede shoes...' And if you're a classy Chuck Berry kind of singer, you've got to do the whole line in one breath to keep the energy flowing.

"Straight after that line I usually faint. Everything goes white. If you haven't eaten for a few days and you haven't had any sleep, you just keel over backwards. But I always get back on my feet for the next line, 'Hey diddle, diddle, I'm playing my fiddle/I got nothing to lose...' That's just such a great line, you've got to stay on your feet for that.

"And we'll always be on our feet. We're gonna take this all the way." **MM**

A change in musical approach

FEBRUARY 8

New faces for Fleetwood Mac.

FLEETWOOD MAC have lost guitarist Bob Welch, who has left the band to concentrate on production work. He has been replaced in the lineup by two new members – Stevie Nicks (who despite the name is in fact a girl singer) and guitarist Lindsey Buckingham. This personnel change means that Mac now have two girl vocalists in Christine McVie and newcomer Stevie.

It is not yet clear how Mac will be affected by this new policy, although it would seem to point to a change in their musical approach. The band are now based permanently in Los Angeles, where they are currently engaged in cutting a new album – which is being produced by their former member, Bob Welch. **NME**

◀ The 101ers at The Elgin pub, Ladbroke Grove, London in 1975. Left to right: Richard "Snakehips" Dudanski, Joe Strummer, and Simon "Big John" Cassell

An Incredible Show

JUNE 22 · **MADISON SQUARE GARDEN, NEW YORK**

Over several nights at Madison Square Garden, the Rolling Stones'
arrangement with Ron Wood continues to pay dividends.

◀ Ronnie Wood, Mick Jagger and
Keith Richards share the vocals
with keyboard player Billy Preston
(second left) on stage in 1975.

NEW YORK: So there's half the island of Jamaica up there –
drums, tambourines, triangles, maracas, talking drums – just
anything that comes to hand, right, and there's this stringy dude
in a denim frock coat and a beret that folks are saying is Clapton
– but from a hundred yards away, who knows?

And Mick's wearing Keith's leather jacket – this is after he's
poured the bucket of water over his head and after the parachute-
silk dragon has spewed confetti and balloons over the front few
rows... Anyway, they're doing "Sympathy For The Devil" for the
first time since... since then, and wow, does it ever sound good.

Feels good, too, what with the house lights up and most
everybody dancing and clapping, and the star-shaped stage
flapping up and down, and fire crackers exploding everywhere,
but I guess the atmosphere at Madison Square Garden is always
pretty... electric, and the Stones' opening night could hardly fail,
could it?

All the same, it took the group a while to get into their stride,
a half-hour at least, the sound so strangled and mangled for
"Honky Tonk Women" through to "Star Star" that listening
wasn't much fun. "You Gotta Move" was the ice-breaker. Jagger,
Billy Preston, Ron Wood, Richards and percussionist Ollie E
Brown locked into uncertain but enthusiastic harmonies – and
Keith, in the absence of Mick Taylor, pulled off a taut and
emotional blues solo.

Technically, of course, neither he nor Wood are world-class
lead players, but they complement each other nicely and the lack
of bone fide virtuoso only underlines all the essential earthiness
that we used to associate with the old *Out Of Our Heads* period.
Plus, Taylor never fitted visually with his shy, student good looks,
while the Face, cigarette glued permanently to his lower lip,
resembles some evolutionary stage between Wyman and
Richards – all three of them, even in expensive silks and leathers,
coming on like Portobello Road hustlers gone ape.

But the overriding impression gleaned from the whole shebang
is that they're having fun. A lot of the macho-sadist excess has
been pruned back, and although Jagger cavorts and leaps and
pouts as much as ever, he seems more like an irresistible clown
than any Lucifer figure. Indeed, at times, he lets the image slide
entirely as he straps on a guitar for "Fingerprint File" and stands
immobile behind the mic stand as Wood and Wyman move to
bass and keyboards respectively.

And these flashes of naturalness are inevitably at odds with the
elaborate props – the notorious giant phallus, the dragon head
and, worse, a sequence where Jagger is raised 30 feet above the
stage on a high-wire, suspended-stirrup affair. Firing on all
cylinders as the vitriolic rock band, the very essence of hard blues
and boogie, such paraphernalia seems exceptionally jive.

But not to bitch overmuch. It's still an incredible show. *MM*

"I don't think Ron knows yet"

DECEMBER 27

The Faces finally fold. Where does this leave Ron Wood?

THE MOST WIDELY anticipated split in rock history finally came to a head last weekend, when Rod Stewart officially announced that he has broken his connections with the Faces.

Stewart said that his decision to leave the group, in order to concentrate on a solo career, was taken after much deliberation. He added that he could no longer work in a situation where the Faces' lead guitarist, Ron Wood, seemed to be permanently "on loan" to the Rolling Stones.

Stewart now intends to form his own band, the lineup of which will be made known early in the New Year. However, it now seems unlikely that Wood will join the new band, as had been widely rumoured in the past.

There has, as yet, been no official word regarding Ron Wood's future plans. It has automatically been assumed that he will now join the Rolling Stones – with whom he toured America in the summer and has recently been recording on the Continent – on a permanent basis.

When *NME* contacted Mick Jagger in Paris on Friday morning, just before he boarded a plane for the United States, he had only just heard of the Faces split. He commented: "I don't think Ron even knows about it yet. All I can say at the moment is that no agreement has yet been signed between the Stones and Ron Wood. There's nothing finalised at all. But as I say, we've only just learned of the split."

It seems logical that Wood will join the Stones. But reports in the national and evening papers last weekend, suggesting that he had already done so, were – at press-time – still premature.

Jagger reaffirmed that the Stones are planning a European tour in the early spring, and expected to include British dates in their itinerary. He said they were aiming at March–April for the tour, but emphasised that no venues are yet set.

The *NME* understands that April 6 is being held for a Rolling Stones concert at Wembley Empire Pool, but that the Stones have not yet given their final approval. *NME*

▶ Rolling Stones new boy Ronnie Wood enjoying a beer and a ciggie

"I'm not into writing songs. I find that real boring"

A scene is developing in New York, and it is led by PATTI SMITH. From art student to factory worker to bohemian poet, she describes how meeting guitarist Lenny Kaye introduced her to the rock'n'roll world as her chosen path.

LAST MONTH THEY caught Patti Hearst – and so ended the biggest man (or woman) hunt in the history of the US. All this is history now, of course, but it'll probably be the subject of at least two best-selling novels in the near future, not to mention a major screen movie.

But perhaps the first outside view of the Patti Hearst case was provided by New York's sparrow-like poetess Patti Smith, then a struggling personality in the underground rock scene of the city. With considerable difficulty, she raised $1,000 and headed for Electric Ladyland Studios in Greenwich Village and recorded a version of the traditional Hendrix classic "Hey Joe".

The inspiration for this move was provided by the words of Randolph Hearst, who on seeing the picture of his daughter holding a rifle, exclaimed to the anxious ears of America: "What are you doing with that gun in your hand?"

Patti Smith's version of "Hey Joe" was a bitch of a record. Opening with a poetic dialogue about the Hearst situation, it gradually flowed into the regular song. It was chock-full of atmosphere and, for topicality, it really couldn't be beaten. Had it received more exposure, I'm sure that Patti Smith would have been an overnight sensation.

It didn't, though, and it never will. About 1,000 copies of Patti's "Hey Joe" were pressed and made available by mail order through her management company and selected record shops down in the

◄ Patti Smith in concert, New York City, 1975

▶ Behind the shades, the "poet of punk" Patti Smith, 1975

Village. According to Patti's manager, Jane Friedman, the project lost around $3,000, even though the singles were sold at $2.50, a mark-up of over 50 per cent on the regular singles' price.

Today it's a collector's item, and no more are available. Also today, Patti Smith stands on the brink of success after a long, hard struggle. This summer she signed with Arista Records, and her debut album is out in the States this month.

Thanks to Clive Davis, the boss of Arista, she is only the second of many artists in this (New York) fringe-rock fraternity to be recognised by a record company. The first, of course, was the New York Dolls, whose recording career slumped after two albums.

But Ms Smith cannot be placed in the same category as the Dolls, or any rock band, for that matter. Some may call her a singer, but she is really an improvising lyricist whose performances rush with crazy momentum as each song, or poem, unrolls. She recites with a musical backdrop, frequently breaking into song as the energy spirals, criss-crossing between the two and, more often than not, making up the words as she stumbles headlong forward.

Her band has been increasing in size over the years. Four years back it was just Patti and her guitarist Lenny Kaye, an occasional rock journalist and walking encyclopaedia on the last two decades of pop in America. Kaye, who three years ago, incidentally, compiled the *Nuggets* album of relatively obscure US singles for the Elektra label, might be described as a free-form guitarist, as he plays random notes at will according to the prompting of Patti's dialogue. They understand one another and, as such, it's doubtful whether any orthodox guitar player would fit.

Pianist Richard Sohl is a similar performer. Like Kaye, nothing he plays can be predicted beforehand.

Recently two other musicians have been added: a second guitarist, Ivan Kral, who like Patti bears a striking resemblance to Keith Richards, and drummer Jay Dougherty. There is no bass player – Patti feels a drummer is ample rhythm.

John Cale was brought in to produce her first Arista album, *Horses*, which is released this month. It was on this topic that we began what turned out to be a very lengthy conversation last week.

"It's a live album," she announced, squatting on the floor. "There's hardly any overdubbing at all. We just went in and did the songs straight away.

"In the studio we went through hell. I asked John to do it for me, I begged him to, and we had nothing but friction, but it was a love-hate relationship and it worked. At first I wanted an engineer-producer, somebody like Tom Dowd, but Atlantic wouldn't let him go, so I figured I'd get a top artist-producer who would act as a mirror.

"The whole thing in the studio was us proving to John that we could do it the way we wanted, so we fought a lot but it was fighting on a very intimate level."

The result is an album that's actually far more melodic than the half-dozen or so occasions I've watched Patti perform in various places in New York. The inclusion of a drummer – Dougherty was brought in immediately before the sessions began – tightens up Patti's style no end. Before, it was often shapeless and without discipline of any kind. Now you can even dance to Patti Smith, or at least some of the tracks.

Even words were improvised in the studio, she says. "I'm not into writing songs. I find that real boring. All our things started out initially as improvisation, but doing them over and over again got them into a formula.

"I can't play anything at all, so Lenny and I work out tunes as they go along. I have words and know how I think they should go, so we just pull it out and pull it out further until we get somewhere."

She and Kaye first got together in 1971. This followed a period of Patti's life when she lived at the Chelsea Hotel, writing poetry and spending time with rock musicians in what she describes as a "tequila split life".

Before that she was at art school, which followed work in a factory in New Jersey, where she was brought up. It was Bobby Neuwirth who introduced her to the changing musical inhabitants of the Chelsea Hotel. (Neuwirth is currently playing on Dylan's tour of New England with Joan Baez.)

"Neuwirth recognised my poetry and immediately introduced me to everybody he knew in rock'n'roll and kept pumping me to work at it. I studied Rimbaud, too, but being surrounded by these rock'n'roll rhythms, the two moved simultaneously."

It wasn't until 1972 that Patti started making regular appearances in New York.

In 1973, Lenny Kaye reappeared following a reading Patti gave on the anniversary of Jim Morrison's death, and from then on things accelerated. Pianist Richard Sohl joined the ranks and gigs followed at anywhere manager Jane Friedman could book them.

Which just about brings us up to where we began: the "Hey Joe" single recorded at Electric Ladyland. It was a deliberate choice of studio, for Patti strongly allies herself with Hendrix, another artist who took his art beyond contemporary strictures.

"We had three hours of studio time, but I just did it like we were on stage. Eventually we had 10 minutes left and no B-side, so I recited this poem and the musicians just joined in and we had it done."

According to Friedman, that "Hey Joe" chapter lost about $3,000 as so many copies were given away to friends instead of being sold. Part of their deal with Arista was a clause that no more could be made, so it'll remain a collector's item forever.

Clive Davis' interest in Patti stems from his days with Columbia, when Patti wrote the lyrics to two songs recorded by Blue Öyster Cult, a CBS act.

The deal with Arista is for five albums over the next three years, and meanwhile she has branched out from New York, playing concerts in California for the first time. In the coming months she will embark on her first proper tour, mainly visiting colleges across the country.

"We're a group now," she said. "We're together and that's it. I'm in rock'n'roll now and I'm proud to be in it." **MM**

◀ Promoting her first album *Horses*, released December 13, 1975

"Seems to have been an overdose"

JUNE 29

RIP, Tim Buckley.

TIM BUCKLEY, the 27-year-old singer and composer, died suddenly in America last week. He had apparently played a gig and returned to his hotel, where he was found dead some hours later. Manager Herb Cohen commented: "It seems to have been an overdose, but Tim wasn't into drugs, so I can only put it down to misadventure."

Buckley played in various country bands and, as a solo singer, worked in folk clubs around Los Angeles. He was signed by Elektra in 1967, subsequently moving to Reprise. Of his eight albums on release in this country, the best-known are probably *Goodbye And Hello* and *Starsailor*, the latter marking a move into avant-garde jazz. His last appearances in this country were in 1974 when he took part in the Knebworth Park concert and headlined a concert at London's Rainbow Theatre. **NME**

ALBUM REVIEW

In Suspended Animation

SEPTEMBER 12

Floyd lack all conviction.

Pink Floyd *Wish You Were Here*

THIS, SPACE CADETS, is IT. You've been waiting for two years for it to arrive, just so's you could snatch it, shrink-wrapped and shining, hot from the deck – Pink Floyd's long-awaited successor to their record-breaking *Dark Side Of The Moon* (in the best-selling album lists for over 30 months and still selling).

Wish You Were Here took six months to record at EMI's new 24-track studio in Abbey Road.

I am not enthralled. I have, also, to admit that its predecessor, despite its enormous popularity, left me equally unmoved. I did try, though, to acclimatise myself to its bleak, emotionally barren landscape. Just as I have tried to entertain the prospect of embracing *Wish You Were Here* as A Giant Step Forward For Mankind, I keep missing the connection, somehow. From whichever direction one approaches *Wish You Were Here*, it still sounds unconvincing in its ponderous sincerity and displays a critical lack of imagination in all departments. It's really all quite predictable, and forces one to the conclusion that for the last two years (possibly longer) the Floyd have existed in a state of suspended animation.

It's really quite alarming that they should have remained so secure in their isolation. While the world turns in destruction upon itself, the Floyd amble somnambulantly along their star-struck avenues arm in arm with some pallid ghost of creativity. *Wish You Were Here* sucks. It's as simple as that.

The omission of two of the songs premiered on their last British tour – "Raving And Drooling" and "Gotta Be Crazy" – is perhaps significant in that it suggests the Floyd have a fundamental lack of confidence in their own material. Similarly, the amount of time they have devoted to this record shouldn't be taken as a sign of their constant search for perfection. Rather, it indicates a lack of determination and resolution.

The constant embellishments and elaborate effects which adorn the album seem merely artificial and contrived. A series of masks and facades to disguise the crucial lack of inspiration which afflicts the whole project.

One thing is evident from the moment the stylus hits the vinyl: *Wish You Were Here* is no progression from *Dark Side Of The Moon*. Just as there has been no real development in the Floyd's music since *Ummagumma*. The slight concept which holds the album together is, essentially, a rather petulant tirade against the

▲ Pink Floyd: left to right, David Gilmour, Nick Mason, Roger Waters and Richard "Rick" Wright, at the Los Angeles Memorial Sports Arena in April 1975

▶ Dave Gilmour onstage at the Sports Arena in April 1975, in Los Angeles, California

◀ Pink Floyd's Richard Wright, a portrait by photographer Barrie Wentzell in 1975

▲ Dave Gilmour, guitar supremo with the Floyd, 1975

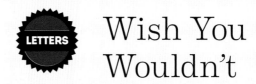

Wish You Wouldn't

OCTOBER 4

From Allan Jones' first abusive, smug and belittling comment, it was obvious what sort of putdown his review of Pink Floyd's *Wish You Were Here* was to be. He states that it took six months to record, and later amplifies this statement by saying this shows "a lack of determination and resolution" and that it "shouldn't be taken as a sign of their constant search for perfection".

But it should! Six months is not a particularly lengthy time for recording an album in this day and age, and the superb production and masterful technical quality of the album surely vindicates this. Maybe the Bay City Rollers did record *Rollin'* in four days, but it's hardly a masterpiece.

CHRIS FERRARY, Coolgardie Ave, Highams Park, London. **MM**

---

rockbiz. The attack is no more than petulant because of Roger Waters' rather dubious qualities as a lyricist. EMI describe Waters' efforts as "penetrating and significant". I refer you and your good judgement to "Welcome To The Machine", which closes side one in a blur of electronic and crowd sound effects. (The Floyd's use of such techniques throughout the album displays as much aural sophistication as a 1967 psychedelic band embarking upon their first concept album.) Elsewhere, we have the same wall-to-wall cliches which have marked almost every Floyd album since *Saucerful Of Secrets*. Rick Wright's dawn-of-man keyboard atmospherics became tedious enough on that album. It's unbelievable that he's not realised since that you can do more with a synthesizer than simulate the winds of time drifting across the face of the universe. The worst move he ever made was trading in his Farfisa for a Mellotron.

As musicians, the Floyd have never made any claims for virtuosity, but here the overall standard of their performance is without exception extremely poor. David Gilmour could never be described as a graceful or inventive guitarist, and it's unfortunate that for much of the time the focus should be on his contributions. He plays with a dogged enthusiasm, but he's too often ridiculously obvious.

Only on the introduction to "Have A Cigar" do the band play with any real vigour. It's not majestic, and it's no profound spiritual experience, but at least it's enough to convince me that they haven't stiffed out completely. Yet. Roy Harper, guesting here on vocals, adds a little more interest to what is really a rather colourless song. Waters' lyrics again are painfully mundane. He's simply unable to invest his attack against rockbiz manipulation with any vestige of urgency.

Sample lyric: "Come in here, dear boy, have a cigar. You're gonna go far, fly high/You're never gonna die, you're gonna make it if you try; they're gonna love you". The title track – dominated by some thoroughly inadequate acoustic guitar and Waters' weakest vocal performance – is curiously lightweight, and almost instantly forgettable "...year after year/Running over the same old ground". sings Waters in the third verse. I know how he must feel.

The Floyd's real attempt at a magnum opus to rival past triumphs is the nine-part "Shine On You Crazy Diamond". This is Roger Waters' epic tribute to fractured genius Syd Barrett.

It was perhaps inevitable, within the context of the album and Waters' lyrical preoccupation, that he should choose Barrett, rock casualty supreme, as a tragic example of creative innocence compromised and all but destroyed by the pressures of the biz. The insensitivity of Waters' lyrics borders on the offensive in that they completely trivialise Barrett's predicament.

I can't honestly recommend it for its musical content, either, although the last four "movements" on side two have a vitality absent from the first five which open side one. For most of the ride it's the usual Floyd panorama of sound, with Wright's congregation of keyboards adding ethereal splashes behind Gilmour's armour-piercing guitar forays. The final effect is not unlike a theme from *Quo Vadis* being piped into a supermarket. Careful with those frozen peas, Eugene.

Wish You Were Here will sell as well as *Dark Side Of The Moon*, of course. And in three years, when the next Floyd album is released, I wouldn't be at all surprised if it's still in the chart.

Crazy, isn't it? **MM**

"A certain Western charisma"

Evolving slowly, with a closed circle around them, the EAGLES are preparing for greatness. But, as one reporter discovers, their jarring personalities may not help them. "I love Bernie Leadon and I hate him," says Don Henley. "You know what I mean?"

O N A CLEAR DAY in Hollywood, Glenn Frey can see from his living room right out to sea, right across the Pacific to Catalina, the island off the coast of southern California. On a not so clear day, he can see layers of orange smog, the product of the internal combustion engine, which is God in this part of America.

Today is clear and the view is quite breathtaking. Certainly conducive to writing those typical Los Angeles soft-rock melodies with which the Eagles have become synonymous.

It doesn't take a fortune teller to predict that 1975 is going to be the big year for the Eagles. They've been clicking their boot heels for three years now, steadily building a reputation in the wake of The Byrds, waiting for the breakthrough that their third album, *On The Border*, has seemingly now brought about. Although it's easing down the charts right now, it's established the band as a force to be reckoned with.

"*On The Border* was the best-sounding record we ever made, but that's also experience. We're starting to learn how to become recording artists, which is a little different from learning how to be a member of a band or how to become a singer-songwriter.

"There're definitely things we've learned slowly over a couple of years of making records. I know when we made *Desperado* we were

◄ The Eagles: Glenn Frey tuning his guitars before a 1975 show in Los Angeles

very conscious of having a group identity running through the songs, and that was something we learned out of doing the first album.

"After doing that one, when we went in to do *On The Border* we tried to bring in the best elements from both the albums. That probably had something to do with it, but I think it was a better album anyway. I think we just progressed and played with a little more confidence. But mainly I think it's that we stayed together."

Another factor which Frey credits as being important to the group's recent success is the introduction of Don Felder on slide guitar. Felder, says Frey, put extra punch into the Eagles' live show, with the added result that they picked up more followers. "I believe in selling records on the road, and I believe that if you work hard and have a good album out, it will sell.

"Since we got Felder in the band we've had a much better second half – the rock'n'roll half – in our shows. The other part – the vocal-harmony softer part – was always real good, but Felder nails down the harder stuff.

"He's like Duane Allman: he drives the band on certain songs. Some slide players, myself included, just slide along with the song, but when Felder plays slide he drives the band and the whole thing revolves around him. So the year that we promoted *On The Border* we had a much better show together."

Desperado was a concept album in as much as many of the tunes dealt with the old West. It seemed curious, I remarked, that a band would travel to England from America to make that kind of record.

"Well," mused Glenn. "I guess you're right, but Clint Eastwood made all those cowboy movies of his in Italy. Some of the best Western movies have been made in Europe. You get a whole new perspective working in England. All of a sudden you're a foreigner, and it put us and LA and everything into perspective. Now I like staying here, although we tried going to Miami for part of this new album. We got some stuff accomplished there, but not nearly as much as we did recording here."

Another factor which possibly aided the success of the last album was their decision to tour with some of the material before it was put

▲ The Eagles pose during a photoshoot in Hamburg, Germany, in February 1975

▶ The Eagles on stage in Amsterdam, Netherlands, in1975.
Left to right: Glenn Frey, Joe Walsh, Bernie Leadon

Rumours of disenchantment

DECEMBER 20

Bernie Leadon quits the Eagles, Joe Walsh steps up.

JOE WALSH has replaced guitarist Bernie Leadon in the Eagles. He will be playing with the band on their forthcoming American tour.

Rumours of disenchantment within the band have been rife for some time and Leadon is known to dislike touring. The choice of Joe Walsh as his replacement, however, is a complete surprise. He has established a considerable reputation as an artist in his own right.

Walsh and the Eagles share the same manager, Irving Azoff, and both acts appeared at Elton John's Wembley Stadium concert last June – a performance which climaxed with Walsh jamming with the Eagles.

A new live album by Walsh will be released in February, and after the Eagles' US concerts, the band will be embarking on a world tour with gigs in Britain on the cards.

Although Walsh is now a full-time member of the band, it seems certain that he will also continue his solo career. **MM**

down on tape. Thus not only were audiences already familiar with the tracks, but the band had an opportunity to work on them before they reached the studio.

"I think we did about five songs on a college tour," said Glenn. "We were out there testing them, mixing them in with the better-known songs. I think it's good to do it that way sometimes, because it forces you to make a presentation immediately.

"It forces you to give a rendering immediately so vocal parts get simplified, and backing parts and guitar parts get honed down to what you can do best to present the song. By the time we get to the studio there's a whole basic sketch already done.

"With this next album we haven't done that, but again this album so far is nothing but our own songs. On the others we usually included a song by another writer or called in a friend, like Jackson [Browne] or John David [Souther], to help on a track. We may do that in the next two weeks, though.

"This is maybe a reason why it's taking longer to make than other albums, but another reason is that Don Henley and I are trying to change the traditional symbolic rock'n'roll lyrics that most people use on albums.

"The songs have been finished for a while but we've sat around thinking whether we ought to change them. All we have to do now is to go in and sing the parts, and that's when it'll begin to sound like an Eagles record. Whenever I hear backing tracks, I can't think of it being the Eagles at all, a long way from 'Peaceful Easy Feeling'."

Last summer, the Eagles backed Neil Young at a Native American benefit concert near San Francisco, an experience which may be repeated this year, and one which Frey recollects with more than a little pride.

"The guy that put it together was our art director, and he knows the native California Indians and he approached Neil Young who said he'd do it. He didn't commit himself until three or four days before the concert, though, because he didn't want it to be advertised.

"We had a great jam on 'Cowgirl In The Sand', with me and Felder and Neil trading solos for about 12 minutes. We hope to make it an annual event as we're doing another one this May. I'm into doing things for them because I figure we're living on their land even if I don't have one iota of guilt about it.

"The Indians knew how to live here properly and a lot of people are starting to think this way and realise their Old West consciousness. I'm into the western civilisation mysticism. Over here people are always turning to the east, but I figure it's all right here if we want to look for it.

"I'm sure some of this Indian and Mexican influence was with us when we were doing Desperado, as we had a great time doing the little links between songs, the banjo and traditional things. I would like to do another concept album, though I'm not sure what the premise would be."

"When Felder plays slide, the whole thing revolves around him"

Frey's song "Best Of My Love" undoubtedly gave *On The Border* sales a boost. It was, he says, an attempt to work off a guitar tuning that Joni Mitchell had demonstrated. "Actually, I got into a totally different tuning and that's how the song ended up.

"I had a little help from John David Souther, who worked on the bridge and rang me up from LA when I was in England to play it over the phone. We actually worked on it over the phone until he came to England to see us. 'Cry Like A Lover' came about the same way, working on the phone over all that distance."

Collaboration with other LA musicians is a way of life in California, as can usually be detected by reading album credits as well as noticing various similarities in the actual music.

"On songwriting, I do it all the time," admits Frey. "If I get something I can't finish by myself, it's always good to take it to someone else. We collaborate among ourselves, but Souther helps us out sometimes.

"It's not so much calling up for help in an emergency as just calling and suggesting we spend an evening writing together and picking up on fragments. The funny thing that we find with the guys in the Eagles and Souther and Jackson is how much we think

alike. Whenever anyone plays something, we tend to pick on it right away."

This summer the Eagles are making their first trip to England in over 18 months. They're tentatively scheduled to appear with Elton John at Wembley Stadium on June 21 along with stablemate Joe Walsh.

"What I like about playing in England," said Frey as we drew to a close, "is the attentiveness of the audience. In America we tend to play to very boisterous crowds, but in England they sit and listen and I just thrive on that.

"We found when we played our first ever gigs in England that being American helped us. Being an American unknown in America is a drag, but being an American unknown in England is cool. We found we had a certain amount of Western charisma. I didn't realise it until people started looking at my cowboy boots and asking where I got them." **MM**

◄ Eagles' Glen Frey (left) and Don Henley (centre) during an interview at Frey's home in Los Angeles, 1975

▼ The Eagles during a European tour in 1975

ABBA // AC/DC // Bob Dylan
Bob Marley and the Wailers // The Clash
Howlin' Wolf // Kiss // Led Zeppelin // Queen
Robert Plant // Sex Pistols // Tom Waits

1976

Euro-pop quartet ABBA increase their presence on charts worldwide, Robert Plant bemoans how much he's giving to the taxman, and Bob Marley survives an assassination attempt.

American glam-rockers Kiss plumb the lowest depths with their stage show, Australian wunderkinds AC/DC show how refreshingly raw heavy rock can really be, and left-field singer Tom Waits talks jazz, Kerouac, and the Beat generation.

But it's in London where the biggest new waves are being created, with the start of a punk explosion triggered by bands like The Clash, and a scandalous TV interview with the Sex Pistols.

"Just a hobby"

ABBA, a pop cottage industry from Sweden, have triumphed at Eurovision, but Britain is initially hostile. "Normally a group like us doesn't make good albums," reckons Björn Ulvaeus, "and that's probably what frightens people off."

THINGS WERE SO BAD in Scandinavia, an *MM* reader there informed us some months ago, that ABBA were regarded as a progressive rock band. ABBA, the pride of the Continent, can afford to scoff at such cynicism, for while they have no pretensions about being a rock band, world reaction to their music during the past year has earned them an aura of respectability from many hitherto sceptical quarters.

They've been in the *MM* singles chart twice in the past four months, first with "SOS" and currently with "Mamma Mia", two magnificent pop tunes; they've had four hit singles in the States' charts, two of them Top 10-ers; they've had hit after hit across the Continent; and down under in Australia, three of their singles are in the Top 10: "Mamma Mia" at No 1, "SOS" at No 2 and "I Do, I Do, I Do..." at No 6.

ABBA, you will recall, first came to prominence during April 1974, when they won the Eurovision Song Contest with the self-penned "Waterloo". Since then, their stature in the rest of Europe has grown phenomenally, but Britain has lagged behind, rejecting their product with a vengeance. Until last year, when the breakthrough was made.

While we were humming and hawing over how ABBA should be approached, the band played it cool, ignored our disregard and stayed home in Sweden, confident that, sooner or later, Britain would come alive to their talent.

And at home they're their own bosses, have their own record label, write, produce and play their own material and make a little fortune. The two male members of the band, Benny Andersson and Björn Ulvaeus, produce six of the artists on their Polar Music label, while the girls, Anni-Frid Lyngstad and Agnetha Fältskog, pass the time away from ABBA by supervising dancing and singing lessons.

"In a lot of ways, ABBA is just a hobby for us," said Benny. "We've had to spend more and more time with the group as it has become so successful. We're our own bosses. Our existence doesn't depend on ABBA being a success, which is lucky. Most groups have to travel to make a living. We don't have that pressure on us, so we can do what we want to do.

"The thing is that England has been a most difficult market for us. We've had hits in Europe, America and Australia, but only Britain has been reluctant. I don't know why. I think the problem was to get rid of the Eurovision reputation, and at last we seem to have done that."

Despite all the hits, though, ABBA are desperate now to get recognised as an albums band, and can't understand why they have not yet achieved that ambition – especially when one considers that many of their recent singles were taken from one album, their second, *ABBA*.

"The singles aren't really representative of everything we do," Benny added. "What I wish is that we could become an albums band. The albums have a lot more to give than just a single. We agree that we write quite simple songs, but they're catchy and there's a lot of effort put into the arrangements. The only thing to get exposure is a single. You see, normally a group like us doesn't make good albums, and that's probably what frightens people off. But we go in and try to record 10 very good singles for an album. People don't notice that.

"It's not really important to us that we have a No 1 single. What is important is that people sit and listen to the music we play and like what they hear." *MM*

▶ ABBA, clockwise from top left: Benny Andersson, Björn Ulvaeus, Anni-Frid Lyngstad and Agnetha Fältskog

"Right out of the blue"

How a chance meeting with BOB DYLAN led theatre director Jacques Levy to co-write much of the *Desire* LP.

THOSE WHO HAVE already acquired a copy of Dylan's new album, *Desire*, will have noticed at least one difference between this and other Dylan records – on seven of the nine tracks Dylan has collaborated with another writer, Jacques Levy.

It is not the first time Dylan has worked on songs with another writer – in the past he's collaborated with The Band's Richard Manuel, George Harrison and, I believe, Johnny Cash, but it's the first time a definite partnership has developed for so many tracks.

Jacques Levy is not a musician and neither is he attracted to the life of a full-time lyricist, even though he has clocked up a success or two in the past. In fact, he's better known in New York as a theatrical director, having worked on about 30 stage productions, including *Oh! Calcutta!*

His friendship with Dylan came about through Roger McGuinn, with whom he collaborated on both "Chestnut Mare" and "Lover Of The Bayou", two latterday Byrds hits, and also on several tracks on the subsequent solo albums by McGuinn. Apart from a few contributions to the lyrics of his stage productions, this seems to be his only experience as a songwriter.

Jacques Levy lives in La Guardia Place, Greenwich Village, and was mentioned in dispatches while Dylan trotted around the folk clubs there last summer. They were often in each other's company, and when the Rolling Thunder Revue hit the road it was Levy who suggested the sequence of songs and a running order for the various combinations of musicians. He directed the tour in much the same way he directs theatre productions.

He lives in a sprawling but elegant loft, a habitation common to New York but hardly seen in England. In effect, it's open-plan living, whose absence of walls creates a huge feeling of space. A PhD in psychology, Levy practised for two years before entering the theatre and now, in

his late 30s, exudes the air of a man to whom life has generally been good.

Levy settled down with a Scotch on ice and a packet of Lucky Strikes and talked openly about writing with Dylan. He was vague on only one subject – whether or not the Rolling Thunder Revue would roll again and whether it could thunder across the Atlantic. There was a chance, he admitted, but he honestly didn't know, no more than he knew whether he and Dylan would collaborate again, or whether the rumoured West Coast Thunder dates would take place.

We began by talking about the events leading up to writing *Desire* and going on the road. "Bob and McGuinn have known each other for years, of course," he began, "and Bob knew all the things I'd written for McGuinn.

"Two years ago we met for the first time on the street here. He was walking one way and I was walking the other, and we both knew who each other was, so we stopped and talked. We spent the evening together, agreed to meet again and maybe work together, and left it

at that. We didn't see each other for a long time until last summer when, again, he was walking around the corner and so was I. We chatted and he came up to the apartment and then, right out of the blue, he suggested I wrote some material for him as he'd liked the things I'd written for Roger."

The first song to come from the partnership was "Isis", though Dylan had already put together the first verse: "He had the general feeling of the song when he came around here but he hadn't got further. We started to work on it at night and by the following morning it was finished. We did it together, going back and forth and trying things out on each other to see what would work and what wouldn't.

"We were having a great time here during July. Bob would write a song, then pick up a guitar and rush around to the Other End and get up on stage and sing it, but it wasn't the right atmosphere to write too seriously, and by this time we both knew we wanted to be serious about writing together."

▲ Dylan arriving for the sound check at the *Last Waltz* farewell concert to The Band, Winterland Ballroom, San Francisco, November 25, 1976

▶ Left to right, Van Morrison, Bob Dylan and The Band's Robbie Robertson singing "I Shall Be Released" at the *Last Waltz* concert

"It was just that thing with us sitting here and obviously connecting"

In August, Levy and Dylan went out to a house on Long Island for three weeks and put together the rest of the songs. The song "Joey" was an old idea of Levy's which Dylan picked up on, motivated especially by conversation during dinner one evening with Marta Aurbach, a New York authoress who is currently working on a book about Joey Gallo, the New York Mafia figure who was gunned down in 1970.

"She and her husband knew Joey well and I knew Joey through them," said Levy. "I spent a lot of time with Joey in that last year he was alive, and Bob became very interested in it all. We were telling stories about Joey, and when we left their house we came back here and started to work on it."

"One More Cup Of Coffee" was purely Dylan's creation, though. It came, according to Levy, while he was living with gypsies in Corsica. "Sara", too, was written by Dylan alone, but again, the idea of the song had been in Dylan's mind for some time: "Bob had been fooling with 'Sara' for a long time. He'd got the choruses down, but the verses were actually written out at this place on Long Island where we stayed. Out there are the dunes and beach and all that stuff mentioned in the song. He would try things out on me, but it was a very personal song for him to write."

Levy is hard-pressed to explain why Dylan should want to take on a songwriting partner at this stage in his career. "I don't think he ever

made up this mind that he wanted to collaborate with someone, and then went ahead and looked for somebody," he said.

"It was just that thing with us sitting here and obviously connecting with each other and throwing suggestions at each other."

When the Rolling Thunder Revue was first mooted, Levy played a prominent role in the planning. He was present at the discussions last summer: "We were taking it seriously, right at the beginning, but we realised that it would be an extraordinary thing to do.

"It seemed like a good idea but a very hard thing to pull off. It was one thing talking about it but another thing actually going out and doing it. Just before Bob left New York at the end of the summer, after we'd done the recording, we sat down and talked about what kind of show it would be and who would be in it.

"I did a loose version of the outline of the show, putting down ideas on paper, things like who would open and who would go next, and what kind of a song would be appropriate at what time, and the big point of how exactly we'd get to the point where Bob came on, and when to play his new material. I sort of switched gears from being a songwriter to a director. I built in the possibility of flexibility, so there were open choices, so it could be varied from night to night.

"I think the secrecy angle was really well handled. There was word around because quite a few people were involved, but the general information wasn't out and the public weren't officially informed that it was going to happen until right before each show.

"There was a deal made with the promoters and they were told that, if any word got out about this, the show would be cancelled. There was, of course, a schedule for the whole tour, but it was only known by a few people."

And the chances of Rolling Thunder reappearing this year? "I don't know. I don't see why it won't. Everybody had a great time, and it's hard for me to imagine that it won't happen again, but I don't know anything for sure at this point."

Or going to England? "Wouldn't that be nice? Sure, there's a chance. There's a chance they could play in Peking."

Levy's first tentative steps into songwriting came when he had the idea of directing a country & western musical for the stage. He enlisted the help of Roger McGuinn, but although they came up with a load of songs, the music never got further than the planning stage. McGuinn did, however, record most of the material and this included "Chestnut Mare" and "Lover Of The Bayou". From then on, Levy and McGuinn met annually to prepare material together.

Levy also wrote a song for *Oh! Calcutta!* and has dabbled with songs for other proposed musicals, but he will not be turning to songwriting full-time despite taking on such an illustrious partner as Bob Dylan. "I like my work in the theatre and I don't want to give that up, and it's hard to imagine people coming to me now asking me to write songs for them.

"I think I'll do some more work with Bob in the future, but it's hard to tell. We'd both like to, and I know that during the tour we were talking about new possibilities for songs, new ideas that came to us." **MM**

◀ Dylan, as part of the legendary Rolling Thunder Revue, playing at the Hofheinz Pavilion on May 8, 1976, in Houston, Texas

Prime influence

JANUARY 10

RIP, Howlin' Wolf.

HOWLIN' WOLF, one of the great names of traditional blues, died on Saturday in a Chicago hospital. He had been in poor health for many months.

Wolf was a seminal blues artist whose work was one of the prime influences behind the British R&B boom of the early '60s. His best-known song, "Smokestack Lightning", was in the repertoire of most British bands of the period, and his influence was acknowledged in 1971 when Wolf recorded *London Sessions*, an album that also featured such luminaries as Eric Clapton, Bill Wyman, Steve Winwood, Charlie Watts and Ringo Starr.

Chester Burnett – Wolf's real name – was born in Aberdeen, Mississippi, on June 10, 1910. His down-home Delta blues style was learned from the example of guitarist-singer Charley Patton.

During the early part of Wolf's career he moved to north Arkansas, where he played alongside such legends as Robert Johnson and Sonny Boy Williamson, picking up some of the latter's ideas on harmonica.

He was leading his own group by 1948, and stated broadcasting in the South the following year. And about this time he began recording in Memphis.

In August 1951, he cut "Moanin' At Midnight" and "How Many More Years", both classic Wolf tracks. He left the South in 1952 when he was signed by Chess Records in Chicago, one of America's pioneering blues labels.

Wolf finally came to Britain in 1964, at the height of the R&B boom. By that time, such songs as "Natchez Burning", "Spoonful" and "Smokestack Lightning" had established him as one of the heroes of a new generation of bluesmen, and his concerts in this country made a tremendous impact on fans and musicians.

His recordings are admired for the band's heavy beat, the raw power of his voice, the simple funkiness of his harp playing and the often arresting quality of his themes and lyrics. **MM**

"His down-home Delta blues style was learned from Charley Patton"

1976

▶ A portrait of Robert Plant as he poses in woods near his home in rural Wales, October 15, 1976

"A pitiful situation"

FEBRUARY 14

Robert Plant blames Zeppelin's tax exile on "an outrageous state of affairs".

NOBODY REALLY EXPECTS Robert Plant has become the first rock superstar to hit out against the British tax system. In an outspoken interview with the *Melody Maker*, Plant said this week: "You can't just sit down and write a song that you're prepared to put out, because you'll be taxed to the hilt. Why the hell should you put out something and come out of it with tuppence?"

Plant, with the rest of Led Zeppelin, is among the ever-growing community of Britain's tax exiles allowed into their own country for only a limited number of days each year. Never before, however, has a rock star so strongly condemned the British tax laws.

Talking to the *MM*'s Chris Charlesworth in New York, Plant claimed: "It aggravates me that people have worked for something for a long time and they've had to leave because of these tax laws.

"New York, grey as it may be, is full of some of the finest English talent, not just music but sports personalities and actors, and anybody who has a flair for something.

"We all want to go home, but there's an outrageous state of affairs taking place in England, an outrageous mishandling of the country's affairs in general.

"It's a very pitiful situation when a lot of the more established musicians have to flee. You only have to go from here, and four skyscrapers down the street there's Mick Jagger. He'd echo the same thing. We're all holed up in little boxes here, looking over Central Park. It's very, very sad. Now, I can just imagine the letters to Mailbag saying, 'Fuck the money and come home', but you have to live with reality.

"It's one thing to forget the money, but there's a moral aspect which is ludicrous. Rock'n'roll is a very lucrative form of making money easily, and just because the government has loused up all the way round, they shouldn't just turn to music or any form of entertainment.

"If it wasn't for this tax, we'd be doing an English tour at least once a year for sure, but even when we did Earls Court we didn't come out with anything." **MM**

He Went of His Own Accord

FEBRUARY 21

Robert Plant's remarks about the British tax laws in your last issue sickened and disgusted me. He seems to believe that the primary motive for creating music is financial and to have an inflated opinion of his own worth and relevance.

The creation of music should be essentially an act of giving, the imparting and sharing of emotional responses. But Plant seems to view it as a manufacturing process with one ear tuned to the sound of the cash till. Has he forgotten that some people still play music just for fun, and that some of his fellow superstars use their privileged positions to help the less fortunate? On the same page as Plant's outburst, for instance, it was announced that Elton John intends to tour for charity.

In addition, if it is true that most rock stars find their work enjoyable and satisfying, they simply do not deserve the huge financial rewards they receive.

Is Plant seriously trying to tell us that he could not live and work in Great Britain and earn as much after tax as the average coal worker or nurse, who works just as hard, and performs just as useful a service for the community as he does? If self-centred superstars feel they must live abroad for tax reasons, all you can really say is – good riddance.

CHRIS DURSTON, Grove Road, Emmer Green, Reading. **MM**

"We're into chaos"

The SEX PISTOLS play their first public date at the Marquee Club in Soho.

"**H**URRY UP, they're having an orgy on stage," said the bloke on the door as he tore the tickets up. I waded to the front and straightaway sighted a chair arcing gracefully through the air, skidding across the stage and thudding contentedly into the PA system, to the obvious nonchalance of the bass, drums and guitar. Well, I didn't think they sounded that bad on first earful – then I saw it was the singer who'd done the throwing.

He was stalking round the front rows, apparently scuffing over the litter on the floor between baring his teeth at the audience and stopping to chat to members of the group's retinue. He's called Johnny Rotten and the moniker fits.

Sex Pistols? Seems I'd missed the cavortings with two scantily clad (plastic thigh boots and bodices) pieces dancing up front. In fact, I only caught the last few numbers; enough, as it happens, to get the idea. Which is… a quartet of spiky teenage misfits from the wrong end of various London roads, playing '60s-styled white punk rock as unself-consciously as it's possible to play these days – i.e. self-consciously.

Punks? Springsteen Bruce and the rest of 'em would get shredded if they went up against these boys. They've played less than a dozen gigs as yet, have a small but fanatic following, and don't get asked back. Next month they play the Institute of Contemporary Arts, if that's a clue.

I'm told the Pistols' repertoire includes lesser-known Dave Berry and Small Faces numbers (check out early Kinks' B-sides leads), besides an Iggy and the Stooges item and several self-penned numbers like the moronic "I'm Pretty Vacant", a meandering power-chord job that produced the chair-throwing incident.

No one asked for an encore but they did one anyway: "We're going to play 'Substitute'."

"You can't play," heckled an irate French punter.

"So what?" countered the bassman, jutting his chin in the direction of the bewildered Frog.

That's how it is with the Pistols – a musical experience with the emphasis on Experience.

"Actually, we're not into music," one of the Pistols confided afterwards. Wot then?

"We're into chaos." **NME**

◀ The 'Pistols Johnny Rotten in typical snarling mode, London 1976

▲ The Sex Pistols backstage in 1976; left to right, Johnny Rotten, Glen Matlock, Steve Jones and Paul Cook

Aggro Chic

AUGUST 29 · **THE SCREEN ON THE GREEN, LONDON**

The Clash and the Sex Pistols play an Islington cinema. Teeth are broken.

IT'S ALMOST FUNNY. Not quite worth an uproarious explosion of uncontrollable hilarity, but definitely good for a wry chuckle or two when it happens to someone else. Trouble is, no one's laughing because all the professional chucklers just found out that the joke's on them.

Any halfway competent rock'n'roll pulse-fingerer knows that this is The Year of the Punk. You got Patti Smith doing Rimbaud's-in-the-basement-mixing-up-the-medicine, you got Bruce Springsteen with his down-these-mean-streets-a-man-must-go stereologues, you got the Ramones as updated Hanna-Barbera Dead End Kids, you got Ian Hunter doing I-used-to-be-a-punk-until-I-got-old-and-made-all-this-money, you got every-body and his kid brother (or sister) crawling out of the woodwork in leather jackets trying to look like they were hell on wheels in a street fight and shouting Put The Balls Back Into The Music.

Ultimately, if the whole concept of Punk means anything, it means Nasty Kids, and if Punk Rock means anything, it means music of, by and for Nasty Kids. So when a group of real live Nasty Kids come along playing Nasty Kids music and actually behaving like Nasty Kids, it is no bleeding good at all for those who have been loudly thirsting for someone to come along and blow all them old farts away to throw up their hands in prissy-ass horror and exclaim in duchessy fluster that, oh no, this wasn't what they meant at all and won't it please go away.

In words of one (or, at the most, two) syllables: you wanted Sex Pistols and now you've got 'em. Trouble is, they look like they aren't going to go away, so what are you going to do with them? Alternatively – ha ha – what are they going to do with you?

In a way, it's a classic horror-movie situation. Dr Frankenstein's monster didn't turn out according to plan but he was stuck with it anyway, Professor Bozo opens up a pyramid/summons a demon/goes up to the Old Dark Mansion despite the warnings of the villagers and gets into a whole mess of trouble. Don't rub the lamp unless you can handle the genie.

The current vogue for Punkophilia and Aggro Chic has created the atmosphere in which a group like the Sex Pistols could get started and find an audience, and – dig it – it is entirely too late to start complaining because they behave like real Nasty Kids and not the stylised abstraction of Nasty Kiddery which we've been demanding and applauding from sensitive, well-educated, late-20s pop superstars.

Anyway, time's a-wastin'. Their gig at The Screen On The Green has already started; in fact we've already missed the first band, a Manchester group called Buzzcocks. All kinds of folks in Bizarre Costumes – the kind of clothes you used to find at Bowie gigs before 'e went all funny like – are milling around the foyer playing the wild

mutation. The occasional celeb – Chris Spedding, who has eyes to produce the Pistols, and Sadistic Mika – is mingling.

Up on the stage it's Party Piece time. A bunch of people, including a chick in SM drag with tits out (photographer from one of the nationals working overtime, presumably with the intention of selling a nice big fat look-at-all-this-disgusting-decadence-and-degradation centrespread) and a lumpy guy in rompers are dancing around to a barrage of Ferry and Bowie records. Every time the lumpy go-go boy does a particularly ambitious move the record jumps. He makes elaborate not-my-fault gestures and keeps dancing. The record keeps jumping.

This goes on for quite a while. Movies are projected on the screen and someone gets creative with the lights. The area near me 'n' the missus reeks of amyl nitrate.

There is nothing more tedious and embarrassing than inept recreations of that which was considered avant-garde 10 years ago. Someone has obviously read too many articles about the Andy Warhol/Velvet Underground Exploding Plastic Inevitable Show. Andy and Lou and Cale would laugh their butts off. This ain't rock'n'roll – this is interestocide.

Sooner or later – later, actually – a group called Clash take the stage. They are the kind of garage band who should be speedily returned to their garage, preferably with the motor running, which would undoubtedly be more of a loss to their friends and families than to either rock or roll. Their extreme-left guitarist, allegedly known as Joe Strummer, has good moves, but he and the band are a little shaky on ground that involves starting, stopping and changing chord at approximately the same time.

In between times, they show Kenneth Anger's *Scorpio Rising*. The Pistols' gear is assembled in a commendably short time with an equally commendable absence of fuss and pissing about and then the

> "The Pistols play loud, clean and tight and they don't mess around"

▲ The Sex Pistols performing at the 100 Club in London '76. Seen here, Steve Jones (left) and Johnny Rotten

Pistols slope on stage and Johnny Rotten lays some ritual abuse on the audience and then they start to play.

Any reports that I had heard and that you may have heard about the Pistols being lame and sloppy are completely and utterly full of shit. They play loud, clean and tight and they don't mess around. They're well into the two-minute-thirty-second powerdrive, though they're a different cup of manic monomania than the Ramones. They have the same air of seething just-about-repressed violence that the Feelgoods have, and watching them gives that same clenched-gut feeling that you get walking through Shepherd's Bush just after the pubs shut and you see The Lads hanging out on the corner looking for some action and you wonder whether the action might be you.

The Pistols are all those short-haired kids in the big boots and rolled-up baggies and sleeveless T-shirts. Their music is coming from the straight-out-of-school-and-onto-the-dole deathtrap which we seem to have engineered for Our Young: the '76 British terminal stasis, the modern urban blind alley.

The first 30 seconds of their set blew out all the boring, amateurish artsy-fartsy mock-decadence that preceded it purely by virtue of its tautness, directness and utter realism. They did songs with titles like "I'm A Lazy Sod" and "I'm Pretty Vacant", they did blasts-from-the-past like "I'm Not Your Steppin' Stone" (10 points for doing it, 10 more for doing it well) and "Substitute" (a Shepherd's Bush special, that) and they kept on rockin'.

"Should I say all the trendy fings like 'peace and love, maaaaaaan'?" asked Johnny Rotten, leaning out off the stage manically jerking off his retractable mic stand. "'Are you all having a good time, maaaaaaaan?'?" Believe it: this ain't the summer of love.

They ain't quite the full-tilt crazies they'd like to be, though: Johnny Rotten knocked his false tooth out on the mic and had the front rows down on their knees amidst the garbage looking for it. He kept bitching about it all the way through the gig; Iggy wouldn't even have noticed. Still, they got more energy and more real than any new British act to emerge this year, and even if they get big and famous and rich, I really can't imagine Johnny Rotten showing up at parties with Rod'n'Britt 'n' Mick'n'Bianca or buying the next-door villa to Keef'n'Anita in the South of France. And if Elton ever sees them I swear he'll never be able to sing "Saturday Night's Alright (For Fighting)" again without choking on his Dr Pepper. **NME**

◄ John Lydon, aka, Johnny Rotten, relaxing backstage after a Pistols gig: London, 1976

NEWS

"The start of a wave"

NOVEMBER 6

The first major British tour for the Sex Pistols tour is planned.

A BIG PUNK ROCK concert starring the Sex Pistols is being planned for London later this month. The show celebrates the release of the band's debut single, "Anarchy In The UK", on November 19. The show will also feature Chris Spedding & The Vibrators, whose "Pogo Dancing" single is available from November 12, together with Suzi & The Banshees [sic] and, from New York, the Ramones and Talking Heads.

The venue has yet to be decided, though there were plans to stage the show at the Talk of the Town, London's traditional cabaret club. This idea was dropped after difficulties over the licensing laws.

The show will be the prelude to the Pistols' first major British tour, exclusively reported in the *MM* last week. The concerts will be co-headlined by the Pistols and the Ramones – who made their British debut at London's Roundhouse earlier this year. Spedding and Talking Heads will also be on the tour.

The 20-date tour, from November 30 to December 21, visits all of Britain's major cities. Among the dates will be a show at London's Hammersmith Palais.

The concerts come as the climax to a triumphant three months for the Sex Pistols, Britain's top punk band. They were one of the big successes at the punk-rock festival in London two months ago, and in October they signed a recording contract with EMI.

In this week's *Melody Maker*, Nick Mobbs of EMI, the man who signed the Pistols, claims: "I genuinely think that they're the start of a wave. I think they're the rare breed of artist; they're total entertainment and in a lot of ways uncompromising in what they want to do."

Mobbs is one of the top A&R directors featured in the *MM*'s Dialogue, which this week discusses the state of British rock.

"The time is right for an act that kids of 16 to 18 can actually identify with," says Mobbs. "The key point is that the group are very young. There's other groups giving entertainment, but this group are only 19-year-olds and because they're young they'll grow and their audience will grow with them.

"In the same way that the Rolling Stones were known as symbols of rebellion when they started, so are the Sex Pistols. The Stones are now the elite of the rock'n'roll establishment and the Sex Pistols are the new people knocking at the door.

"To a lot of kids, the Stones and groups from that era don't mean a thing. They're too old for a start, all over 30, and the kids want some young people they can identify with.

"A lot of people criticise the Sex Pistols for not playing well, but they've only been together for about eight months. I think a lot of kids watch them and think, 'Yeah, I could get up there and do that, let's form a group'.

"Again, that hasn't happened for a long time because groups are too good; the musicianship has been so high that kids of 16 have been put off. But already, there are about 12 groups in London directly inspired by the Sex Pistols." *MM*

"Say something outrageous..."

DECEMBER 1

The Sex Pistols appear on *Today*, an early-evening news show. An unexpurgated transcript appears in *NME*.

THE INTERVIEW THAT started the controversy took place on Wednesday December 1 on Thames Television's early current-affairs programme *Today*. The actual interview lasted one minute 40 seconds, after a short introduction by Bill Grundy and a 40-second clip of the Pistols on stage. Our recording started a few seconds after Grundy's introduction as he faced the four members of the band seated in the studio. Standing behind the Pistols was a group of fans.

The following is a transcript of what ensued.

GRUNDY (To camera) ...Chains round the necks and that's just the fellas, innit? Eh? I mean, is it just the fellas? Yeah? They are punk rockers. The new craze, they tell me. Their heroes? Not the nice, clean Rolling Stones... you see they are as drunk as I am... they are clean by comparison. They're a group called the Sex Pistols, and I am surrounded by all of them...

JONES (Reading the autocue) In action!

GRUNDY Just let us see the Sex Pistols in action. Come on, kids...

(A film clip of London Weekend's documentary on punk broadcast the previous Sunday came on the screen)

GRUNDY I am told that that group (hits his knee with sheaf of papers) have received £40,000 from a record company. Doesn't that seem, er, to be slightly opposed to their anti-materialistic view of life?

MATLOCK No, the more the merrier.

GRUNDY Really?

MATLOCK Oh yeah.

GRUNDY Well tell me more then.

JONES We've fuckin' spent it, ain't we?

GRUNDY I don't know, have you?

MATLOCK Yeah, it's all gone.

GRUNDY Really?

JONES Down the boozer.

GRUNDY Really? Good lord! Now I want to know one thing...

MATLOCK What?

GRUNDY Are you serious or are you just making me – trying to make me – laugh?

MATLOCK No, it's all gone. Gone.

GRUNDY Really?

MATLOCK Yeah.

GRUNDY No, but I mean about what you're doing.

MATLOCK Oh yeah.

GRUNDY You are serious?

MATLOCK Mmm.

GRUNDY Beethoven, Mozart, Bach and Brahms have all died...

ROTTEN They're all heroes of ours, ain't they?

GRUNDY Really... what? What were you saying, sir?

ROTTEN They're wonderful people.

GRUNDY Are they?

ROTTEN Oh yes! They really turn us on.

JONES But they're dead!

GRUNDY Well suppose they turn other people on?

ROTTEN (Under his breath) That's just their tough shit.

GRUNDY It's what?

ROTTEN Nothing. A rude word. Next question.

GRUNDY No, no, what was the rude word?

ROTTEN Shit.

GRUNDY Was it really? Good heavens, you frighten me to death.

ROTTEN Oh all right, Siegfried...

GRUNDY (Turning to those standing behind the band) What about you girls behind?

MATLOCK He's like yer dad, inne, this geezer?

GRUNDY Are you, er...

MATLOCK Or your grandad.

GRUNDY (To Sioux) Are you worried, or are you just enjoying yourself?

SIOUX Enjoying myself.

GRUNDY Are you?

SIOUX Yeah.

GRUNDY Ah, that's what I thought you were doing.

SIOUX I always wanted to meet you.

GRUNDY Did you really?

SIOUX Yeah.

GRUNDY We'll meet afterwards, shall we? (Sioux does a camp pout)

JONES You dirty sod. You dirty old man!

GRUNDY Well keep going, chief, keep going. Go on, you've got another five seconds. Say something outrageous.

JONES You dirty bastard!

GRUNDY Go on, again.

JONES You dirty fucker! (Laughter from the group)

GRUNDY What a clever boy!

JONES What a fucking rotter.

GRUNDY Well, that's it for tonight. The other rocker, Eamonn, and I'm saying nothing else about him, will be back tomorrow. I'll be seeing you soon. I hope I'm not seeing you [the band] again. From me, though, goodnight.

Today theme. Closing credits. ***NME***

1976

▶ Tom Waits performing at the
New York club The Bottom Line, in
December 1976

"I'm a legend in my own mind"

**Kerouac, Moondog, Symphony Sid... a chat with
TOM WAITS has historical references, and vivid
contemporary touches. "I don't like the Eagles," he
says. "They're like watching paint dry..."**

I CAME IN on the southbound flyer, then hoofed it halfway across town to see Tom. From a nearby window drifted the sound of Billie aqua-freshing "The Man I Love", Prez singing long, thoughtful phrases and making it, really making it. Was it really like that? Hell, no. But when you're booked to interview Tom Waits, the Brian Case of singer-songwriters, then it's best to get in the mood.

Waits is in town for a gaggle of nights at Ronnie [Scott]'s. That his gig seems a well-kept secret I'll agree – just another chapter in Waits' as-yet-unwritten biography, *The Last Of The Big Time Losers*. The guy's had three albums released so far. The first was deleted after just a fly's life, while the second never received a UK pressing. And the third, a live-in-the-studio double, got slammed by reviewers who never had a chance to ease on into Waits via the more accessible preceding duo. Three strikes in a row then.

Writing-wise he's been luckier. It's become fashionable to include at least one Waits song on an album. However, our hero claims this trend doesn't exactly keep him in Savile Row suits – not as though sartorial elegance has ever been a strong line with the Californian,

"I've got my own tastes, and I have to say that most of the performers on the circuit don't"

whose bum-of-the-year appearance has brought forth accusations of gimmickry from non-believers.

"I'm not a household word – I'm just a legend in my own mind," croaks Waits in a voice that's broken out of Alcatraz and got shot up in the process. "Still, I've come a long way since I was a dishwasher and had a good job sweeping up. I once worked in a jewellery store and when I quit I took a gold watch. I figured they weren't gonna give me one 'cos I'd only been with them six months anyway."

Back to those cover versions, though.

"I don't like any of 'em."

Not even the Eagles' version of "Ol' 55"?

"Naw – I don't like the Eagles. They're about as exciting as watching paint dry. Their albums are good for keeping the dust off your turntable and that's about all."

Eric Andersen then? After all, Andersen's included Waits' songs on his last two albums.

"Naw – I don't like Eric Andersen either."

He takes the copy of Andersen's latest Arista project, which I proffer, and reads the sleeve notes, punctuating the singer's own poetic album jottings with the words "Rod McKuen" every few seconds. I remark that even if Waits has a low opinion of Andersen's output, the reverse would not appear to be true.

"Yeah, right. But I still don't like him. I wish he didn't like me. We had a fight once because he was messing about with my girl. Y'know something? It's really difficult to hit a guy who likes you, so I wish he didn't.

"I guess I shouldn't badmouth anybody, though. I mean, who the hell am I? Still, I've got my own tastes and I have to say that most of the performers currently on the circuit don't, with the exception of a few, fall into that category."

Many of the people Waits actually admires are long gone... Kerouac, Lenny Bruce, Lester Young, Tim Buckley. While others, like Zoot Sims, Al Cohn, Charlie Mingus and Thelonious Monk, remain as living reminders of the time when New York's 52nd Street was the hub of the music world; all bop, berets and goatees. Waits himself sports a 35-year-old goatee on his 27-year-old chin. His threadbare cap seems even older.

Talk about Kerouac's *Visions of Cody* ("I've got a first edition that's signed by Jack"), Moondog, the legendary blind street musician who once made an album featuring the sounds of the New York streets, Symphony Sid, the DJ who once preached *Bird and Diz* from tiny Bronx radio station WBNX, or King Pleasure, the singer who taught the world vocalese, and Waits latches on, swapping story for story.

He digs the whole beat-generation scene ("I was something of a misfit during the '60s") but resents any suggestion that his act is any part of the current boom in nostalgia. He shudders when I toss

around names like Bette Midler (who recorded Waits' "Shiver Me Timbers" on her last LP) or The Pointer Sisters.

"The whole thing is rampant y'know. Those people who go in and enjoy Manhattan Transfer don't know who the hell Lambert, Hendricks and Ross are. Music is not a big part of most people's lives. When it stops becoming something you do and becomes rather what you are – then you begin to understand what's important historically. I don't see anything I do as being nostalgic – I feel very contemporary.

"The thing is to do something that's not necessarily here today and gone tomorrow. But most people don't care about that, they're under a lot of social pressure. When getting laid depends upon what you've got in your record collection, then you gotta have all Top 10 hits – that's the way it is."

Interviewing Waits is both easy and difficult. It's easy because he's an inveterate raconteur, a mainman on words, a sultan of scrabble. But the difficulty arises when he opts for being Waits the entertainer, testing whole routines on unsuspecting journalists waiting merely for the short answer. Already he'd thrown two monologues my way – one being a hilarious (but true) story involving Waits himself, his '54 Cadillac, Ed Begley Jr and a girl from Persia who couldn't speak English ("I hadda pinned up against a wall, trying to explain things to her"). Another being a tale called "Rocky And Charlie Dutton" that's likely to appear on what Waits terms his fourth, coming (geddit?) album. It takes a little time to get him back on course again.

So tell us about your backup band, Tom.

"Well, I've got Frank Vicari on tenor sax, Dr Huntingdon Jenkins III Jr on upright bass and Chip White on drums. Vicari's being playing since he was about 13 years old. He used to line up outside Birdland when he was a kid... the only white tenor player lining up with a whole lotta black cats – just for a chance to sit in, listen or hang out. Since then he's played for Woody, Maynard Ferguson... lots of others."

Waits has always had a penchant for useful tenor players – people like Tom Scott and Al Cohn, once of Herman's great '48 Herd, along with Zoot Sims and Stan Getz.

"Yeah, I had Tom Scott on one of my albums – but that was before I found out I could get anyone that I wanted. Tom's OK but he's too young and too stylised, more like a rock tenorman, not really what I'd call a jazz player, though he can play jazz. He did some nice stuff on the soundtrack of a movie called *Taxi Driver* that's very big in the States. Al played with me for a couple of weeks once and I hope to have him on my next album if everything fits in with his

▶ Tom Waits being driven to a photo shoot during a visit to London in May 1976

◄ Portrait of Tom Waits, photographed near the Portobello Road in London, May 25, 1976

schedule. I admire him and his style. And he drinks about a quart of Johnnie Walker Red Label a night – though how he does it I just don't know."

Though Waits plays some guitar and a reasonable line in gin-soaked piano, he describes himself as a pedestrian musician. "I'd never cut it as a sideman, I just accompany, that's what I do. I'm glad to have my band with me, they're a real high-voltage bebop trio. I've been on the road for about five years now but I've never been able to afford a band until recently – and even now I can't afford it, I just pay through the ass."

Reminiscences next – about the time he tried to get a gig with a then unknown Al Jarreau at the Blah Blah Club in LA ("A real toilet, that place"), about Maria Muldaur explaining to Martin Mull just how much an ancient necklace had cost her ("Just imagine what you'd have paid if it had been new," said Mull in mock wonder), and about the multitude of American tradenames and expressions that proliferate throughout Waits' albums...

"Muckalucks are carpet slippers, a Peterbilt is a truck and Stacey Adams once were a very prestigious shoe... If you had them on, then nobody messed with you and you could go anywhere. Staceys stayed ahead of current affairs and were considered extremely hip. By the way, the shoes I'm wearing are called Ratstickers!"

It's retaliation time, so Waits begins writing down some of the British expressions he hasn't heard before. "You call them French Letters here?... or Packets Of Three? Yeah, I'll have to remember that."

One last question then. Is there anyone in this wide world who he'd actually like to cover his songs? "Ray Charles... and I'd like Cleo Laine to do one. The thing is, though, that people never record the songs I'm really proud of. There are songs I do every night and the magic is still there – but there are others that you can ambush and beat the shit out of until they just don't water any more for you.

"I've got a lot of new songs – 'A Bad Liver And A Broken Heart', 'A Briefcase And The Blues', 'Frank Is Here', 'Whitey Ford'... and a lot of these haven't been written yet but I've got the titles and I'll be glad if somebody covers them.

After a brief discourse regarding that next album – which is likely to be called *Pasties And A G-String* – the subject moves finally to the ineptitude of some country rockers. "Those guys grew up in LA and they don't have cow shit on their boots – they just got dog shit from Laurel Canyon. They wouldn't last two minutes in Putnam County, that's for sure. If somebody gets shot and killed there on a Saturday night, the Sunday papers say he just died of natural causes!"

At which point I, in the words of Waits himself, made like a hockey player and got the puck outta there. *NME*

Bob Marley and the Wailers
"Roots, Rock, Reggae"

JUNE 22

As Scrooge was haunted by Marley's ghost, so it seems that rock critics must be haunted by his substance. Having resolutely sung his praises for some years, reviewers are faced with Marley's vast popular success. What was once the preserve of the select few has caught on with the masses. And this poses a dilemma. There's no prestige in supporting an overdog. Who wants to live on Mount Olympus if it's packed with picnic areas?

The inevitable result is mixed reviews, thus denying kudos to the army of latecomers. You know the sort of thing: "I dug The Wailers when their music was still valid."

The irony, of course, is that Marley's music has become less commercial, rather than more, over the last few albums. Where *Catch A Fire* had a thick layer of studio cosmetics, *Rastaman Vibration* is largely stripped of such disguises, and undeniably closer to JA. **NME**

▶ Bob Marley on stage during 1976, photographed by Bob Gruen

Queen
"You're My Best Friend"

MAY 18

There was no way they could top the grand guignol of "Bohemian Rhapsody", and it's as well they didn't try. One brilliant operetta is enough. When the second one comes out – all complexity and pidgin Italian – the public is bored, they've heard it all before. So, instead, a potential summer classic. John Deacon's melodic chunk of True-Life Romance. Gorgeous vocals from Freddie, peerless harmonies, exquisite loose-stringed guitar from Brian May. Possibly the finest thing they've done, but then everything they've done has been fairly fine. **NME**

ABBA
"Dancing Queen"

AUGUST 15

The original exponents of pop autopsies, Benny Andersson and Björn Ulvaeus continue to produce themselves and their pre-programmed grand design. The title, in using the word "dancing", is as hip to the prevailing zeitgeist as were all those earnest hacks of last year, when to have "rock'n'roll" somewhere in your book-phrase was a guarantee of covering studio time and pressing costs. The word "Queen", too, is closely associated with money. **NME**

The Lowest Depths

MAY 16 · HAMMERSMITH ODEON, LONDON

The Kiss phenomenon – fake blood, fireworks and all – fails to impress the critics.

MAN, KISS HAD everything; every single effect in the book. They had a perfect lighting system; dry ice; smoke bombs; a fire-eater; a huge lighted insignia; sirens; confetti that simulated a blizzard; guitars; drums. EVERYTHING.

But what Kiss hadn't got at their Hammersmith Odeon gig on Sunday night was a feeling for music. They depended on their bland pyrotechnics to win over this English audience and, admittedly, they seemed to do that. But it was all so nauseatingly contrived that the showmanship meant nothing. I comfort myself in the knowledge that the audience were battered into submission by the sheer fantasia of it all.

I remember what their manager Bill Aucoin said in last week's *MM*: "When you're running around the stage like Kiss do, you can't be overly critical about every note you play." An admission of their pathetic musical ability if ever there was one.

First, let's look at the image on which they stake their reputation. There's the facial makeup and leather gear that's obviously calculated to outrage. This semblance of outrage is apparent in everything they attempt to do. Bass player Gene Simmons is well to the fore. He's the guy who breathes fire in one song and a couple of minutes later starts spitting blood as he pumps out a bassline. He also sticks his tongue out a lot and, like his comrades, poses. Of the entire band, I reckon he must feel the most stupid.

Rhythm guitarist and vocalist Paul Stanley almost matches Simmons for this distinction. He's the "link man", hollering out his lines like a man possessed. As well as that, he's about the worst guitarist I've ever heard.

Ace Frehley, the lead guitarist, I had a little sympathy for. A few times, just a few, he looked as if he was well into what he was doing. To the others, it seemed to be just another gig.

Musically, Kiss sink to the lowest depths. The wall of noise only partially hides their musical inadequacies: for the entire night they slammed out mindless riff after mindless riff, and it's a reflection on their mediocrity that they all sounded the same, apart from "Detroit Rock City", which I quite liked.

And don't give me the line that that's what heavy-metal bands are about, because that's just a feeble excuse. I can honestly state that at no stage during the 80 minutes Kiss were on stage did my nerves tingle at anything they did. And that is simply because there was no feeling in what they were doing, no sense of purpose. They were ice-cold.

Please bar me the intellectual argument that Kiss are a parody of all that has gone on in rock for the past 10 years. No way. Even parodies have talent. I pray that Kiss will not have the same superficial effect on this country as they have in America. They're boring. *MM*

Today's Punks, Tomorrow's Establishment

NOVEMBER 27

I'd like to know why the world is so worked up and surprised by the arrival of punk rock, as it was bound to come. OK, it's a load of crap and anyone with hands can play it, but the same was true of early rock'n'roll and English reggae. Both of these types of music attracted the violent element of their generation – the rockers and the skinheads – and today punk rock attracts our violent element: the punks, I suppose they're called.

The thing is, given two to four years, the 19-year-old musicians will be 22, 23 and no longer relevant to the new violence generation.

They will become the thing they despise now, the establishment. Unlike bands like the Stones, The Beatles and the Floyd, they won't survive with their own generation because they have no talent and they won't progress from punk music because they can't. So real music lovers just be patient; punk rock will kill itself with its own hate of establishment.

CHRIS WHITAKER, Ongar, Essex. *MM*

▶ Kiss giving it all at one of their over-the-top concert appearances in 1976

Punk: The Truth

DECEMBER 11

In reply to Chris Whitaker's letter. I would like to say that it's not what the punk bands are playing that matters, it's what they are saying.

I've been involved with music now for about 16 years, and one thing I've learned is that music and truth go together hand-in-hand. For too long now we've been inundated with bands who are very technical, very clever, very polished, but shy away from the important issues of life and cover them up with technical wizardry and pretentious lyrics that have no relevance.

Now I'm not knocking good music, but let's have good music and truth together. You may think punk bands lack talent; this may be true in the musical sense, but there is no lack of honesty and truthfulness in what they do, and this must surely be the rarest talent of them all.

Thank you, punk rockers; it seems the Age Of Aquarius isn't dead after all.

GEOFF GRAHAM, 2 Tudor Road, Camp Hill, Nuneaton, Warwickshire. **MM**

"I like to rip it up"

AC/DC's triumphant residencey at London's Marquee Club showcase an Australian band with a raw and ribald take on rock'n'roll. Audiences go wild. And that's before they've seen the "human kangaroo". Really, you don't want to know.

THOSE PUZZLED BY the Status Quo phenomenon should beware. AC/DC, from the same rock family, could wreak similar havoc, but they will only realise their full potential if, amid all the raucousness that inevitably surrounds power-chord bands, they better organise their assaults.

But whatever they do lack in presentation at the moment, the band is certainly making great strides towards becoming a major attraction, as was suggested by their Monday-night residency at London's Marquee Club. When I caught the band there last week, they had just broken another house-attendance record, which, I'm told, they'd set themselves the previous week.

AC/DC have been tagged as an Australian band, though three of the members – brother guitarists Angus and Malcolm Young and singer Bon Scott – are Glaswegians, with only the rhythm section of drummer Philip Rudd and bassist Mark Evans being children of Melbourne.

◀ AC/DC at the Shepperton film studios, near London, in 1976

"I don't like to play above or below people's heads"

Although I'm sure that the gig I saw at the Marquee, where sweat was shed by the bucketful, was an off-night for the band – sound troubles (twice) brought the gig to a halt – they did enough to show that they're a good boogie band, with apparently no pretensions about being anything else.

But I was left hoping, somewhere around the middle of their set, that they'd shatter the uniformity of riff, vocal and solo (in that order), which all tended to become much of a muchness after a while, and widen the scope a little.

The potential is there to do it if they'd only harness and direct the music, and vocalist Scott and punk guitarist Angus Young have certain charismatic qualities. Scott, with his moody stare and distinctive Scottish voice, could be a first-class frontman instead of,

as he strikes me, a poor cross between Alex Harvey and Stevie Marriott. His enthusiasm did seem a trifle contrived at times.

Seventeen-year-old Young, with his schoolboy uniform (discarded after the fourth number of the set because of sauna-bath conditions), has hit on the really good gimmick of looking like a rock'n'roll Norman Wisdom, only more backward.

Though not a great guitarist (solos over the one-minute mark became, to say the least, repetitive), he's a great showman. Where do AC/DC go from the Marquee in murky Wardour Street? Judging from the wild reaction of their audiences, they could just about slip comfortably into Status Quo's shoes once they have pulled their socks up. **MM**

The Same Old Boogie

APRIL 30

AC/DC's debut fails to spark excitement.

AC/DC *High Voltage*

ANY NEW BAND that opens its first album with a song that goes, "It's a long way to the top if you wanna rock'n'roll," is asking for trouble. And it's particularly apposite in the case of AC/DC, whose musical development is still at the raw stage. Not that there's anything wrong with punk rock, of course, but if Lenny Kaye of the Patti Smith band, and acknowledged expert on these matters, can claim that his group aren't punk because they don't have a Farfisa organ, then there's no reason for AC/DC's lack of originality to be lauded.

Their main fault lies in the instrumentals: it's the same old boogie, the same old sub-metal riffs you've heard a thousand times before. Too many of their songs sound the same. Still, there's hope. The lyrics have a brashness and lack of sophistication that's always useful in the heavy branch of rock. Best of all is the suitably laboured punning and innuendo in "The Jack", a song which only the naive will think is about playing cards.

This track is evidence that AC/DC (said to be Australia's most popular hard-rock band) have some potential. But then so did fellow Aussies Daddy Cool (arguably the best rock'n'roll revival band around – and long before most everybody else got in on the act), and what happened to them? **MM**

Assassination attempt

DECEMBER 3

Bob Marley shot at home. Attack possibly "politically motivated".

REGGAE SUPERSTAR BOB MARLEY was the victim of an assassination attempt last week. Gunmen shot their way into his home in Kingston, Jamaica, on Friday night, but Marley suffered only a slight arm wound in the raid.

His manager, Don Taylor, threw himself between Marley and the gunmen as they opened fire. He was shot five times and is now on the critical list after an emergency operation. It is thought he may be permanently crippled as a result of his injuries. Marley's wife, Rita, was wounded and clubbed during the attack, but she was released from hospital after treatment.

Speculation suggests the attack was politically motivated. There will be a general election in Jamaica in three weeks' time, and Marley, despite his allegedly apolitical stance, had accepted an invitation to appear, together with The Wailers and Burning Spear, at a concert benefit for the Island's current premier, Michael Manley. The invitation followed the release of a new Marley single, "Smile Jamaica", in which he extols the virtues of the country despite its recent history of political violence. *MM*

▶ Bob Marley fronting the Wailers in 1976, at a concert in Voorburg, Holland

Blondie // The Clash // Elvis Costello // Elvis Presley
Fleetwood Mac // Keith Richards // Lynyrd Skynyrd
Marc Bolan // Ramones // Sex Pistols // The Stranglers
Television // Tom Petty and the Heartbreakers

1977

The Ramones show us what American punk is all about with their new album, while Blondie glamorously upstages fellow New Yorkers, Television. In the UK, Elvis Costello signs with Stiff Records while the new wave is spearheaded by The Clash, The Stranglers, and most notoriously the Sex Pistols.

Meanwhile, representing the old guard, the Stones' Keef gets busted (twice!). And sadly, the world of rock says a tearful goodbye to T. Rex's Marc Bolan, half of Lynyrd Skynyrd, and with 100,000 fans attending his Graceland funeral, the uncrowned King of Rock 'n' Roll Elvis Presley.

"We ain't geniuses"

The RAMONES talk about their second album, *Ramones Leave Home*, which like the first is packed with two-minute songs. No time to dwell on the finer points, therefore, as becomes clear in this brief encounter after the record's New York launch party.

NEW YORK: The evening began, somewhat ominously, with a slow ride in an antiquated elevator whose door didn't close. Ten floors later, its passengers emerged in Redfield Sound, a small rehearsal studio on West 20th Street where a buffet meal was served with champagne. Nuggets was playing quietly through studio speakers, an apt choice since Lenny Kaye, who compiled these relatively obscure tracks onto one album, was prominent among the throng.

The occasion was the first public hearing of the Ramones' second album, *Ramones Leave Home*, which, after the invited listeners had been given an opportunity to get suitably wired on alcohol and/or pungent smoking mixture, was played very loudly to the assembled guests.

Three of the Ramones were present, Johnny, Dee Dee and Tommy, all dressed in the obligatory jeans, tennis shoes and leather jackets. Joey, the singer, is currently in hospital, where he may have to have an operation on his ankle; he was represented by his brother. Also on hand was John Camp, the bass player for Renaissance, whose music seems at the absolute opposite end of the music spectrum to that of the Ramones. Significantly, Camp declined to be photographed with the three Ramones present. Renaissance, of course, record for Sire in the US, as do the Ramones.

While sophisticated would not be quite the right word, the Ramones' second-floor effort is a good deal less raw than their first. Greater attention has been paid to the production, which makes the overall picture a lot less amateurish than before. They've discovered echo, and this takes away that rather flat, droning vocal sound and adds immensely to the numerous guitar riffs.

Once again there're 14 tracks that make up just over 30 minutes, and consequently each song averages out at just over a couple of

▶ The Ramones (left to right): Johnny Ramone, Tommy Ramone (front), Joey Ramone (back), Dee Dee Ramone, photographed in England, May 19, 1977

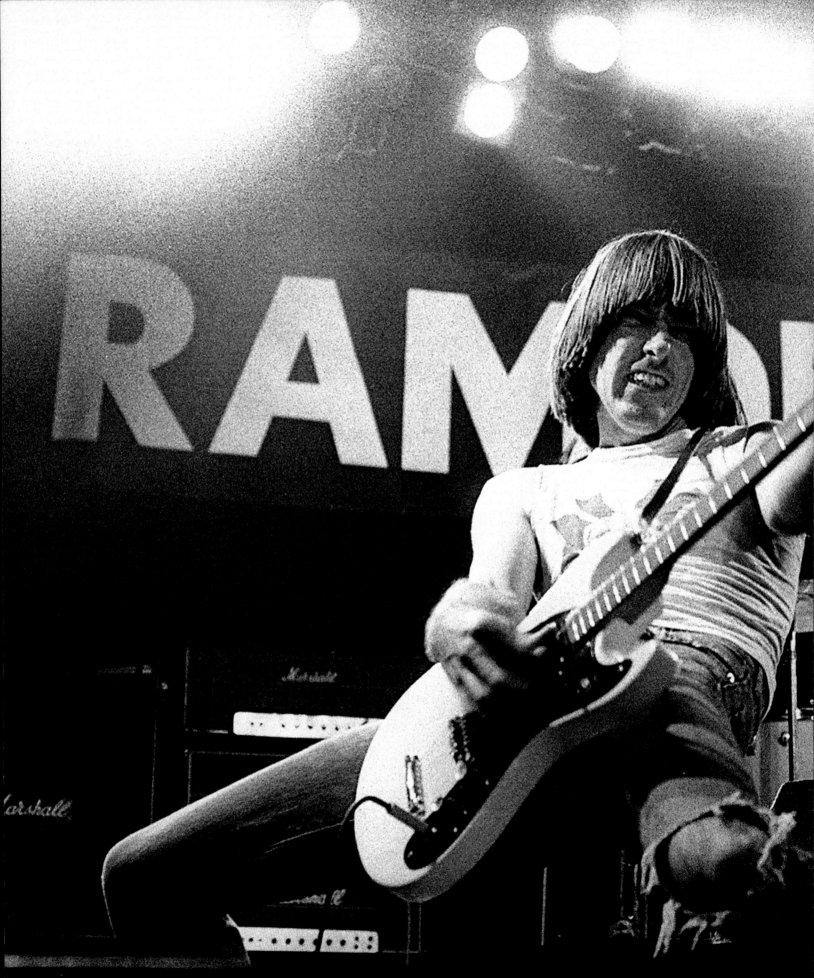

◄ December 21, 1977: On stage at the Apollo, Manchester, the Ramones during a UK tour, with Johnny on guitar and Joey singing

◀ Joey Ramone fronting the Ramones at a gig at the Palladium in New York City, October 6, 1977

▲ The Ramones (left to right): bassist Dee Dee, drummer Tommy, singer Joey and guitarist Johnny, near the Bowery in New York, April 1977

Ramones "Sheena Is A Punk Rocker"

MAY 28

FOR THE TIME being, this is available as a 12-incher with a cute picture sleeve, T-shirt offer, green stamps, chance to win a three-year subscription to *New Society* and all manner of specialised weirdness like that, but I'm reviewing this off a plain old seven-incher and it still sounds sufficiently monstrous. Monstrously charming, that is. "Sheena Is A Punk Rocker" is a heart-warming love song with references to surfboards and discotheques and it's got harmonies and a chorus and... and... Look, all the Ramones' songs sound like hit singles and then don't sell, but this song is so flat-out delightful that not even the dull-as-bleedin'-ditch-water Brit-public will be able to resist it. The sheer charm and essential niceness of Dolly Ramone's four horrible sons is gonna win out. And even if it doesn't, there's always the double B-side of "Commando" (from the last album) and "I Don't Care" (never previously released) to cop the sympathy vote. Me, I like "I Don't Care" because of the beautifully soulful way in which Joey Ramone lists all the various things he doesn't care about. "Heart-warming" just isn't the word, though I haven't the faintest idea what is. ***NME***

minutes. There are no guitar solos, no slow songs and just one non-original, "California Sun". The urgency is still there and on at least one track you can hear Dee Dee Ramone's frenzied count-in which stands out so much in their live shows.

Coupled with their new-found studio inventiveness is the use of vocal harmony, hitherto scorned in favour of vocal unison. One track sounded uncannily like the early Who, in the days when Roger Daltrey was experimenting with a not-quite-falsetto vocal style, while another reminded me of the Stones, circa *Between the Buttons*, probably because the instrumentation was sparser than usual.

But the majority of tracks exude that manic, urgent approach to an instant flash of song that marked the first album. Ideas are never developed, just exposed, flat and brutal, over before they've almost begun and only occasionally memorable. So many instant tracks played so fast back to back make it extraordinarily hard to differentiate between one and another, especially when the mix favours the guitarist rather than the singer.

I didn't catch one title, apart from "California Sun", yet the lyrics seemed to deal with boy/girl relationships rather than violence or glue-sniffing – a gesture that will surely find sympathy with people who make up radio playlists.

"We spent at least twice as long making this album as we did on the first," guitarist Johnny Ramone told me after the album had been played. He could not, though, remember just how long that was: "Most of November, I think."

Despite the punk image of the Ramones, Johnny, like his colleagues, is an amiable enough fellow even if he is not too bright. It's difficult to prise more than a couple of sentences from his reluctant mouth.

"We like to get the idea of a song across quick, leave out all the slack and play fast," said Johnny when I commented on the length of the

tracks. "We try to write a song a day when we're due to record. We'll get up in the morning and say, 'Let's write a song today,' and get on with it. Sometimes it takes 30 minutes and sometimes it takes the whole day. Then we rehearse it to get it right until we play it on stage.

"We even had a few songs that we didn't even bother to record, and one that we recorded but left off the album. We wanted to keep it to 14 tracks."

Johnny was particularly vague about the cancelled British tour with the Sex Pistols. He had wanted to go over but manager Danny Fields decided against it and the group seem to have little say in business matters – probably a wise state of affairs.

"I enjoyed the last time we went to England," said Johnny. "I remember playing the Roundhouse on July 4, Independence Day, and that was fun. It seemed that the dates on this last tour weren't so good, so Danny cancelled it, but we're due back in February or March."

The Ramones will play some dates in New York over the Christmas period provided that Joey's ankle has healed up, then spend early New Year in California before coming to England.

At the end of the evening a young, dark-haired girl opened her blouse to reveal a perfect figure. The gesture, largely unnoticed, was enough. We spent the evening prodding each other with safety pins. ***MM***

An ominous shadow

FEBRUARY 27

Keith on heroin-trafficking rap in Canada.

ROLLING STONE KEITH RICHARDS and his girlfriend Anita Pallenberg have been busted in Toronto on heroin charges. In Richards' case the charge is the very serious one of "possessing heroin for the purpose of trafficking", an indictment which carries a maximum life sentence.

All of the Stones had gone to Canada to complete their new live album. On the arrival of Richards and Pallenberg, Anita was arrested at Toronto International Airport and charged with possession of hashish and heroin. Police said 10 grams of hash were found, along with a spoon which, after laboratory analysis, was said to show traces of heroin.

It was as a result of the ensuing week-long investigation that Royal Canadian Mounted Police and provincial officers from Ontario on Sunday raided Keith Richards' hotel room and, allegedly, discovered an ounce of heroin worth approximately £600 at street prices. Keith was arrested and taken to the home of a Toronto Justice of the Peace. He was released on $1,000 bail to appear in court on Monday next week. Anita was due to appear in court today (Thursday).

The Stones had gone to Toronto planning to hire a local club in

which to record material for their upcoming double live album. The *NME* understands that three sides of material are already in the can, comprising cuts from their 1976 US and European tours (including Knebworth).

The double live album – due late spring/early summer – will be the Stones' last under their deal with WEA, prior to the switch of Rolling Stones Records to EMI in the UK.

At press time, representatives of the Stones were insisting that the group would remain in Canada to complete the live-album project.

Richards' bust is by far the most potentially serious ever experienced by the group, and comes only weeks after his UK drugs conviction in Aylesbury.

The two events together – if the one is proved and the appeal on the other is unsuccessful – must now cast an ominous shadow over the Stones' future ability to enter the United States (with Keith) to tour. *NME*

▲ Accompanied by press agent Paul Wasserman, Keith Richards arrives at City Hall, Toronto, to face drug charges on March 7, 1977

The Clash
The Clash

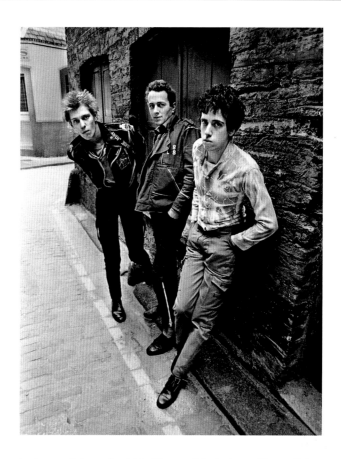

APRIL 8

BY AN ODD quirk of fate, this debut album by The Clash came into the *MM* office on the same day as The Beatles' *Live at Hamburg*. Both found their way on to the record player and the somewhat surprising reaction was that The Beatles album induced derisory laughter, while The Clash produced requests for even louder volume.

The lesson from that is not that the *MM* is full of punk-rock freaks – not a safety-pin among us (honest) – nor that we don't like The Beatles, but that in the '70s punk rock has the vitality which many now esteemed bands had when they were first starting. And it sounds a lot more fun, especially when you're not listening too closely, than triple-album concepts.

It would be ludicrous, of course, to judge The Beatles by what is little more than a bootleg; probably even more ludicrous to expect The Clash to achieve even more than one-tenth of what the Fab Four did. But it at least shows that at one time they – and the Stones, and The Who, and all the other establishment bands – sounded pretty rotten. They weren't adept at their instruments (to say the least; you ought to hear George Harrison on Hamburg), they hit bum notes, their harmonies were flat; all the faults we lay at the punk rockers' door.

Yet they had an energy that overrode all those considerations, and a defiance of the status quo. The attitude was: if you want to hear note-perfect music, go to a classical concert.

The same applies today, except that in many cases you can substitute "rock" for classical. It all boils down, of course, to what exactly you do want. Personally, I care neither for the reverential neo-classical shows of the Pink Floyd, nor for my turntable to be filled all day with the extremely restricted music performed by The Clash and their cohorts.

Punk rock strikes me as an experience to be savoured in small doses and, if on record, then at a high volume and preferably while doing something else. A closer examination, I find, leads to headaches, thanks to the tuneless repetition of chords at a breakneck pace.

The Clash, if you can believe it, manage to make the Stooges sound subtle. A shame that the instruments have the upper hand, because lurking beneath the racket are some interesting lyrics, snatches of which it's possible to hear if you listen carefully (not recommended).

It's here that The Clash, and others of their ilk, justify their existence. Just as in the pre-Beatles era lyrics had degenerated into "moon in June" romantic slush, so has the standard of today's pop-song lyric gone back into a moronic slump?

By it's very definition, "popular" music should not just be for the people, but about them, too. The Clash do exactly this, chronicling the ideas, frustrations and problems of disaffected youth in songs like "Remote Control", "Cheat" and "48 Hours" – these are the kind of themes that ought to be in the chart (if someone could write a tune for them, of course).

Particularly impressive is the sneering denunciation of the employment prospects faced by the young in "Career Opportunities".

Some commentators will no doubt find the most significance in the only non-original on the album, a cover of Junior Marvin's big reggae hit of last year, "Police And Thieves" (you know, rebellious white youth links with angry blacks to create a potent political force, blah, blah, blah), but I shall leave that for the sociologists, except to say that it's a musically creditable version.

As an album, *The Clash* is pretty much what you'd expect: raucous, basic, and should go down a treat with the Blank Generation. Thank God I'm "too old" to have to enjoy it. *MM*

▶ Portrait of Paul Simonon (left)
and Joe Strummer of The Clash,
photographed in Paris in April 1977

1977

SINGLE REVIEW

Sex Pistols "God Save The Queen"

MAY 27

RAMALAMAFA FA FA! Just in case there was any danger of forgetting that the Pistols are a rock band instead of just a media hoax/guaranteed talk-show laff-getter/all-purpose scapegoat or whatever, here's a record which actually managed to squeak its way past the official guardians or our morality and may well be in your shops any minute now. It may even stay there long enough for you to buy it. It comes out on Saturday and it'll probably be banned by Monday, so move f-a-s-t.

The "real" title of this song is "No Future", but it's received so much notoriety as "God Save The Queen" that now it's called "God Save The Queen" so that you can get what you ask for when you ask for it. And what you will get when you ask for it is a remorseless, streamlined crusher of a single that establishes the Pistols' credentials as a real live rock'n'roll band. Up front,

star of stage and screen Johnny Rotten (the singer) gets to grips with the already oft-quoted lyric in the inimitably charming manner that has made him the darling of international cafe society. "We're the future/You're the future/NO FUTURE!" he leers, except that there is a future, you're it and if you don't take it, then you've only yerownass to blame...

Anyway, buy it. Buy it whether you like the Sex Pistols or not. If people try that hard to stop you from hearing something, then you owe it to yourself to find out why. Besides, since 1977 marks the Queen's ascent to cult-figure status, maybe the reason that punx dig her so much is that she's a shining example to all of us. How many of you dole-queue cowboys can get that much bread for posing all year? Gabba gabba hey! Which reminds me... ***NME***

Sex Pistols
Never Mind The Bollocks, Here's The Sex Pistols

OCTOBER 28

WHAT ARE YOU waiting for? True love, school to end, third world/civil war, more wars in the third world, a leader, the commandos to storm the next aeroplane, next week's *NME*, The Revolution?

The Sex Pistols album!

Hail, hail, rock'n'roll, deliver them from evil but lead them not into temptation. Keep them quiet/off the street/content.

Hey, punk! You wanna elpee-sized "Anarchy" single? You wanna original "Anarchy" black bag? You wanna bootleg album? You wanna collect butterflies?

Very fulfilling, collecting things... very satisfying. Keep you satisfied, make you satiated, make you fat and old, queueing for the rock'n'roll show.

The Sex Pistols. They could have dreamed up the name and died. The hysterical equation society makes of love/a gun = power/crime shoved down its own throat, rubbed in its own face. See, I'm just as repressed and contaminated as the next guy. And I like the Sex Pistols. Aesthetically, apart from anything else. Three of them are very good-looking. And the sound of the band goes...

"I don't wanna holiday in the sun/I wanna go in the city/There's a thousand things I wanna say to you..."

All very Weller, but is this a Jagger I see before me? No, it's the singles, all four of them – "Anarchy In The UK", "God Save The Queen", "Pretty Vacant" and "Holidays In The Sun" – constituting one third (weigh it) of the vinyl. Of course, there are other great songs.

This in no first-round knockout. This is no Clash attending the CBS Convention; no Jam voting Conservative; no Damned fucking an American girl with a Fender bass; no Stranglers distorting Trotsky and Lenin for their own cunt-hating, bully-boy ends. No, this is the Sex Pistols. The band which (so I'm told – I wasn't there in the beginning) started it all.

Great songs like "Submission", a numb-nostrilled "Venus In Furs"/"Penetration"/"I Wanna Be Your Dog", in form hypnotic, in content writhing. Pain through a dull, passive haze. Is that a whip in your hand or are you abnormal?

"Submission/Going down, down, dragging her down/Submission/I can't tell you what I've found." Smack?

Geeks? What a mystery and who grew up on the New York Dolls? Dogs yelp as the drill continues. Most unhealthy and ya like it like that? Well, it grows on you. A bit like cancer.

▲ Johnny Rotten fronting the Sex Pistols at a concert in Eindhoven, Holland, December 1977

▶ The Sex Pistols on stage in Copenhagen, Denmark, July 13, 1977

Great songs like "No Feelings": "I got no emotion for anybody else/ You better understand I'm in love with myself/My self, my beautiful self." Ah, solipsism rules, as Tony Parsons used to say before he got wise. Good dance tune, anyway, while "Problems" says it all: "Bet you thought you knew what I was about/ Bet you thought you'd solved all your problems/But YOU are the problem".

Whatcha gonna do? Vegetate? Listen to the Sex Pistols album? Great songs gone, ineffectual flicks of the wrist like "New York", which probably has David Johansen quaking in his heels, and "EMI" – you guessed it, they're bitching.

"You're only 29/You gotta lot to learn". In spite of this inspired opening, "Seventeen" rambles a little and the guitars do go on a bit. "I just speed/That's all I need".

Whaddya think so far?

Well, I've saved the best bit for you to linger over. You've already heard two songs the band co-wrote with Sid Vicious (as opposed to Glen Matlock, The True Pop Kid): "EMI" and "Holidays In The Sun". Here's the third. It's called "Bodies".

"She was a girl from Birmingham/She had just had an abortion/She was a case of insanity/Her name was Pauline, she lived in a tree/She was a no one who killed her baby/She sent her letters from the country/She was an animal/She was a bloody disgrace/Bodies/I'm not an animal/Dragged on a table in a factory/Illegitimate place to be/ In a packet in a lavatory/Die little baby screaming/Bodies/Screaming fucking bloody mess/ Not an animal/It's an abortion/Mummy/I'm not an abortion/Throbbing squirm/Gurgling bloody mess..."

What? Good God. Was I shocked! Did I jump! Is that what they wanted, to shock people? Smart boys. Do they mean it? Is it satire of the most dubious kind? Did John's Catholic schooling leave its mark? I don't know where "Bodies" is coming from and it scares me. It's obviously a gutter view of sex/dirt/blood/reproduction and if the song is an attack on such a mentality it's admirable.

But, as with "Holidays In The Sun", Rotten never allows himself to make a moral judgement and, going by things he's said, he seems refreshingly capable of making them. I wish he would. I wish he would say that East Germany is presently organising itself better than West Germany – or vice versa, if that's what he believes. I wish the Sex Pistols had said in "Bodies" that women should not be forced to undergo such savagery, especially within a "welfare" state.

I'm sick of unlimited tolerance and objectivity, because it leads to annihilation. I wish everyone would quit sitting on the fence in the middle of the road. I think "Bodies" will be open to much misinterpretation and that to issue it was grossly irresponsible.

Many of these songs (under new names) also crop up on their bootleg album – plus "Satellite", in which the Pistols give the finger to the provinces, and "Just Me", which has a non-existent tune and frightening words: "You wanna be me/Didn't I fool you?" The singing is done with much less expertise. Rotten sounding sick to death. It's a much better record.

I don't really know anything about music, but the Sex Pistols seem to play as well as anyone I've heard, and I've heard Jimi Hendrix and Pete Townshend records. I never knew what was meant by "guitar hero" – it sounds like the kind of phrase a mental retard might mouth. "Guitar hero" – you mean as in "war hero", that kind of thing?

Why should anyone wish to play more usefully than Steve Jones, or drum more elaborately than Paul Cook, or play better bass than Sid Vicious? What purpose could it serve to outdo them?

So what are the Sex Pistols?

For the tabloids, a welcome rest from nubiles (sex and violence in their name alone and drugs too, if you count Rotten's speed dalliance); for the dilettantes, a new diversion (Ritz has a monthly punk column); for the promoters, a new product to push; for the parents, a new excuse; for the kids, a new way (in the tradition of the Boy Scouts, the terraces and one-upmanship) in which to dissipate their precious energy.

Johnny Rotten, Oliver Twist of this generation. "I wanna some MORE, Malcolm!" *NME*

FIRE EXIT

June 1977: Johnny Rotten (aka John Lydon) and Sid Vicious, outside the Portobello Hotel, London

NEWS

"Only advertised locally"

DECEMBER 17

The Sex Pistols plan to tour. Discreetly, to keep "local objections down to a minimum".

ON FRIDAY THIS WEEK the Sex Pistols kick off on their first official British tour since their debut *Anarchy In The UK* dates. The band will be playing a straight run of 10 dates, finishing on Christmas Day, but there is the possibility of a further show being added for London audiences on Boxing Day.

While the concerts have been officially confirmed by Cowbell, the band's booking agency, and booked openly in the Sex Pistols' name, there is still some secrecy about the exact location of the venues and the final bookings will only be advertised locally within a few days of the shows.

Cowbell's John Jackson said that the details of the venues and concert dates are being kept a last-minute secret, even from Virgin Records, the band's record company, and from the group themselves. Despite the secrecy, Jackson still fears problems from local authorities, but he has worked out a complex strategy involving two alternative "tours" if local authorities or police revoke licences at the last minute.

"The shows will be advertised locally as the Sex Pistols, but the advertising will be very close to the date to keep the possibility of local objections down to a minimum and to ensure a fair distribution of tickets. The tickets for the first show will go on sale the day before the concert."

Jackson confirmed that the 10 shows will be played in the following areas of Britain: North London, East Anglia, the West Country, Merseyside, two in North Yorkshire, East Midlands, two in the West Midlands, and one south of London outside the GLC area. One show that has already been advertised and sold well is at Bristol's Bamboo Club on December 21.

Tickets for the shows cost £1.75, although one promoter has been offering them at £2.50. Jackson said that anyone who has paid more than £1.75 for a legitimate ticket will get the balance refunded when they go to the show. *MM*

"He won admiration"

SEPTEMBER 16

On the brink of a comeback, Marc Bolan is killed in a car accident.

MARC BOLAN'S LADY, GLORIA JONES, had still not been told of his death on Tuesday, when his funeral took place at Golders Green. She was still in shock after an operation on her fractured jaw, but was said to be recovering and resting comfortably. The couple's 20-month-old son Rolan was being looked after by Marc's parents.

Bolan died when the Mini in which he was passenger, with Gloria at the wheel, crashed into a tree in Barnes, South-West London, last Friday morning. They were returning home after a late meal at a West End restaurant with Gloria's brother, Richard Jones, who was following behind in his own car. The crash occurred at a notorious accident black spot, on the far side of a hump-back bridge and on a wet surface.

Bolan himself did not drive and had never held a licence. He had also emerged from a self-confessed period of drug taking and hard drinking, sparked by his decline in popularity and his divorce. He gave up both drugs and drink when Gloria came into his life, and was poised – both mentally and professionally – for a major comeback.

The first step in his direction was his own Granada TV series, which he completed filming shortly before his death – screening of the final show, with the full consent of his family, is next Wednesday (28). His TV producer Muriel Young said this week, "He won the admiration of everyone in the studio. He really cared about his show, his colleagues and his music." And plans were already being laid for Marc and T. Rex to headline a major tour at the end of the year.

EMI Records were planning to release a compilation album titled *Solid Gold T. Rex* on October 14, consisting of a dozen of his hit singles which he had chosen himself. The LP will still be coming out, but it's possible that the title may now be changed, and that it will become a commemorative set. Bolan's publicist said there is "a fair amount" of new T. Rex material in the can, though there are no immediate plans to issue any singles.

Bolan's peak was in 1971–73 when, after a relatively fruitless period fronting John's Children, he and Steve Took expanded their Tyrannosaurus Rex duo into a quartet – and T. Rex was born. They had a string of No 1 hits with "Hot Love", "Get It On", "Telegram Sam" and "Metal Guru"; four No 2 successes with "Ride A White Swan", "Jeepster", "Children Of The Revolution" and "Solid Gold Easy Action"; and four other Top 10 entries.

During that period, Bolan was one of the hottest properties on the British scene. But his success took a tumble when he became

"His greatest ambition was to have another No 1"

a tax exile in America, where he was unable to emulate his British achievements. There followed a period in limbo, but as Bolan started his fightback, he once again stood on the threshold of the big time.

He headlined a short tour earlier this year, with The Damned as guest artists, but he was hoping for more substantial developments in the coming months. His greatest ambition was to have another No 1 hit, but tragically it was never to be realised. **NME**

Elvis Costello, with a Fender Jazzmaster guitar, posing during a photoshoot for the cover of his debut album, March 1977

"I'm not askin' anybody for charity"

Introducing, on Stiff Records, ELVIS COSTELLO, a sharp-eyed laureate of the new wave. "I'm not an arbitrator of public taste or opinion," he says. "I don't have a following of people waiting for my next word."

ELVIS APPROACHED STIFF RECORDS last August: he arrived at their office in West London with a tape of his songs and the response of Jake Riviera and Dave Robinson (also manager of Graham Parker) was immediate and enthusiastic.

They signed him to the label, in fact.

"There was no phenomenal advance," he laughs. "They've bought me an amp and a tape recorder. I'm glad that they're not subsidising me to any greater extent. I don't want to be put on a retainer and spend my time ligging around record company offices like a lot of other musicians.

"I don't want any charity. I want to be out gigging, earning money. I don't want anything for nothing. I'm not askin' anybody for their fucking charity. I went to a lot of record companies before I came to Stiff. Major record companies. And I never asked them for charity. I didn't go in with any servile attitude.

"I didn't go in and say, 'Look, I've got these songs and, well, with a bit of patching up and a good producer I might make a good record.' I went in and said, 'I've got some great fucking songs; record them and release them.' Stiff were the only ones that showed that kind of faith in me.

"They let me do it. I'm still working, right. I'll only give up the job when I start working with a band."

Elvis mentions, mischievously, that none of the musicians that contributed their services to his album are credited on the sleeve (Nick Lowe gets a production credit on the label, though). It transpires that this was El's idea of a caustic comment upon the contemporary state of the music business – an industry for which Elvis has very little admiration or respect.

He had a caption, in fact, prepared for the sleeve of his album, which would have read: "No thanks to anybody." Unfortunately, The Damned got there first when they had printed on the sleeve of their album: "Thanks to no one." El didn't want anyone to think he'd copied the idea, so it was abandoned.

"The people who were directly involved with the album know who they are," El explains, "and they're not the kind of people who'd be worried about credits and namechecks. Equally, the people who were instrumental in stopping me from recording before know who they were, and I wanted to remind them that I hadn't forgotten them.

"Like, I went around for nearly a year with demo tapes before I came to Stiff, and it was always the same response. 'We can't hear the words.' 'It isn't commercial enough.' 'There aren't any singles.' Idiots. Those tapes were just voice-and-guitar demos. I didn't have enough money to do anything with a band. It was just a lack of imagination on the part of those people at the record companies. I felt as if I was bashing my head against a brick wall, those people just weren't prepared to listen to the songs.

"It's a terrible position to be in. You start thinking you're mad. You listen to the radio and you watch the TV and you hear a lot of fucking rubbish. You very rarely turn on the radio or TV and hear anything exciting, right? And, all the time, you know that you're capable of producing something infinitely better.

"But I never lost faith. I'm convinced in my own talent, yeah. Like I said, I wasn't going up to these people meekly and saying, 'Look, with your help and a bit of polishing up, and with all your expertise

"I hate hard-rock bands.
I hate anything with fucking extended solos"

and knowledge of the world of music, we might have a moderate success on our hands.'

"I was going in thinking, 'You're a bunch of fucking idiots who don't know what you're doing. I'm bringing you a lot of good songs, why don't you go ahead and fucking well record them.' They didn't seem to understand that kind of approach.

"No, it didn't make me bitter. I was already bitter. I knew what it would be like. I had no illusions. I have no illusions at all about the music business. It was no sudden shock to be confronted by these idiots. I didn't ever think that I was going to walk into a record company to meet all these fat guys smoking big cigars who'd say something like, 'Stick with me son. I'll make you a STAR.'

"I'm not starry-eyed in the slightest. You can tell what all these people are like instinctively. You just have to look at them to tell that they're fucking idiots. But I don't want to come off sounding like I'm obsessed with the music business.

"I couldn't give a shit about the music business. They just don't know anything. That's all you've got to remember. They're irrelevant. I don't give any thought to any of those people. They're not worth my time." Elvis, who by this time seems to be metamorphising before my very eyes into the superhuman guise of Captain Verbals, is telling me about his album. It was recorded, he says, on his days off from work (he is a computer analyst in Acton), over a very brief period.

He was fortunate, he readily admits, that Nick Lowe was so sympathetic a producer: their respective ideas were entirely compatible and there were few arguments about the sound and instrumentation employed.

All the songs were written within weeks of the first session; "Less Than Zero", his first single, was written three days before it was recorded, for instance. Elvis just says he felt inspired and excited. The hits just kept on coming, as it were. (*My Aim Is True*, incidentally, is the first album I've heard for ages that sounds as if it is essentially a collection of Top 10 singles.)

"I just love the sound of the album," Elvis enthuses. "'Cos I love things that sound great on the radio. 'Less Than Zero', I thought sounded great on the radio. The record isn't for people with fucking great hi-fis. I'm not interested in those people, or that kind of mentality. I don't want my records to be used to demonstrate fucking stereos in Laskys. I just want people to listen to the fucking music.

"I don't want to be successful so that I can get a lot of money and retire to a house in the fucking country. I don't want any of that rock'n'roll rubbish. I don't want to go cruising in Hollywood or hang out at all the star parties. I'm not interested in any of that. It's the arse end of rock'n'roll. I'm just interested in playing.

"I want to put a band together as soon as possible and get out on the fucking road. We're auditioning people this week. We're looking for young people. People that want to get out and play. Putting a band together is the most important thing at the moment.

"I think it might be difficult getting the right kind of people and I can imagine us wading through a right bunch of idiots. The group sound I want will be a lot sparser than the album sound. I just want bass, drum, guitar – my guitar – and for keyboards we'll probably go for a Vox or Farfisa sound.

"I want to get away from the conventional group sound. I'd say that I want a kind of pop-group lineup, but people might take that as something lightweight or trivial. But it will be a pop lineup in the sense that it won't be a rock band.

"I hate hard-rock bands. I hate anything with fucking extended solos or bands that are concerned with any kind of instrumental virtuosity. I can listen to maybe 15 seconds of someone like The Crusaders, say, before I get very bored. I know how good they are because everybody keeps telling me how fucking marvellous they are. But I get bored.

"There are going to be no fucking soloists in my band. The songs are the most important thing. I want the songs to mean something to people. I don't mean by that that I want them to be significant. It's just that too much rock has cut itself off from people. It's become like ballet or something. Ballet is only for people who can afford to go and see it. It's not for anybody else. You don't get ballet going on in your local pub.

"There's a lot of rock music that's become exclusive and it's of no use to anyone. Least of all me. Music has to get to people. In the heart, in the head. I don't care where, as long as it fucking gets them. So much music gets thrown away. It's such a fucking waste.

"That's why I like and write short songs. It's a discipline. There's no disguise. You can't cover up songs like that by dragging in banks of fucking synthesizers and choirs of angels. They have to stand up on their own. With none of that nonsense. Songs are just so fucking effective. People seem to have forgotten that.

"Like, people used to live their lives by songs. They were like calendars or diaries. And they were pop songs. Not elaborate fucking pieces of music. You wouldn't say, like, 'Yeah, that's the time I went out with Janet, we went to see the LSO playing Mozart.' You'd remember you went out with Janet because they were playing 'Summer In The City' on the radio."

You will have gathered by now that Elvis is committed to success; he's not, however, altogether sure when that success will be achieved.

"There are a lot of people," he says, "who should be successful. If ability had anything to do with success, then there would be a whole lot of obscure people who'd be famous and there would be a whole lot of famous people who'd be lingering in obscurity."

Was there anyone, I wondered, that he would like to see becoming famous? "Yeah," he replied. "Me." **MM**

Elvis Costello pictured in Holland as he was leaving a radio show in 1977

Craft And Precision

APRIL 2 · BIRMINGHAM ODEON

The latest-lineup Mac score an impressive victory at their first UK concert.

THEIR TECHNICALLY IMPECCABLE performance was rewarded with a series of standing ovations, and by the end of the set half the audience were out of their seats, crowding the stage and dancing in the aisles.

That in itself was something of a triumph since Birmingham audiences have never been noted for enthusiasm on this scale. For Christine McVie, it must have been a particularly emotional experience; it marked her first performance in her hometown for seven years.

Fleetwood Mac played for around 90 minutes, dovetailing old and new songs with craftsman-like precision. Only at one stage did they allow their faultless pacing to slip, when they encored with the slow-moving "Hypnotised"; but by then most of the audience would probably have been content to listen to Stevie Nicks read the football results. The band's performance was a pleasant surprise for me because neither of their two recent hit albums, *Fleetwood Mac* and *Rumours*, offered the excitement of earlier work from previous lineups of the band.

On stage, however, they were an entirely different proposition. Lindsey Buckingham was excellent, both vocally and, more particularly, on guitar; there was a notable solo at the end of "The Chain", while on acoustic guitar he performed a particularly engaging version of "Never Going Back Again".

On the latter he was joined by John McVie, playing a giant-sized acoustic bass guitar. McVie was calmly impressive throughout, his assured work with drummer Mick Fleetwood born of a decade of playing together. Fleetwood, looking manic with his mouth leering open for most of the night, played one of the nicest drum solos I've heard for a long time on "World Turning". He left his kit, strapped on an African talking drum, and took stage centre to beat out a delightfully novel rhythm.

Christine McVie kept her keyboard work pure and simple most of the time, and her best moments came when she gave full reign to that excellent mellow voice on "Oh Daddy". By comparison Stevie Nicks was much more raucous, but she displayed a tremendous vocal range and an enthusiasm which one rarely sees on stage at the moment. I was less enamoured of her stage movements: she seems to think she is an exponent of modern dance, but her posturing belonged more to a Hammer horror rising-from-the grave sequence than to the dance theatre of Harlem.

However, her raunchy antics caused a stir among the male section of the audience, some of whom seemed to enjoy her costume changes more than the music. The warmest responses of the evening were reserved for "Go Your Own Way", "Over My Head" and an exceptional turn by Buckingham on the old favourite "Oh Well".

I have just two reservations about the new Fleetwood Mac. Firstly, they're not nearly as adventurous as they might be. I reiterate that they belong to the Peter Frampton progressive–school, which is currently lucrative but scarcely stands exposure for any length of time.

Secondly, none of their work sticks in the mind for longer than about 15 minutes after hearing it; that indicates shallowness. However, if they can maintain the sort of technical standard in concert that they attained in Birmingham, their success in Britain is assured. *MM*

Fleetwood Mac taking a break in 1977.
From left to right: John McVie,
Christine McVie, Stevie Nicks, Lindsey
Buckingham and Mick Fleetwood

"They played adequately"

JUNE 19 · **RAINBOW THEATRE, LONDON**

An under-amplified Petty and co. are upstaged by some hungry young Rats from Dublin.

OK, LET'S START with some facts. Tom Petty & The Heartbreakers hit the music scene with a creditably impressive debut album a few months back. Some say it was the best debut they had heard in an age, and while I reckon that is a trifle expansive, it is certainly a neatly produced album with a handful of fine songs.

The band was packed on board the recent Nils Lofgren gravy train, and took the laurels from right under the jaded Lofgren's nose. Good for them. Then came this headline tour, ending up with Tom P and the boys at London's Rainbow on Sunday night.

Given these facts, I just cannot understand the tumultuous reception given to the band. They played adequately enough, doing a very fair cover job of the main songs on the album and letting rip on some older material, but it was nothing to go berserk about.

For a start, it was under-amplified – a rare event – with Tom's soft voice often well below the level of the guitar line. Then came the songs themselves. A good half of the show featured the best tracks from the debut album, with songs like "American Girl" and "Strangered In The Night" showing the band at their full commercial appeal.

They worked well together, Mike Campbell's lead guitar keeping strictly to the record over the rhythm section of Ron Blair on bass and Stan Lynch on drums. Campbell's guitar was one of the main points of interest. He plays with control and as much subtlety as the fairly limited structure of the music allows, his tone and feedback control colouring his crisp solos.

Keyboard player Benmont Tench is a careful player, using his synthesizer effectively to add atmosphere to the gentler songs and the electric piano to beef up the rockers.

But all this, plus Tom's bounding rhythm work and aforementioned vocals, did little to mask the fact that the other half of the band's material was bland and uninspired, lacking musical excitement or lyrical appeal.

For my money, the evening was made by support band The Boomtown Rats, a bunch of Dublin lads led by Bob Geldof who play with a finely honed combination of attack, pace, energy and crisp musicality.

Their music is R&B derived, reminiscent at times of the early Stones, Chuck Berry, the Feelgoods… you get the message. Twin guitars cut and thrust, spitting chords and sneaking out spiky solos while the rhythm section moves like someone is putting the boot in at a regular four to the bar.

Out in front, Geldof, a tall, strangely animated figure, at times a dead ringer for an arrogant Jagger, kicks, runs, dives and generally hurls himself around the stage, cutting to the mic with split-second precision to deliver his vocals with guts and power.

You may have seen it all somewhere before, but the precision and energy of this band make them a whole new experience. **MM**

NEWS

Three dead, three injured

OCTOBER 20

Southern rock band Lynyrd Skynyrd decimated in a plane crash.

AT 9.02PM LOCAL TIME on Thursday, October 20, in remote woodland in south-west Mississippi, Lynyrd Skynyrd ceased to exist. The whole band were involved in an air crash, killing three of their members and critically injuring another three, so adding to the string of recent tragedies.

The band's lead singer Ronnie Van Zant died, along with their newest recruit, guitarist Steve Gaines (who joined last year) and his sister, Cassie Gaines, one of the three backing vocalists. Also killed were personal manager Dean Kilpatrick and the two pilots, while two of the road crew died subsequently in hospital.

Gary Rossington (guitar), Leon Wilkeson (bass) and Billy Powell (keyboards) were seriously injured and, on Monday, were still on the critical list. Guitarist Allen Collins and drummer Artimus Pyle were also injured, as well as the other backing singers, but they are said to be recovering.

The plane was on charter to Skynyrd, and was carrying the full band and their road and lighting crew. First reports suggest that it ran out of fuel and clipped some trees as the pilot tried to crash land.

The band's latest album, with the unfortunate title of *Street Survivors*, was officially released here by MCA the day after the crash. And because of this, MCA have no immediate plans for a memorial or compilation album. In America, the LP went gold on the day of release.

Skynyrd had just started a massive four-month tour of the States to promote the album. It opened on October 15 and was due to run until mid-February, and they were on their way to a concert on Friday (21) at Louisiana University in Baton Rouge when the disaster occurred. Their British promoter Harvey Goldsmith had just returned from America, after signing them for a major British tour in March.

They were discovered by Al Kooper, and made their name as support on The Who's 1973 US tour. They first toured Britain as support to Golden Earring, and were so successful that they finished by headlining their own Rainbow concert.

They have since continued to grow in stature – touring here several times – and in the last *NME* Poll were voted one of the world's Top 10 rock bands. **NME**

REVIEW

Pop-pulp
vs Prayers

MAY 28 · **HAMMERSMITH ODEON, LONDON**

YC cool crosses the pond as Blondie support Television.

BLONDIE'S DEBBIE HARRY frantically shimmies and shakes across the stage limelight, furiously rattling a pair of shiny maracas, and I sigh sadly, wishing they were mine.

You look good in black – fashion notes are an off-the-creamy-shoulder mini-dress, night-nurse tights and stiletto leather ankle boots from which project the silk-clad sparrow legs of the type of non-stop-dancing NOO Yawk City bud that Tom Wolfe eulogised in the "Peppermint Lounge Revisited" section of his *Kandy-Kolored Tangerine-Flake Streamline Baby*.

The World's Greatest Mouth cries "SURF'S UP!" at the start of Blondie's celebration of summer, "In The Sun", a number that's the equal of the type of Golden Old'un that Brian Wilson used to knock out on a lazy afternoon with his piano parked in the sand box. That song's typical – a joyous, updated synthesis of Beach Boys, Spector, Orlons, Daytonas, early Motown, the very *crème de la crème* of the most timeless *American Graffiti* pop-pulp that every poured out of a cruising car's radio.

· It's exhilarating Amerikana, and even though the furthest West I've ever been is Ealing Broadway, I could almost taste the back-seat-drive-in love and the ketchup-soaked cheeseburgers sizzling on an open grill...

Debbie looks like a peroxided 16-year-old ponytailed cheerleader who got a job turning tricks on Times Square during the vacation. The angelic countenance, absorbed in her speeding-sideways dance steps, turns vicious as her painted nails claw the air for the Patti Smith-inspired "Rip Her To Shreds".

Her Mop Top Muppet band ploughed through "Get Off Of My Cloud" on Saturday and "Louie Louie" the next night for the intro to the opening track on their *Private Stock* album, "X Offender", a child-like paean to a perverted cop who's into rubber boots, if you see what I mean. It's the tragic story of a jailed man and the girl who waits for him.

The notion that the band should stick to small clubs and avoid the larger halls is smashed as the descendant of every enigma from Monroe to Piaf to Ronnie Spector gets bathed in blue lucid spotlight for "Look Good In Blue" done soft and sultry. *West Side Story* derivative finger-snapping choreography with Debbie torching it into the footlights with Doomed Lover angst.

▶ Debbie Harry performing with Blondie during their British tour with Television; the Free Trade Hall, Manchester, May 26, 1977

"Television may have 10 times the talent of Blondie, but they ain't half as much fun"

"For Iggy!" Debbie cries and they rip through their tribute to The Pop, "Detroit".

"In The Flesh" was only performed on the Sunday, which was bad strategy as they should do it every night. Not a dry eye in the house as Debbie purrs, murmurs and sighs.

It's Blondie's newest single and it would mean a lot to me if you all go out and buy it.

I bite my toenails in anguish as "Man Overboard" is followed by "Rifle Range", with Debbie getting gunned down and dying the Bogart, flat on her back and twitching with the throes of Sudden Death.

But when she bounces back for "I Didn't Have The Nerve To Say No (Dear)", a sort of porno "God Only Knows", I know that everything's gonna be alright.

The band leave the stage (sulky bastards, her musicians; not the type of boys Debbie should mix with at all), then get brought back for two numbers that display real fire – killer versions of "Heatwave" by Martha Reeves & The Vandellas and The Daytonas' "Little GTO".

The difference between Blondie and Television was the difference between hanging around an amusement arcade and going to church. Honest, I think that the *Marquee Moon* album is great. But the two weekend gigs that Tom Verlaine's Television played at Hammersmith Odeon were like sitting at the Maharishi's feet or gazing respectfully at the Crown Jewels – or watching Pink Floyd if they had any good songs.

"Prove it, Tommy boy!" an irreverent prole bawled, and I assumed he was talking about the album track of the same name. But when the song had come and gone and he continued shouting, "Prove it, Tommy boy!" I realised he was challenging Verlaine to live up to the hyperbole of his build-up.

On the album, Verlaine's frighteningly intense music carries some warmth, passion and SOUL. There was a paucity of all those qualities during these two gigs. It was cold, heartless and joyless, and they played with the technical perfection of a sophisticated computer. When they started with the first tracks on the album, "See No Evil" and "Venus", I thought they were gonna run straight through the album because they didn't have the energy to change the tracklisting around.

When a man as talented as Verlaine can write something like "Venus", perhaps the finest love song since Dylan's "Love Minus Zero", there's just no excuse for playing with as much sexuality, love or affection as a necrophiliac.

Between numbers, Verlaine savours the role of distant, cool, patronising Star. Unsmiling, unmoving throughout, he introduces

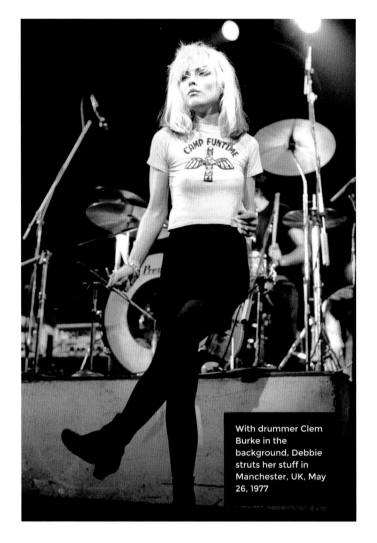

With drummer Clem Burke in the background, Debbie struts her stuff in Manchester, UK, May 26, 1977

each song in a short slur of words, all indistinguishable except for the title.

Meanwhile, everybody's sitting round watching Television. It made me think that the Television/Blondie tour and the Ramones/Talking Heads tour should swap support acts for everyone's benefit.

While not in the same league as songs on the album like "Friction" or "Prove It", the old Ork single "Little Johnny Jewel" got the best reception simply because it's certainly the most esoteric number the band do.

"Marquee Moon" alone comes across as visually impressive as it is on vinyl, with guitarist Richard Lloyd and Verlaine cutting jagged, incisive structures through the air as TV's transparent axe reflected beams of coloured light that looked like the music FELT.

On that occasion the music touched me inside. The rest of the time it was how I imagine a Grateful Dead concert to be.

"Knockin' On Heaven's Door" is dire, and it's not until the encore of "Satisfaction" that the audience stand up from their chairs and Idiot Dance.

"WALLY!" somebody has the amusing and appropriate audacity to bellow, and then the bouncers start playing Gestapo Warriors and it ain't funny.

As the fishbloods leave the stage, I reflect that Television may have 10 times the talent of Blondie, but they ain't half as much fun. I think I'm in love. *NME*

The Stranglers
Strangers IV (Rattus Norvegicus)

APRIL 15

JUST ABOUT THE ONLY predictable thing about rock is that, as soon as something new comes along, there's always someone willing to jump on the bandwagon. Even more predictable is that punk rock/new wave is going to get more than its fair share of these jerks, simply because it is a genre without rules and regulations.

The Stranglers strike me as one such group attempting to cash in. On the face of it, they've got all the punk credentials: the name, the musical incompetence, even a gig supporting Patti Smith. But one look at this album is enough to let you know where The Stranglers are at – or, perhaps, where their record company would like them to be at.

There's a beautifully designed sleeve and inner sleeve, a special label with The Stranglers' rat logo and even – try and hide the groans – a free single. ELP should be so lucky! As a special bonus for us lucky reviewers, there's a bundle of press cuttings, fax, pix and info, a press release that's magnificently mistyped and – here comes the real killer – a card from their press-and-public-relations consultant.

This is the music of disaffected youth, struggling against a hard business that won't give them a break? Smells more like hype to me. The music on the album confirms that The Stranglers have little or nothing to offer. They're singularly lacking in all of the virtues that new-wave bands like The Clash, The Damned and the Pistols have as their saving grace; they're about as energetic as a slug, and their lyrics, far from providing an outlet for the frustrations of today's young, are the same old tripe used by most of the bands the punks love to hate – but with a few naughty swear words thrown in.

Here's an example of the wit and wisdom of The Stranglers from "Peaches": "Strolling along, minding my own business/ Well there goes a girl now, 'hi'/She's got me going up and down/She's got me going up and down/ Walking on the beaches looking at the peaches/Well I've got the notion girl that you've got some suntan lotion in that bottle of yours/ Spread it all over my peeling skin, baby, that feels real good/All the skirts lapping up the sun/Lap me up".

All this is delivered in the usual arrogant tone, as though it

were something momentous, and over a stunningly boring keyboard-dominated riff. It has been suggested that The Stranglers resemble The Doors: an insult if I ever heard one. It's true that the opening cut, "Sometimes", sounds like it's based on the "Light My Fire" organ solo; yet they are more akin to a late-'60s Detroit band, SRC, through their use of keyboards, but without half the Americans' style in exploiting doom-laden chords, nor even anything as remotely cheeky as combining "Hall Of The Mountain King" with "Beck's Bolero".

In truth, The Stranglers are no more than a cut-rate version of '60s American punk bands, but with none of the fizz that made that music so enjoyable. About the only thing they do well is write the titles to their songs; "Grip", "Down In The Sewer" and "Ugly" promise something more interesting than a succession of deadening riffs and a noticeable lack of ideas. The only sense in which The Stranglers could be considered new wave is that no one has had the gall to palm off this rubbish before. **MM**

NEWS

Buried near the grave of his mother

AUGUST 18

Elvis Presley is laid to rest. Celebrities pay their respects.

ELVIS WAS BURIED last week in the Presley family vault near the grave of his mother, after dying from heart failure. An estimated 100,000 fans had passed in mourning by his open coffin.

Among those who came to say farewell to a legend were actors Burt Reynolds and John Wayne, a one-time co-star and friend Ann-Margret, and Caroline Kennedy, daughter of the late President.

The pallbearers at the funeral included Joe Esposito, Presley's road manager, his doctor Dr George Nichopoulos and his record producer, Felton Jarvis. The service was conducted by a friend of Presley's: Ohio evangelist Rex Humbard.

The King (Until The Next One)

SEPTEMBER 10

Without trying to diminish the contribution Elvis made to rock music, it is ridiculous to say he invented rock'n'roll. Like any invention, there is always more than one person on the advent of breakthrough, but Elvis happened to be the first in his mould. If it hadn't been him, it would have been somebody else. So all that rubbish about there being no Cliff Richard or Beatles without Elvis is pure drivel.

It is also ridiculous comparing the record sales of Elvis with those of The Beatles. He released three or four times the quantity of discs that The Beatles released (91 singles to 21 [sic]); the only comparison that can be made is the quality of their respective songs, and in that field The Beatles will never be equalled, let alone beaten. The Beatles could have had 100 No 1 hits, but quality not quantity was their trademark.

Unfortunately for Elvis, he was not a composer or a gifted speaker, and it is music that lives on, not people. In future the names of Lennon/McCartney will ring out as composers, and I doubt if Elvis or The Beatles will be mentioned in name, apart from the odd book or film.

As for the behaviour of the Elvis fans, they have not acted in a way befitting the King of Rock'n'Roll. It is a shame that any person dies, but I would have been old enough to act in a responsible manner, and not go crying all over the place. I don't think Beatles fans would act in this way, and we are closer to them and their music here in Britain.

It is funny how people who have slagged Elvis off for years are now singing his praises in print. The real truth is that Elvis reigned until about 1963, but since then he has been about as important to music as flypaper. Every era has a King, but since The Beatles, we haven't had any.

So the King is dead, long live the next King. RIP, Elvis.
JOHN HALL, Manchester. **MM**

◀ Memphis, Tennessee: The cortege of limousines making their way to Elvis Presley's funeral on August 18, 1977

▲ Elvis' final resting place, the family vault at Forest Hill Cemetery, behind a sea of flowers on the day of his funeral

Blondie // Bob Dylan // Bob Marley
Devo // Kate Bush // Keith Moon // Meat Loaf
Rush // *Saturday Night Fever* // Sex Pistols
Sid Vicious // Siouxsie and the Banshees

1978

Disco is celebrated in the spectacular movie *Saturday Night Fever*, Bob Dylan turns out to be unusually talkative during his UK tour, and Bob Marley hopes to end turmoil in Jamaica with a landmark peace concert.

In Britain, a fresh young Kate Bush makes an exciting debut, while the Sex Pistols implode and Sid Vicious is arrested for murder. Old fans Siouxsie and the Banshees step forward to take their place. And riding a fine line between pop and punk, Debbie Harry and Blondie come up with their *magnum opus*, in their sublime third album *Parallel Lines*.

No Word-of-mouth Movie

Saturday Night Fever is a phenomenon, a winner for star, soundtrack artists and producers alike. Nothing, it turns out, was left to chance.

THE STARTLING RISE to popularity of *Saturday Night Fever* has been widely portrayed as a traditional success story – the rise of a brand-new superstar in the form of John Travolta, whose mugshot currently adorns the front covers of publications as diverse as US gossip rag *The Star* and the political heavyweight *Time*.

Far more interesting in many ways, however, is the story of how *Fever* was developed into a media goldmine which is now, according to *Variety*, "building into a music industry all by itself".

As *Thrills* predicted in January, music movies have come of age with a vengeance in 1978. In recent weeks in America, *Fever* has

topped the film charts, with five tracks from the album taking up no less than half the US Top 10 singles in one recent week.

The financial facts are staggering. Leaving aside the astronomical amounts of money the movie itself is grossing, the album has already sold 6 million copies, and is now selling at the rate of a million copies a week, with a projected final sale in sight of 12 million copies – which would make the double-record set the biggest-grossing album of all time (*The Sound of Music* is still holding the record for biggest-selling soundtrack album at 16 million copies to date, but that is only a single album).

All the album tracks (the Bee Gees and other RSO artists aside) were licensed from other companies on a deal which means that, if *Fever* does reach the 12 million mark, the licensees will walk away with a cool $360,000 per track.

For those artists, this is only the beginning, of course. Many of these tracks, like "Boogie Shoes" by KC & The Sunshine Band, have

been re-released as singles and are now themselves climbing the charts. Obviously, the album will also stimulate sales of each artist's other recordings. Apparently, a number of companies refused to license songs for inclusion in the soundtrack album. They must be kicking themselves right now.

The Bee Gees, who wrote eight tracks for the album, stand to split $1 million on publishing rights alone. Between them they also sang, wrote or produced all the five *Fever* singles recently residing in the US Top 10, a feat which betters even The Beatles at their peak and which should allow the Gibb brothers to retire for life, should they wish to.

The mastermind behind this financial bonanza is Robert Stigwood, who has managed the Bee Gees since their career began in the mid-'60s and is now poised to become one of the most powerful figures in the music business. *Saturday Night Fever* was handled with consummate marketing skill. This was no word-of-mouth movie. Travolta was already a small-screen star via his Fonzie-like role in

◀ Publicity art featuring John Travolta, for *Saturday Night Fever*, released in December 1977 and one of the big movie hits of 1978

▲ John Travolta dancing with co-star Karen Lynn Gorney in a key disco club scene from *Saturday Night Fever*

"*Fever* is a precursor of things to come: the industrialisation of popular culture"

the American sitcom *Welcome Back, Kotter.* This, combined with the movie's eminently commercial disco music, backed by some extremely hard-sell advertising techniques, enabled the package to scale new financial heights of *Jaws*-like proportions.

Having successfully launched the film via a massive in-cinema campaign, the Stigwood organisation went on to spend a phenomenal amount on TV advertising for the album – a quarter of a million dollars in Europe alone.

This reflects current industry trends – movies sell albums and singles, which in turn sell movies. Soundtrack albums dominated the recent Grammy awards (America's music-biz equivalent of Oscars), and are currently making huge dents in the "straight" album market. Biggies to date are the two *Star Wars* albums (soundtrack and spoken word) and *Close Encounters*, all of which are currently approaching platinum status.

Nobody understands this present shift in the industry better than Robert Stigwood, and he is now about to capitalise on it in a way that is going to make even the *Fever* earnings look like chicken feed.

For a start, he has two more major music movies all ready for release later this year. First will be *Grease*, an *American Graffiti*-style '50s pastiche based on a long-running Broadway smash, which once again stars John Travolta, this time teamed with Olivia Newton-John.

Shortly afterwards will follow *Sgt. Pepper's Lonely Hearts Club Band*, which features the Bee Gees and Peter Frampton (to name but two), and which will be accompanied by a double-album package of 30 Beatles songs recycled for mass public consumption.

As if those two potential money mountains were not enough, Stigwood has even more tricks up his sleeve. With the *Saturday Night Fever* and Bee Gees money flowing in, he is now moving into American TV.

He is developing six new television projects, mostly written by writers new to the medium and each one full of crossover possibilities for feature film, record or book developments.

Three of these are specifically music-orientated.

Baby Needs Shoes, a two-hour musical comedy specially designed as a perennial Christmas item, is scripted by Ian La Frenais and Dick Clement of *Porridge* fame, and features music and lyrics by Paul Williams, who will also act. The songs from the show will be released as an album on RSO.

Music Inc. is a four-hour mini-series on the music industry, focusing on the saga of a fictional group and featuring original music. It is due to begin production in August for 1979 release.

The Golden Oldies is a half-hour sitcom created and written by Henry Edwards, who wrote the screenplay for the *Sgt. Pepper* movie. It's about a senior citizens' rock band and is described as a kind of *Happy Days* for the Geritol set.

Whether any of these will provide any worthwhile music is doubtful. But we have now entered an era where large corporations are increasingly intent upon developing entertainment packages which appeal to the lowest common denominator and can readily be translated from film to TV to record to book. Stigwood is blazing a trail which all the other corporations are eagerly following.

In this respect, *Saturday Night Fever* should be seen for what it is – a new mass-market innovation and a precursor of things to come: the industrialisation of popular culture. **NME**

▲ The poster for *Saturday Night Fever*, with Travolta striking the iconic pose which became forever identified with the film

▶ Michael Lee Aday, better known by his stage name of Meat Loaf, strikes a charismatic pose while touring with his album *Bat Out Of Hell* in March 1978.

Meat Loaf *Bat Out Of Hell*

FEBRUARY 18

NOT SINCE JIM MORRISON has there been such a self-conscious writer of rock songs as poetry as Jim Steinman, who has penned all the material on this album.

His words almost leap right off the lyric sheet and screech in your ear, "This is Art!", so eager is he to impress with his knowledge of the various forms of verse. Thus we get the three-part "Paradise By The Dashboard Light", which includes alternate stanzas by "Boy" and "Girl". And there's a snatch of spoken verse before "You Took The Words Right Out Of My Mouth" that appears to be there for no reason in particular.

Sounds like some kind of elaborate joke, doesn't it? Yeah, that's what I think, especially on examining the lyrics closely and discovering that at least two of the songs betray an impish sense of humour; "You Took The Words Right Out Of My Mouth" and "For Crying Out Loud" are both based on literal interpretations of those two phrases.

But the clincher is that Todd Rundgren is at the controls, arranging everything in the most overblown manner possible. He and his band, Utopia, also supply most of the instrumentation; if it had been left to Steinman, one suspects that they wouldn't have had much to do, as the tunes aren't up to much; Rundgren, however, finds work for all by filling up every space in the music with sound.

However, there is a saving grace in this pretentious rubbish – the title track, an aggressive song about a motorcycle crash (into which Steinman injects every urban nightmare cliché in the book), which goes so far over the top one can only marvel.

Not for nothing is this album on the Epic label. *MM*

ALBUM REVIEW

Joyfully Insistent

AUGUST 28

Devo's Eno-produced debut album is provocative fun.

Devo *Q: Are We Not Men? A: We Are Devo!*

Well, here it is at last. The eagerly awaited first 12-inch slice from that Akron workforce known as Devo. So many promotional gimmicks have been mounted (the album, for instance, comes in no less than FIVE separate vinyl colourings), so many legal wrangles have had to be ironed out, so many claims and counterclaims have been made both by journalists and the Booji Boys themselves that even the starting point becomes bewildering.

Hence, the only feasible way to approach the situation is to try and forget most of the column inches that have gone before.

Devo may be experts at myth-making and media manipulation with their constantly evasive concepts, but the proof of a good spud always lies in the consumption. And let me say straight away that this is one helluva fine debut. It may not seem so at first. You'll have

to play it loud and often for the power and surprising intricacies to strike home.

Also don't get annoyed when you see that the tracklisting includes the four songs that began the whole Devo craze. "Satisfaction", "Mongoloid", "Sloppy (I Saw My Baby Gettin')" and "Jocko Homo" have been remade and remodelled in such a way that, although they might not always be as effective as the original versions, are forcefully DIFFERENT.

What impresses immediately is the QUALITY of the sound that the band, together with producer Brian Eno (yes, him again!), have achieved. If you're expecting the artfully contrived inaccessibility of, say, The Residents, you'd be very wrong. Devo work on a powerful, abrasive cut and thrust, which also happens to be utterly danceable. It may be fanciful, but they remind me of an updated and mutated version of The Yardbirds circa '65 (remember them?). The guitar sound frequently recalls the early full-bloodied shriek of Jeff Beck and the stop-start nature of some of the songs finds a loose parallel in ancient Yardbird anthems like "Heart Full Of Soul" and the double A-sided "Evil Hearted You"/"Still I'm Sad". That is just a thought and not a cast-iron reference point in any way whatsoever.

They locate everything in rough-edged rock'n'roll with the result that what is in fact pretty complex can sound exasperatingly simple and joyfully insistent. The deliciously jerky rhythms, the weird time signatures, the sense of pinhead theatricality, the deliberately questionable images (which come from a mixture of infantile abuse, domestic Americans, the urban mire we apparently inhabit and pseudo-science) plus Mark's wildly declamatory vocals all manage to mesh into a compact unit. They can even be very funny.

So in a song like "Too Much Paranoias" the synthesized breaks (imagine possibly the sound of a thousand rusty mattress springs) become part and parcel of the number's juddering momentum (here I go again). I guess you could say that the style complements the content as Mark yelps with deadpan hysteria: "There's too much paranoias/My mother's afraid to tell me the things she is afraid of".

It all surges along, throwing in surprises at unexpected junctures while being firmly welded together by fat-slap drums (mixed well to the fore) and a pneumatic bass in particular. Somehow, the effect is crazy, tough, nimble, alert and provocative all at the same time. Really, I'm not kidding!

You can best see the process in operation on the new versions of the two singles. They are generally faster, sharper and more drilled, with that packing-case drum sound once again up in the foreground. Sometimes it's for the best, sometimes not.

As far as I'm concerned, nothing can equal the original garage version of "Satisfaction", however cleverly synchronised the Mark II effect might be. "Jocko Homo", on the other hand, is easily on a par with its predecessor.

However, current fave of the new material has to be "Gut Feeling", which starts on a beautifully ringing guitar pattern only then to build layer upon layer. Mark enters with typically disdainful words (beware of taking ANY of them too seriously): "Something about the

way you taste makes me want to clear my throat..." The song continues to expand until it lurches into a second thrash called "Slap Your Mammy". Pure petulance, it's designed simply and solely to annoy, I'm sure.

Call them puerile, call them pig-headed, call them distasteful, call them wilfully calculating. All these criticisms will be made, and this is enough potential ammunition for any silver-tongued shaman to build an acid case for the prosecution. I'm on the defence, and enthusiastically so. Devo may not monitor reality as suburban robots, but they still are a smart patrol. *MM*

◀ A typically quirky shot of Devo, taken in New York City in October 1978

▲ Lead singer Mark Mothersbaugh performing with Devo at the Old Waldorf in San Francisco, November 20, 1978

1978

◀ Bob Marley in the middle of his headline performance at the One Love peace concert

Guns, Ganja, Love

APRIL 22 · NATIONAL STADIUM, KINGSTON

Bob Marley returns to Jamaica for a huge concert that aims to end the island's political civil war. The Rastafari movement gets a boost, too.

BENEATH RASTAFARIAN BANNERS and a full Caribbean moon, Jamaica's two leading politicians – Prime Minister Michael Manley and opposition leader Edward Seaga – shook hands on stage at Saturday's "One Love" peace concert headed by Bob Marley. Assembled for the sight were nearly 200 of the world's press, including camera crews and journalists from America, Europe and Cuba, and upwards of 20,000 people, who half-filled the massive National Stadium where the concert took place under heavy police and military guard.

Held to commemorate the 12th anniversary of the visit of Emperor Haile Selassie to Jamaica, and to raise funds for the Peace Movement, the concert took place in an atmosphere of devotion and optimism, an emotion given further dimension by the massive nationalist slogans surrounding the arena: "Build Jamaica With Discipline", "Unite Struggle Produce", etc.

Besides the politicians going through what was evidently a prearranged ritual, the audience was also witness to the sight of the top-ranking gunmen from the previously warring ghettos of West Kingston embracing each other and dancing together like excited football fans. These were two men like Bucky Marshall and Claude Massop, who a few months ago were facing each other down over gun barrels. Since last January, when suddenly "peace broke out", they have been working together in the Peace Movement, and these last few days had given press conferences at Marley's former home in Hope Road, Kingston, where the singer himself had been gunned down in December 1976.

This was the first time Marley had set foot in Jamaica since that incident. On the bill were some of the cream of Jamaica's musicians. First off, Lloyd Parks and We People provided the backing for a stunning salvo of talent as The Meditations, Dillinger, The Mighty Diamonds, Culture, Dennis Brown, Trinity, Leroy Smart and 10-year-old Junior Tucker all delivered excellent sets, with the zany Culture outstanding. Althea & Donna also came on to sing… guess what!

Around this time, the only disturbance of any real size took place, when a number of people decided to storm the McDonald tunnel entrance. An hour of violent skirmishes followed before the police and heavily armed soldiers sealed the entrance, but not before about 200 people had entered.

The next two acts – Jacob Miller & Inner Circle and Big Youth – provided completely different interpretations of the Rasta and reggae heritage. Miller was wildly energetic, lewd and comic with his populist anthems; youth, cool, elegant and devotional.

During Miller's set, Marley and Seaga arrived and, shortly after, Killer Miller donned a riot policeman's helmet and paraded along the stage smoking a spliff and singing "Peace Treaty Is Coming Home Hurrah" to the tune of "When Johnny Comes Marching Home".

It's unlikely that any of the political dignitaries present took exception to Miller's buffoonery, but many were evidently ill-at-ease during a Peter Tosh set that was strictly "no jesterin'".

The former Wailer, clad in a black judo suit and guerrilla beret, interspersed his set with lengthy oratorical denunciations of social injustice and paeans to black pride, and directed a harangue at Prime Minister Manley personally on the subject of Jamaica's ganja laws before playing "Legalize It", which he dedicated to "all those who have been humiliated for an ickle draw of jah herb".

Just to rub salt in establishment wounds, he smoked a spliff on stage while a dread blew clouds of ganja from a chalice stage front, defying arrest by the many assembled soldiers and policemen. The ferocity of Tosh's malevolent and obscenity-studded diatribes were more than matched by the set he played, with Tosh standards like "400 Years", "Burial" and "Stepping Razor" being given dazzling workouts by a band which boasted the finest rhythm section on the island in Sly Dunbar (drums) and Robbie Shakespeare (bass), who was this critic's choice as man of the match.

Recently signed to Rolling Stones Records in the US, Tosh was watched from the wings by Mick Jagger, who witnessed that the Stones have acquired a dangerously powerful foil for their upcoming American tour. The previous day, Jagger described the peace concert as "very important".

It was left to Ras Michael and the Sons Of Negus to consecrate the stage with a stately set of Rasta drums and chanting before Bob Marley & The Wailers belatedly took the stage for the finale. It was interesting that, of the three original Wailers, Tosh was adopting a vigorous rebel image, Marley was working alongside the establishment, and Bunny Wailer was conspicuous by his absence.

Clearly under some strain, Marley put in an energetic and almost desperate performance for the assembled media host. After opening with two Rastafarian hymns, he ran through a selection of "Natural Mystic", "Natty Dread", "Rastaman Vibration", "War", "Jamming" and "Trenchtown Rock" before the ritual of joining together the politicians.

In many ways, it was a moment of paradox and anticlimax, but besides attracting welcome funds for the Peace Movement – a movement which clearly matters enormously to ordinary Jamaicans – the concert proves that Jamaica's future is intimately bound up with the doctrine of Rastafari. **NME**

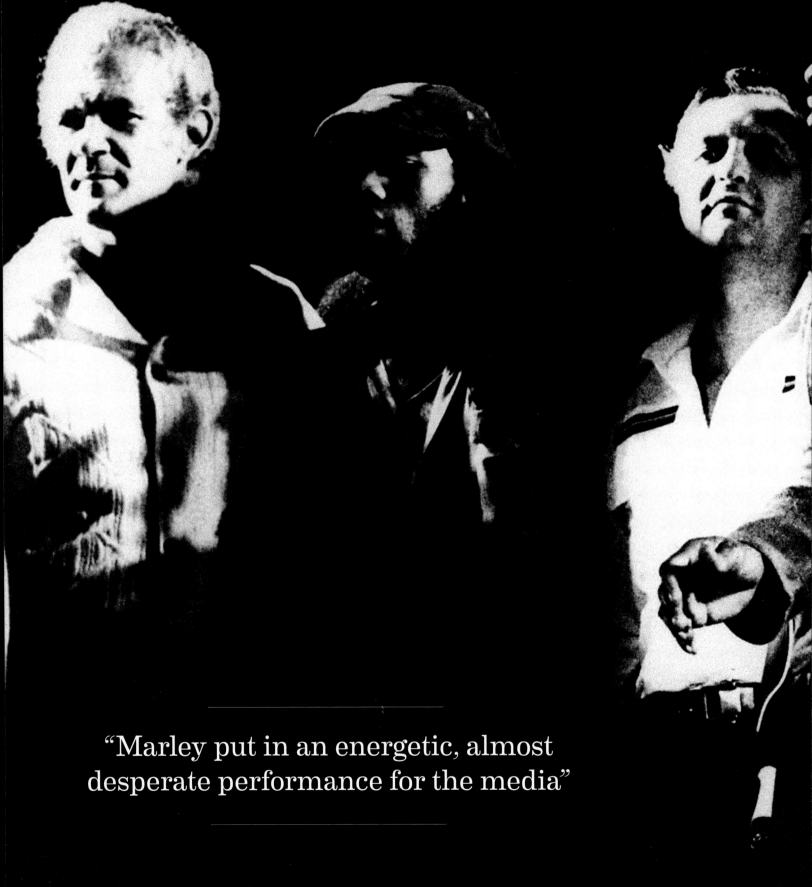

"Marley put in an energetic, almost
desperate performance for the media"

◄ April 22, 1978: Bob Marley and the Wailers at the One Love peace concert in Kingston, Jamaica, with Prime Minister Michael Manley (far left) and his political opponent Edward Seaga (third from left)

The 19-year-old Kate Bush pictured shortly after dramatically bursting on to the music scene in 1978

"I prefer to take a risk"

Introducing KATE BUSH, the most original voice of 1978. From mime and Lindsay Kemp, to her introduction by a family friend to the music business, the singer is following a unique path. "I'd like my music to intrude," the stealth new-wave fan says. "It's got to."

BY NOW, THE VOICE of Kate Bush will have made a full-frontal attack on the brains of the nation. Attack? Not an unreasonable word when you consider the strange, weird quality of Ms Bush's vocal, captured in all its resonant glory on her first single, "Wuthering Heights".

Whether attack is construed as compliment or insult is down to the individual, but after an initial reaction of shock – as one reacts to all things foreign – I've grown to like "Wuthering Heights" and am presently engaged in learning the finer delights of her competent, if occasionally erratic, first album, *The Kick Inside*.

But first – an introduction to the unknown name and face that is suddenly being hailed as a major new singer-songwriter in Britain. Kate Bush is 19, comes from Kent, is now resident in South-East London, has a pretty face with curves to match, and is more intelligent than the usual singers who have emanated from EMI in such dramatic fashion in the past. The girl has a mind of her own and is not averse to forcefully presenting an opinion (an asset in itself).

She comes from a "good" family. Her father is a GP and she had quite a comfortable childhood. The family itself was always musical, specialising in English and Irish traditional and playing around local folk clubs.

Kate, however, never performed outside the confines of home and was content to learn the basics, starting piano at the age of 11 and quickly finding that she could write her own songs. School was St Joseph's Grammar School, in Abbey Wood, but apart from her early period in the classroom, it held little fascination.

The explanation in hindsight: "I found it wasn't helping me. I became introvert. I guess it was the teachers' system, the way they react to pupils, and I wasn't quite responsive to that."

"When I write songs I really like to explore the mental area, the emotional values"

Nonetheless, Kate quit school at the age of 16 with 10 O-levels, specialising in English and Music and showing an unusual interest in Latin, although she found it an incredibly difficult language to master.

"The reason I left was that I felt I could do something more in tune with my purpose – music."

This she was able to do with the help of an inheritance from an aunt who died. Effectively the money gave her the security to become her own boss and follow her own mind. At one time, just before leaving school, there was an ambition to become either a psychiatrist or a social worker. Both careers made sense to her as an alternative to her first love.

"I guess it's the thinking bit, trying to communicate with people and help them out. The emotional aspect. It's so sad to see good, nice people emotionally dis-served, screwed up, when they could be so happy."

She couldn't have pursued the ambition because she was lousy at physics, chemistry and maths. She agreed that the careers she fancied, psychiatry, social work or music, were in direct contrast. Music is completely self-indulgent and the other is almost charitable.

"I know what you mean. The only reason in the first place that I did think of those things was that I in no way thought that my music could be a career because it's so difficult to make it. It's all a matter of timing and contacts and talent... and luck. I never thought I would have a chance to do that, so I deliberately tried to have a career-orientated ambition, something I could hold on to.

"The reason I chose those sort of things is that they are, in a way, the things I do with music. When I write songs I really like to explore the mental area, the emotional values. Although in a way you can say that being a psychiatrist is more purposeful than writing music, in many ways it isn't, because a lot of people take a great deal of comfort from music. I know I do. It makes you feel good.

"The really important thing about music is that all it is, is a vehicle for a message, whatever your message is. I'm probably a lot better at being a songwriter than I would be a psychiatrist, for instance. I might have people jumping out of windows now."

She thinks, then, that her music is a therapy?

"Oh yes, it's very much a therapeutic thing, not only for me. That's a really good word. It really is like a therapy. The message I would like people to receive is that if they hear it and accept it, that's fantastic.

"If they let it into their ears that is all I can ask for, and if they think about it afterwards or during it, that is even more fantastic. There are so many writers and so many messages, to be chosen out of all of them is something very special. The messages? Things that maybe could help people, like observing the situation where an emotional game is being played and maybe making people think about it again."

It's very glamorous to make a statement like that but how true did she think it was?

"It's easy to say everything. Really, all I do when I write songs is try and write something that affects me – something that I feel does have a solution or something that is unexplored. It really is just self-expression, and although I know that a lot of people will just say it's a load of rubbish, I would like to think that there is a message and maybe people will hear it."

On leaving school, Kate took up dancing, because she felt it was an art parallel to music, "another pure art form in as much as it's free". The show that inspired her was *Flowers*, a Lindsay Kemp performance at the Collegiate Theatre, London, three years ago. Kemp's mime attracted her and the next day a perusal through *Time Out* magazine uncovered an advertisement for classes by Kemp.

Kemp made an instant impression on Kate, displaying an ease in communication that she had never experienced before. He taught her the importance of disciplining the body before attempting to mime. The association with Kemp lasted only six months; he went off to perform professionally in Australia and she moved on to another class.

She reacts vehemently but positively to my comment that mime appeared to be an upper-class art.

"No, I wouldn't call it an upper-class thing at all. It's probably further away from the upper class than anything else, because they probably find it hard to be free as they are so caught up in all their status problems, and the same probably goes for working-class people in a lot of ways because they always feel this alienation from other people."

Because of her inheritance, Kate didn't have the trauma of desperately searching for a job on leaving school. However, she had decided her career would focus on music... long before.

"The money did enable me to think that I could do it, because I was obviously worried about leaving school and finding myself nowhere. I had strong feelings in not having little securities like a nice little job. I wanted to try and do what I wanted and if it went wrong, OK, but at least try to do it."

During this time, Kate had been staying at home writing songs and accompanying herself on either guitar or piano but not daring to let anyone outside the sphere of family hear her work. Then a friend of the family, Ricky Hopper, who had worked in the music business, heard her material, took an interest and started flogging tapes around the music biz, with little luck. The big break came when Hopper contacted an old friend of his from Cambridge, Pink Floyd's Dave Gilmour.

Gilmour came and heard and liked. Gilmour suggested recording proper demo tapes. He put up the money – "an amazing thing" – for the studio, found Kate a good arranger and the songs were recorded

A studio shot of Kate Bush taken by Beverley Goodway in 1978

properly. From there it grew. Gilmour introduced Kate to a friend, Andrew Powell, noted for his work with Alan Parsons, and he was to produce the album.

The voice? Ah yes, that voice. Kate is genuinely bewildered at the response her vocal has evoked. She refutes suggestions that she deliberately "cultivated" the voice. "Honest, I just opened my mouth and it came out."

And then came the album. "Wuthering Heights", by the way, emphasises her unique high-pitched vocal more than any other track. Usually, she comes across as a stranger concoction that resembles a Joni Mitchell-Noosha Fox mongrel, which is a fascination in itself. It's a very promising debut, and that it has spawned a hit single already is a surprise to Kate.

"I was so involved with all my artistic frustrations that I never thought of having a hit. I was thinking of all the things that I wanted to be there musically that weren't and vice versa.

"The battle is with yourself, because there's your expression going down there and there's no way you can change it. It's there forever. It is very frustrating to see something that you have been keeping transient for years just suddenly become solid. It's a little disconcerting... but exciting."

At this early stage in her career, Kate appears uncannily aware of the dangers of an early hit. She is determined that her work in music remains an art.

"You see people who are into the glamour and the ego of it and not the work, and really work's what it's all about. It's not anything to do with ego.

"Music is like being a bank clerk. It's still work, only a different channel of energy." **MM**

"I didn't kill her"

OCTOBER 12

Snapper Joe Stevens phones a report from Rikers Island, where Sid Vicious is held for murder.

RIKERS ISLAND is a heavily guarded remand centre and short-term jail situated in the Hudson River, not far from LaGuardia International Airport. The prison population consists of blacks and Puerto Ricans. The Island has a tough reputation, and is supposedly a drug-trafficking centre.

Accompanied by Sex Pistols manager Malcolm McLaren and Sid Vicious' mum Ann Beverley, I met Vicious in the prison hospital wing. When we told him that, according to both London evening papers on Friday, Sid had "confessed" to Ms Spungen's murder, he angrily denied the reports.

"When the fuck did I make a confession?" he retorted. "I was well out of it, mate!"

Over the course of our visit, Sid detailed his version of the events that took place in room 100 of the Chelsea Hotel between Wednesday evening and Thursday morning. His story is as follows:

He remembers waking up sometime during the night and seeing Nancy sitting up in bed fingering the knife they had bought earlier in the day, ostensibly to protect themselves from junkie scavengers who hung around the methadone clinic Sid frequented. Sid dozed off again before he could ask Nancy what she was doing.

His next recollection is of waking up a few hours later and seeing blood all over Nancy's side of the bed.

"There was blood everywhere. On the sheets, on the pillowcase, all over the mattress and the floor leading into the bathroom. My first thought was that she had been killed."

He stumbled into the bathroom and found Nancy – still breathing – slouched under the bathroom sink. After a futile attempt to revive her, Sid ran out into the lobby yelling for help.

He then ran into the room and called the hotel reception desk, saying, "Get an ambulance up here quick! I'm not kidding!"

Minutes later it wasn't an ambulance but the police who had arrived. When they saw the scene, they turned to the dazed ex-Pistol – who, it was later revealed, had at the time been taking Tuinal – and said, "Listen kid, why'd you do that?"

"Why did I do what?" replied Vicious.

"Why'd you kill the girl?"

"I didn't kill her."

"If you didn't kill her, why can't you look me straight in the face?"

"All right," retorted Vicious, "I'm looking at you straight in the face. I didn't kill her, mate."

The two cops laughed at Vicious' denial, then pushed him up against the wall face first and handcuffed him.

According to police, Nancy died of "a stab wound inflicted after midnight on Wednesday". They later recovered the weapon, a large folding knife with a black wooden handle, and are said to be investigating reports that an unidentified young man had been with the couple until 4am that morning.

Vicious was meanwhile taken to Rikers Island. The following day he appeared in court, where he seemed understandably distressed and not a little disconnected. He was charged with second-degree murder under his real name, John Simon Ritchie, and bail was set at £25,000 – much to the dismay of New York's finest, who had expected bail to be denied.

By this time Malcolm McLaren had arrived in New York – Vicious is still contracted to him – telling the British press before he left that "one of the reasons I want Sid out is to record a new album in New York. With a bit of luck, the money from the record might pay for the trial."

McLaren engaged the respected New York law firm of Pryor, Cashman, Sherman & Flynn to represent Vicious. Estimates of the legal fees likely to be involved are in the region of $100,000.

McLaren also engaged some private investigators to follow up, among other leads, a theory that the death had some connection with the activities of a Puerto Rican gang that has recently take over drug operations on the Lower East Side, who sometimes congregate in a bar near the Chelsea Hotel.

Soon after his court appearance, Vicious was moved to the hospital wing of Rikers Island, where he is undergoing heroin detoxification. On Sunday, Sid's mother Mrs Ann Beverley arrived in New York armed with a sleeping bag and obviously ready for a long siege. We went to see Sid in hospital.

When Mrs Beverley – a very cool-headed lady who spent time on the hippie trails when Sid was 10 years old – started getting a bit soft with her boy, Sid said, "Listen, I'm not a mama's boy. I'll fight my own battles."

Sid seemed to be unaware of the pressures building up around him, of the fact that the US courts will probably be only too happy to make an example of him to any aspiring punk desperadoes. And, of course, Nancy's death is taking its emotional toll.

That same day, Nancy's body was buried in her parents' home city of Philadelphia. On Monday, Virgin Records telegraphed the bail money to McLaren in New York, and Sid was released on Tuesday morning.

If, when the case is heard, Vicious is convicted, the absolute minimum time he will spend in prison, with parole, is seven years. The maximum is 25. *NME*

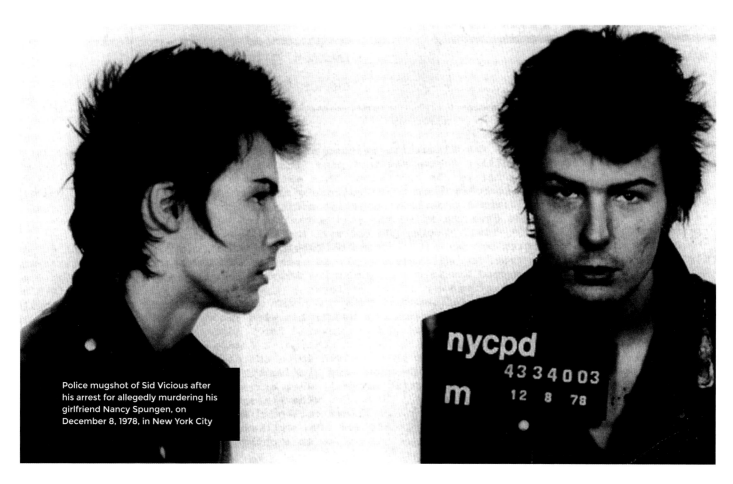

Police mugshot of Sid Vicious after his arrest for allegedly murdering his girlfriend Nancy Spungen, on December 8, 1978, in New York City

nycpd
m 4334003
12 8 78

Sid Vicious and Nancy Spungen relaxing alongside Glen Matlock and Rat Scabies in London, 1978

"Careful – The Place Will Burn Down!"

JUNE 20 · EARLS COURT, LONDON

Bob Dylan plays five nights in London. "Finding these players gave me a chance to develop all the old stuff," he says.

"I'M GLAD THESE songs mean as much to you as they mean to me." Bob Dylan said that.

He said it to his adoring audience on the final night of his six-concert stretch at Earls Court, London – just after he had sung "It's All Right Ma, I'm Only Bleeding". He got a heroic reception, and he thanked us. Warmly.

The Dylan of old used to treat his songs and his audience with virtual disdain. Ten years ago, to have imagined him admitting any real care for them would have been unthinkable. That comment spoke volumes for the man's maturity.

The same new quality was evident later. An hour or so after that final show, Dylan was talking to my colleague Max Jones and me and one of his remarks ran roughly like this: "Doing these concerts here has made me realise about British audiences. They're really something different – they actually come for the words and for the songs. That's what's missing back home. There, they tend to come for…"

The event?

"Yeah, not so much the music, more the sideshow."

For committed Dylan diehards like me, it was all a little hard to swallow; at all his concerts he had been diplomatically thanking his audience. Tonight, he had confessed that the songs meant a lot to him. Now he was getting close to talking about wonderful British audiences. My mind floated back to an *MM* interview with David Bowie recently in which David had said he had been disillusioned by Bob's quote to him: "Wait till you hear my new album." Bowie said, in effect, that he could scarcely take that kind of Las Vegas cliché from Dylan, of all people.

All this was a far cry from the monosyllabic Dylan of yore. Ten or more years ago, a "yes" or more likely "no" would have been regarded as a major political speech. Now, he was looser, talking to the *MM* about anything, from his current musical inclinations, reminding us and himself about his roots and registering unmistakably sincere delight at what had happened to him in Britain.

Max Jones, a cohort of Bob's since long before the musician exploded on to the world stage, commented on the extent of the band's involvement in Dylan's stage act today, and Bob expounded immediately with great enthusiasm.

He had taken ages, he said, to find the right musicians, but was now elated at what they'd done for him and for the old material. "They're all the same songs," he said, in what seemed to me a direct quote from his Albert Hall speech in 1966.

"The songs will go on for ever. People like them done over and over, and me, too. But finding these players gave me a chance to develop all the old stuff. I enjoy them this way and people seem to, as well."

If we wanted them sung as on the record, he added, go and listen to the albums. He managed that famous half-smile.

We talked of the soul and blues inflections in certain passages of his act, notably in "Going, Going, Gone", which closed the first half, and "I Shall Be Released", which carried a definite gospel flavour and even theatrical hand gestures by Bob.

"What I like about the band is that I can get everything I want from them – blues, soul, country, Cajun, American mountain music – everything. This is not just a rock band. Soul has always been in me and I've been listening to Red Prysock, the greatest horn player I've ever heard. And then years ago I used to go to the Apollo [in Harlem] and listen to Bobby "Blue" Bland – I went there night after night.

"Lonnie Johnson and Muddy – these people are the guys I've come up with, so the soul element is a natural."

Mention of the girl back-up trio of Helena Springs, Jo Ann Harris and Carolyn Dennis – introduced jokingly onstage by Dylan as variously "my cousin, my fiancée, my ex-girlfriend" – seemed to stick a very slight glint in Dylan's eye as he stood talking to us just outside the backstage canteen.

We commented on their visual appeal, as well as vocal quality, and Dylan said that he was getting round to thinking that that aspect of the show was a "bit Las Vegas".

"But there's nothing wrong with a bit of sex in the show, is there?" asked the painfully honest Max Jones.

"I turned round in Japan and saw a pair of breasts on stage. I thought then that something's gotta be done about this," replied Dylan, enigmatically.

Getting back to the music, he said that on some nights – but not on this final one – he had included "To Ramona", and this was another example of how thrilled he was with the soulful violin-playing of David Mansfield. "I think he's the best guy around on that instrument, but they're all special to me."

He said it had taken him a year to put the band together, and many of his arrangements had been conceived and executed by Steven Soles, the tasteful guitarist/vocalist who also fronts the critically acclaimed Alpha Band.

Throughout the week, Dylanologists had been collecting anecdotes and comparing shows. On his final night, he had been more communicative than ever. His "thank you's" had been voluminous. At the end of Mansfield's mind-blowing solo, which ended "All Along The Watchtower", Dylan crept up to the mic amid fantastic applause,

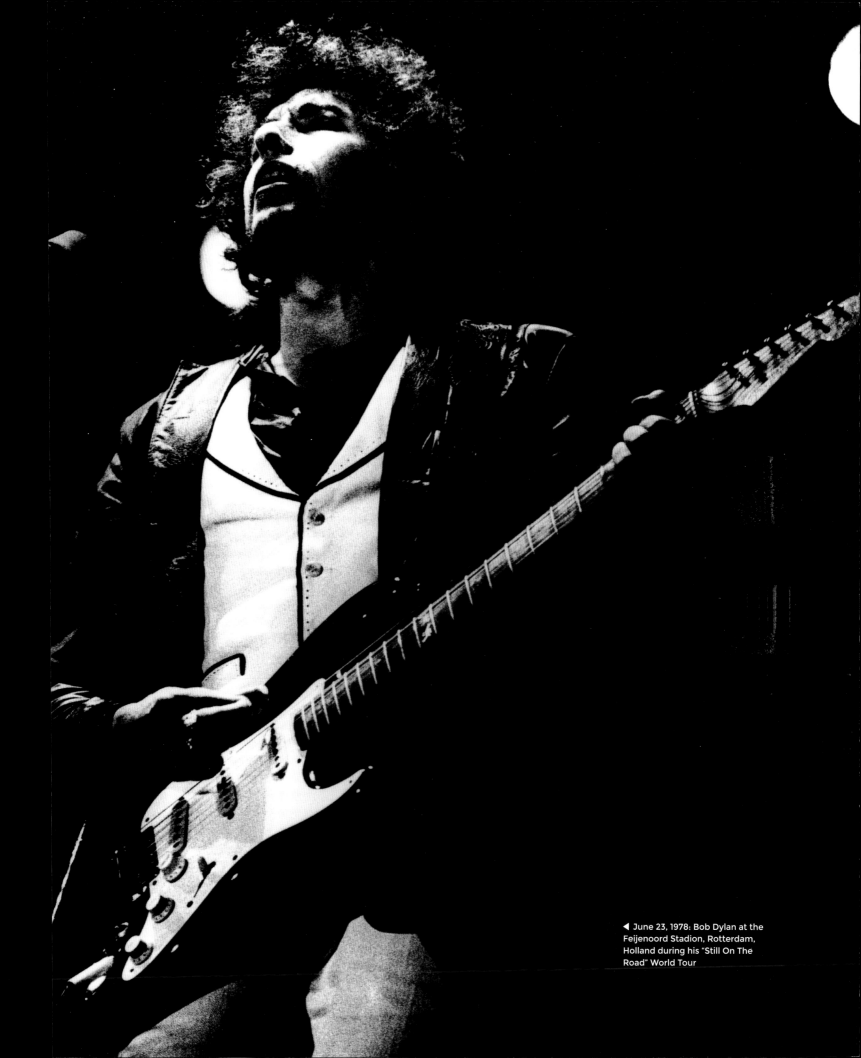

◄ June 23, 1978: Bob Dylan at the Feijenoord Stadion, Rotterdam, Holland during his "Still On The Road" World Tour

"Lonnie Johnson and Muddy are the guys I came up with, so the soul element is natural"

and said drily, "I taught him that solo." Before that performance, Dylan said: "This song is dedicated to the late Jimi Hendrix."

Introducing the heavily orchestrated version of "Ballad Of A Thin Man" – which gave him the cue for more animated gestures than ever, acting out the role of interviewer and musician as in the storyline – Dylan said, "I wrote this song 15 years before the ballad of 'Short People' [an aside alluding to Randy Newman's recent hit]." We were left to make what we wished of the remark.

Sparklers, candles stuck into drink cans and cigarette lighters had combined to set Earls Court alight long before the end of the show was in sight on Tuesday, and Dylan was moved to say, "Careful with those lights – the place will burn down."

Musically, this final night was special for many reasons different from those which made every concert remarkable. Different lines of his songs came over with fresh force.

"Tangled Up In Blue", read so majestically under a solo spotlight on nights one and four, was not so dramatic or meaningful on the final show, because Bob's innovative ideas with bonding the notes weren't so hot (but it's worth mentioning here that Dylan below his best is still incomparably superior to his nearest competitor).

Songs that clinched the final night were "Just Like A Woman", handled with every ounce of persuasiveness and delivered with surprising gusto by Bob and the band. Never, if ever, has the song been so brilliantly blown apart and knitted together to make a beautiful, meaningful tapestry of words: "She makes love just like a woman… and she breaks just like a little girl", never sounded more potent than in the hands of their author.

There are those who prefer his original, simpler versions. But like Dylan says, a good song should be able to stand redefining, or else it's dead. And his harmonica solo was a riveting joy, bringing the ecstatic crowd to its feet with a mighty roar. "It's All Right Ma, I'm Only Bleeding" was another standout. Again, he shook the old version from the *Bringing It All Back Home* album to the foundations and spat out the song in one hell of a hurry.

It gained urgency from the treatment, and the band rocked away handsomely behind the garrulous storyline, but there was no mistaking his own enjoyment of this recycle, and there was no mistaking the crowd's response to the line that became curiously finger-pointing to himself: "I got nothing, Ma, to live up to…" Untrue, of course, but he was doing it with aplomb.

"Shelter From The Storm" was excellent, too – but on this, my third attendance of Dylan at Earls Court, I was struck by the power of one particular song from his new album, *Street-Legal*. This was "Señor (Tales Of Yankee Power)". Brooding and sinister, the lyrics are, on close inspection, as desperately evocative of a mood as anything he's written – "Can you tell me where we're heading… Is it Lincoln Country Road or Armageddon?" – and we are left to surmise the target at which he points his finger yet again. At a directionless America, presumably.

It's a haunting, bluesy song, the microphone touching the right spots to wailing effect, and Dylan's voice reminding us of much of his

early work. "This place don't make sense to me no more… Can you tell me what we're waiting for, señor?"

Splendidly meaty stuff, as is his assumed song of his recent broken marriage, "Baby Stop Crying".

Musically, then, there were highlights aplenty, and each observer will carry his or her own highlights of Dylan's concerts in the memory for a good few months.

Offstage, and backstage, it seemed a fairly orderly week, with Dylan's much-touted interest in British reggae arousing excitement among the national press.

The singer did no formal interviews; hardly surprising in view of the fact that when he emerged early in the week from the Royal Garden Hotel, Kensington, a national foot-in-the-mouth type yelled, "You're doing it for the money, aren't you, Bob?"

That incredible piece of insensitivity reduced everyone's interview chances from nil to nil-plus. And anyway, oddly enough, most artists do perform for money. Dylan, unlike some, actually earned his.

So Dylan came and conquered, and enjoyed [reggae band] Merger at Dingwalls, propped up by bodyguards, and talked informally to Max Jones and me. Dylan went for dinner with Robert Shelton, the American writer who first noted his appearance at Gerde's Folk City in New York, in 1961, and then gave Dylan the first ever review – in the *New York Times*. (Shelton is still at work on the definitive biography, and plans to complete it after *Blackbushe*.)

Dylan also phoned Shusha, the discerning Persian folk singer who has recorded some of his songs and who closes her act with "Forever Young", just like Dylan. He told her how much he liked her work, and that she should perform in America.

Shusha, who saw his final concert and was naturally impressed, found Dylan in articulate mood and seemed to have struck up an intelligent friendship with an artist she has studied for a long time.

The only moment in which Dylan made a mistake with an audience was when he said, "Goodnight – see you tomorrow," not realising that most of the people at Earls Court would not in fact be returning the next night.

But if, as I suspect, that was his only error of communication during a stupendous performance, then the world's most important rock artist clinched it impeccably.

Here were no ordinary occasions. A seer of the '60s, his reputation blurred for some by the mere passing of time, had come to test our patience. And he emerged not just unscathed, but with a greater reputation. Because he risked everything by recycling the songs. And he'd proved they still stand up.

When Dylan said, then, after the final show, to the *MM* that he was genuinely energised by the British reaction, it was patently sincere and no Hollywood jive.

In America, remember, Bob Dylan's records are rarely played on the radio and he does not have the same legendary status as here; it appears that we take musical poets more seriously. A mind-blowing week it had been. *MM*

◀ Bob Dylan performs on stage in the Feijenoord district of Rotterdam, at the football stadium usually known by its local nickname "De Kuip", June 23, 1978

"We feel things more than anyone else"

After the success of "Hong Kong Garden", SIOUXSIE AND THE BANSHEES offer the lowdown on their debut LP... It's not an easy ride. "The best thing would be if couples sat down by the fireside and listened to it."

THE TITLE OF *The Scream* relates to the cover artwork, and to the music inside.

Steve: "We wanted something that would sum up the first album, so we went right back to the name of the band and that's where we got *The Scream* first of all."

Siouxsie: "The words 'The Scream' can apply to every song on the album in different ways. People have different ways of screaming out for help. It just sums it up."

John: "*The Scream* was a lot of suffocated passion coming out."

And that is exactly what the front sleeve portrays. Two bodies are submerged under water, locked in that nightmarish split second of blind panic when drowning suddenly becomes a real possibility.

▶ A slightly confusing picture of Siouxsie and the Banshees, taken in 1978

▲ Siouxsie Sioux performing on stage at the Rainbow Theatre in London, 1978

Siouxsie: "There was a film called *The Swimmer* with Burt Lancaster and there's a bit where the camera's partially submerged and he's swimming through that crowded pool right at the end..."

John: "You know the panic when you swim through a crowded pool, you haven't got room to move, you can't swim properly, so you keep stopping and getting to the bottom..."

Siouxsie: "And the screams of kids having fun in the pool is really ear-piercing. Lancaster was swimming all through that, so I thought it'd be great to get that claustrophobic feel for the photo without the sound..."

Kenny: "Just taking that little moment. It usually only lasts for a few seconds and is almost like you whole life pattern in front of you."

Being an unrepentant hunter of these kind of offshoots. I wondered if a painting by Edvard Munch, also called *The Scream*, had had any bearing in the matter.

John: "I think it was to do with that picture vaguely."

Siouxsie: "No, we found out later that there was a picture called *The Scream*."

John: "No, we knew already."

Siouxsie: "Well, I didn't. And we saw it but we thought it was too obvious, too one-dimensional to just have the face screaming."

This dovetailing idea also comes through strongly in the way the songs slide in and out of one another. While each one is decidedly separate, there is an amazing continuity between them all. Listen, for example, to the climactic finish of "Jigsaw Feeling", when Kenny's acrid drums suddenly finish and a distant guitar sequence gradually introduces "Overground".

Steven picked up the point: "We stuck 'Switch' at the end because it's the most recent song and it's like a pointer for where maybe the music is going."

"Switch" is certainly the most adventurous cut in terms of structure, but John slightly modified the position: "We're suggesting that we're capable of that but not that they're all going to be as complicated as that from now on."

Siouxsie came in: "I can't see that every song we do is necessarily a progression – they're all very different and should be taken on their own... The main link between the songs is that they are different but they're all linked in that they are extremely powerful – whether they're slightly laid back on purpose to show controlled power or just let loose to show we can... just feel things more than anyone else can.

"There's not one song on the album that we think, 'Oh dear, we put that on to fill in a gap.' They're all powerful and... great. I don't mean that in an egotistic, maniac way..."

The band didn't seem to have much difficulty choosing which songs to include and in what order.

Steven: "There was only one song left off that before we went into record it we thought might be on it. That was 'Make Up To Break Up.'"

Much of their original repertoire, including stage faves like "Captain Scarlet" and "Love In A Void", was excluded, though "Carcass" and "Helter Skelter" remain in newly aligned and ferocious form.

Kenny: "There was three-quarters of an album's worth of songs left over that were so old. We chucked all the dead wood out."

Does that mean that those early numbers are forever outlawed?

Siouxsie: "They're dormant at the moment. The only time we'd ever redo them or something was when we felt something for them.

John: "When the Buzzcocks came out with 'Spiral Scratch', if we had come out with something like that at the time, then you wouldn't have expected those songs to be on this album, but because we haven't, they still expect to see all the old songs on it." Message understood.

The album was recorded in a week, but mixing took seven. The band and Steve Lillywhite (with sporadic assistance from Nils) produced. Why Lillywhite, whose name adorns innumerable Island albums?

Steven: "We were desperate. We got an American guy that Polydor had recommended to do the first session with 'Hong Kong Garden' and 'Voices' and he did 'Hong Kong' really badly. So we had to re-record it, and re-record it very quickly. Nils went down to the Johnny Thunders sessions and heard Steve producing and liked that."

Siouxsie: "We were so desperate and we were adamant about not having someone who would try and run the show. A lot of producers are very able but they always leave their mark stamped all over everything. We just wanted to be confident that they could get the basic sounds on everything at least."

So the real testing time came at the mixing stage?

"We had to re-record 'Hong Kong Garden', and very quickly"

Siouxsie: "A lot of that [seven weeks] is down to communicating with someone who doesn't really think on your level."

John: "Steve obviously doesn't think like we do and it took him time to start settling in to some sort of pattern. He didn't even do it in the end – obviously there's a lot of give and take. You just cannot get somebody into the band, in seven weeks, however graphically you might try and describe a thing."

The sound that emerged is strong, abrasive, visceral and constantly inventive, with a thrust that makes the spaces equal partners to the notes. Possible blood relatives to the Banshees in this respect (and maybe in textures as well) are The Velvet Underground, Wire, Can and Pere Ubu. The combination was blueprinted?

John: "It's got to be. It's got to come from a passion. The words have to as well. But music is just that much more raw. Speech is a lot more developed than notes. You can't say as much with a note as you can with words."

I'd have thought the exact opposite.

"If you isolate a note and you isolate a word... I think it should be much more equal, and I think it's much more equal in this band than it is in any other I can think of. But, for most people, music is something to catch people with, and the words are lost, the icing on the cake. And the music isn't something that has to be thought about because it's all 12-bar stuff that any fool can play. It's so simple, some of the stuff that most bands play. The chart stuff – a lot of it is just practice makes perfect, which is something that can never been said about this band."

With the exclusion of some sax snorts on "Suburban Relapse" and "Switch", nothing was imported to boost their regular lineup. They'd never felt any desire to do that, especially on a debut.

Siouxsie: "We'd only use something else if it added; not just for the sake of saying we had an organ on such a thing."

Steve: "Most bands usually do that when they're playing bigger places and they feel they have to have another person or couple of people to make it seem like a really good show. Even Bowie does it. He has violins and things which are totally superfluous to his music."

John played the sax segments.

"I don't play exactly. I play sax the same way I play guitar, in fact a bit better because I haven't got as many inhibitions on a sax. I had two lessons to teach me how to blow it and where to put my fingers roughly and that was it. It's the same attitude to that as the guitar, but with all the guitarists around you can't help but pick up things. With sax it was easier in some ways, but then it's a very difficult instrument to do different things on. You can't make it sound different – it either squeaks or plays a right note. And I decided I never wanted to squeak."

To return to the mix, I suggested a similarity with something that Eno had written two years ago. Eno argued that rock was first of all structured like a hierarchy of events. There was the bassline which varied little and on top of that the rhythm instruments which were marginally more flexible although they still had to carry the chords. Then you have the lead guitar and vocals, which carry the biggest opportunity for change.

People like Bo Diddley, The Who and The Velvet Underground, however, threw spanners into this ranking system and experimented with ideas like using all the instruments in the rhythm role. This sparked off some healthy disorientation. Eno's point was that he wanted to constantly shuffle the two approaches and thereby create a "perceptual drift". The result is that you're not sure what you're supposed to be listening to, and all the instruments seem to travel in parallel lines that actually meet or intertwine or bounce off one another.

Anyway, if bass and drums are already laying down a rhythm, why should the drums follow slavishly behind? They can develop in another direction. Equally the voice can be as much an instrument and a vehicle for words. It seems to me that this is precisely the Banshee method. They agreed.

The Banshees began with less than minimal musical knowledge and, through a ferocious determination have carved out a sound and vision that is entirely their own. The secret is actually utterly simple. Steven unintentionally gave it away: "You don't think about old forms. You pretend that you're the first person ever to put pen to paper and ever to play guitar."

Siouxsie expanded: "We're trying to get rid of more and more of the taboos musically; it was such a natural release and progression."

Steven again: "And that can be dangerous, because people start suspecting you of being self-consciously avant-garde."

Siouxsie: "We're very aware of that, which is probably why we hardly like anyone. There's a lot of new bands that appear to be quite progressive and there's a lot that aren't. Yet they're all in the same vein in a way because it's all fake. They live the life of being an artist. Those big stereotypes."

John agreed. "There's NO intrinsic taboos. I'm thinking about trying slide guitar. Slide is like, OK, 'orrible country & western stuff, but if you say I'm not gonna use this or that, you're obviously limiting yourself terribly. Just use everything and anything you can, in the right way."

Kenny: "The best thing for this album would be if couples sat down by the fireside and listened to it. It's those sorts of people who need to listen to it." *MM*

Siouxsie and the Banshees. From left Siouxsie Sioux, Kenny Morris, John McKay and Steven Severin

▶ Debbie Harry at the Record Plant studio in New York, during the recording of Blondie's *Parallel Lines* in the summer of 1978

Blondie *Parallel Lines*

SEPTEMBER 23

BLONDIE'S THIRD ALBUM seems designed to cater for two distinct requirements: a) to satisfy the near-hysterical cries for the pure pop of the band's debut album; and b) to consolidate their popularity with the hard-rock audience that helped chart the second set, *Plastic Letters*.

Presumably, that is the significance behind this album's title. *Parallel Lines* emerges as an interesting endeavour by Blondie to keep two yelping hounds at bay without sacrificing any artistic integrity and even hinting on one track ("Fade Away And Radiate") that their musical future lies far from the commerciality of the first two albums.

Having subjected the album to intense scrutiny (ie, I've had a tape for a couple of weeks and played it nightly), I'm of the opinion that the compromise between the first and second album is a healthy one and should ideally serve to confirm Blondie's importance in the present and future.

Mike Chapman (you must know Chinnichap) has been called in to handle the production (Richard Gottehrer directed the first two albums), which is a commendable and ambitious attempt by the band to crystallise their pop attitudes. But I have to say that Blondie are no Sweet, Smokie or Mud, and are really not suited to the discipline Chapman obviously wields in the studio.

For starters, I'm not too enamoured of his handling of Deborah Harry's vocal. He forces a strict delivery that is uncharacteristic of her usual casual, street-corner drawl.

On the other hand, there are choruses on the album ("Hanging On The Telephone" and "Pretty Baby" especially) where voices have been tightened to capture that magical Ronettes-like poppiness. To his credit, though, Chapman has pushed Blondie's lucrative pop sensibilities to the fore, exaggerating hooks (which perhaps explains why Debbie Harry's vocal is mixed so high) and making what were very commercial songs even more magnetic.

This works best on "Hanging On The Telephone", the brilliant "Pretty Baby" (a Number One smasheroo if I ever heard one), "11:59", "Sunday Girl" and "I'm Gonna Love You Too", all of which are of a pop excellence that qualifies them for singles and would be more appropriate as a 45 than the dull (in comparison) "Picture This". Another obvious single is

the disco-flavoured "Heart Of Glass", which has, naturally, bass and keyboards prominent against Debbie's beautifully seductive vocal.

Generally, there is a consistency in the band's writing that, in retrospect, may have been previously missing. With the rock songs, the pushy "One Way Or Another", the nonchalant but deviously potent "I Know But I Don't Know" (with Infante duetting with Harry on vocals), "Will Anything Happen", a panic-stricken rocker, and "Just Go Away", with Debbie at her bitchiest ("If you talk much louder, you could get an award from the Federal Communications Board"), Blondie further exploit their growing interest in hard, melodic rock.

That leaves one track, "Fade Away And Radiate", the most testing composition Blondie have yet recorded. Not only does it challenge their own capabilities, but the song is a radical departure from what the band's fans (who get what they want here otherwise) expect. It features Robert Fripp on guitar.

My immediate reaction was to recoil in surprise at the shock shift, but I've since found that the track has a haunting, hypnotic appeal and, with each subsequent listen, I've appreciated it more.

This album will consolidate Blondie's UK popularity. The next, I suspect, will test their audience's loyalty. **MM**

► Debbie eye-to-eye with a snake backstage, before a 1978 Blondie concert in Philadelphia

Short, Sharp Bursts Of Power

FEBRUARY 20 · HAMMERSMITH ODEON, LONDON

Rush triumphant.

RUSH'S ALBUMS BETRAY a band with a sight more erudition than could reasonably be expected from a heavy-metal trio, particularly of the Canadian School, whose pupils' intellect has in the past appeared restricted to counting up to three for the chords. Rush titled their live album *All The World's A Stage*, and quote liberally from Kubla Khan in "Xanadu" on their latest, *A Farewell To Kings*.

The audience at London's Hammersmith Odeon on Sunday night didn't, however, look the sort who would appreciate the finer points of the Swan Of Avon or Samuel Taylor Coleridge. Scattered around the stairs on beer-soaked carpets like bundles of denim rags waiting for the wash, they poured into the auditorium at lights-out with all the grace of stampeding buffalo.

At the sound of the first chord being struck, they turned into a pack of baying hounds, streaming down to the front on espying their quarry, and there proceeded to twitch, strum imaginary guitars, shake clenched fists, flash peace signs, and generally display all the symptoms of a crowd of headbangers reaching nirvana.

Rush, to their credit, refused to be drawn. Their music, naturally, contains all the elements necessary to smelt heavy metal, but they vary the alloy by mixing in more uncommon ingredients. Alex Lifeson gets to strum an acoustic guitar occasionally, Neil Peart selects tubular bells and triangles from his magnificent array of percussive devices, and Geddy Lee coaxes suitably mystic sounds from a synthesizer.

Their songs, too, veer from short, sharp burst of power, like "Lakeside Park" and "Closer To The Heart" to multi-section pieces like "Xanadu" (which, unfortunately, chopped and changed a little too much for comfort) and "2112". In a word, they have flair. There is confident, thoughtful playing from Lifeson; there are Lee's eerie, high-pitched vocals (he runs Pavlov's Dog's David Surkamp close); and Peart's solid underpinning, undemonstrative but crucial in a band without a full-time bassist (a shame he had to spoil it with a gratuitous drum solo at the end – but that's showbiz).

Their stage show, too, avoids the usual excesses of the genre: intelligent use of lighting rather than the customary three-ring circus, though they did show a proclivity for setting off thunder-flashes at dramatic moments. Still, I'm sure Shakespeare would have bunged a few into *As You Like It* if they'd been available. They'd have loved that down at the Globe. *MM*

"Too much of everything"

SEPTEMBER 7

RIP, Keith Moon, found dead in his Mayfair flat.

AFTER THE DEATH of Keith Moon on September 7, The Who confirmed this week that they plan to go ahead with their various projects – including the idea of a handful of selected live shows at the end of the year.

They have not decided how they will replace Moon in concert, nor have definite dates been set, but the band have not ruled out the possibility of the shows using a drummer who is close to the group, or session players.

"I think the only thing I can say definitely is that there will not suddenly be an announcement like, 'The Who name their new drummer,'" said the band's press officer, Keith Altham.

"If they decide to go ahead with the concerts, they will have to work out the percussion side, and it is inconceivable at the moment that they would want to enlist a new member. I would think it would be session people, or perhaps someone closely connected with the band."

In the meantime, work goes ahead on the various Who projects. The finishing touches are being put to the soundtrack of the movie *The Kids Are Alright*, which traces the Who story and is due for release at the end of the year, and casting has just started for *Quadrophenia*, the film of the album to be directed by Franc Roddam with Pete Townshend as musical supervisor. Townshend may provide music for the film with Roger Daltrey and John Entwistle.

The next plan is the filming of *Lifehouse*, scripted some years ago by Townshend and the inspiration for much of the music on *Who's Next*. Filming is due to start next year.

The inquest on Moon, who was found dead at his Mayfair flat, opened this Monday at Westminster Coroners' Court, and was adjourned for a week. It is understood that the tablets found by his bedside were Heminevrin, prescribed as sedatives and also used in connection with withdrawing from alcoholism and combatting epilepsy.

"Keith used them to help sleep, and it looks as if he took too many of them – he always took too much of everything," said Altham. **MM**

▶ "Moon the Loon" as Keith Moon was dubbed, photographed in London after he had moved back to the UK from Los Angeles in 1978

Chrissie Hynde // The Clash // David Bowie
The Jam // Joy Division // Lou Reed // Lowell George
Pink Floyd // Pretenders // Sid Vicious
The Specials // The Who

1979

Despite huge crowds still turning up at open-air festivals for early-70s rockers like Led Zeppelin, there's a club-based mod revival afoot, led by The Jam – on their first US tour – and Coventry ska maestros The Specials, launching their own 2 Tone label with a new band from London, Madness.

Post-new-wave Manchester outfit Joy Division treat the world to some *Unknown Pleasures*, Chrissie Hynde fronts the Pretenders with a feisty confidence, Lou Reed and David Bowie come to blows, while the original punk scene is dealt a death blow – literally – with the passing, in horrific circumstances, of the genre's *enfant terrible*, Sid Vicious.

"It's actually happening"

Introducing THE SPECIALS, a band whose mixed-race lineup is not a policy – just a way of life.

ROCK FOLLIES, SERIES 3. Scene: a London pub. The band is on stage, pumping out fast body rhythms, rock energy fuelling an urgent, irresistible package of ska roots, bluebeat blood and modern fire that hits the audience in the hips. Delirium on the dancefloor.

Back from the dancers, a phalanx of record-company talent scouts and executive bigwigs stand shoulder-to-shoulder, absorbing the music and assessing its effect on the audience, trying to imagine them in a studio, possibly seeing the first album cover, calculating sales chances and breakthrough potential. To their right, more people press forward to see the band over the heads of the furiously skanking dancers. Among the observers is Mick Jagger, in town trying to organise his divorce on his home territory. His face shows a relaxed but definite interest in the group on stage.

The band finish their last encore, the record-biz folk gather in huddles, knowing the battle is hotting up and the auction is on as various meetings with the group are arranged. One company is recognised as the leading contender, but the others express quiet confidence in the size of their chequebooks. Fade.

Back to reality and the scene is still the same – only it's not part of a scriptwriter's fantasy. The pub was London's Greyhound in Fulham, the date was Tuesday last week and the band was The Specials, also known as The Special AKA.

"I find it all a little incredible – it's just like *Rock Follies*. In fact, I'd like to see that series again, because this time round it won't seem so incredible. It's actually happening to us."

The speaker is Sir Horace Gentleman, a van driver by day and bass player with The Specials by choice.

"I'm still incredulous about it – it's amazing that it's happening to us," he continued.

▶ The Specials photographed on the roof of the Odeon cinema, Coventry in 1979; left to right, Lynval Golding, John Bradbury, Terry Hall, Jerry Dammers, Neville Staple, Roddy Radiation and Horace Panter

"The Rolling Stones used black music to start off, and they seem to have got on OK"

While its certainly the dream of most aspiring bands to be pursued by the heavyweights of the rock biz, including personal attendances by the likes of Jagger, Horace and The Specials are reacting with a caution that borders on reserve.

The hunters are headed by Chrysalis, and strong runners include Warner Bros., Island, CBS and Virgin, with Arista and A&M still in the field. Temptation for any band, but The Specials know what they want out of a record deal, and they aren't going to compromise for less. A distribution deal for their 2 Tone label is the plan, with the freedom to record as they want and sign other groups of their choice.

The Specials' emergence as one of the leading lights in the resurgence of ska as a popular live music shows them standing at the crossroads of a fascinating mix of musical and social forms. The seven-man Coventry band was formed out of the musical fire of punk and heavy reggae – the tension between the two is still evident in the striking power of the band on stage – and the last couple of months have seen the growing of a devoted column of London skinheads who crowd the front of every Specials show and throw up

◀ Neville Staple (left) clowning with fellow Special Jerry Dammers, 1979

a barrage of "rude boy" chants. The two-tone ethnic lineup of the band also gives a vivid but natural example of racial unity, a theme extended in a song like "Doesn't Make It Alright" – "He may be black, I may be white/But that doesn't mean we have to fight".

Questions to the band about the racial mix surprise them – they live it, don't analyse it – and the frontline of Terry Hall (cropped hair and street-kid vocal power) and Neville Staple (dancing force) consolidates any doubts about the intensity of the band's existence.

The Specials were formed in mid-1977, when keyboard-player and chief songwriter Jerry "General Dankey" Dammers, rhythm guitarist Lynval Golding and Horace teamed up after acquaintance at college, followed by the arrival in early 1978 of guitarist Roddy Radiation, from a punk outfit called Roddy Radiation & The Wild Boys; Terry Hall from Squad, a second-generation new-wave band; and Neville. Drummer John "Brad" Bradbury joined just after Christmas, initially just to play on the sessions for their debut single.

Much mouth work got the band the support spot on last summer's Clash tour and a meeting with Bernie Rhodes, then Clash manager. He impressed the band with his ability to converse, but a potential management agreement was never concluded. "The Clash, Bernie's number-one sons, were in the process of breaking away from him and he sent us to Paris for a club residency. It was dreadful, the whole thing, like a Peter Sellers disaster movie," Horace explained.

Since then the band have been managing their own affairs, with financial help from a Coventry businessman after Christmas to finance the single. Now publicist Rick Rogers is helping with management and the group is looking at its future every night.

"We started playing punk rock and heavy reggae because they were the elements in the band at the time, but it didn't work," said Horace.

"Both sides have compromised, and the logical step is into ska and bluebeat. Ska has that offbeat that the mods used to dance to, then it got slowed down and became rock-steady, and then reggae. Ska started in New Orleans, broadcast from the radio stations that were picked up in Jamaica.

"It seemed fitting that New Orleans is also where R&B started, and that gave rise to the British rock'n'roll scene. The Rolling Stones used black music to start off, and they seem to have got on OK. Now we're trying to find our own direction from the ska and bluebeat roots."

Some of the traditional ska material featured in the band's set – such as "Guns Of Navarone" and "Skinhead Moonstomp" – is culled from their early listening days. Or as Horace put it, "I've been beaten up many times to the sound of "Liquidator" and "Long Shot".

Mention of being beaten up brought the conversation around to the band's new skinhead following.

"It started a couple of months back. We played the Lyceum with The Damned and the UK Subs, and the Subs have a skin following, who now come to see us.

"They've been great, but before we realised they were OK, I was a bit scared. There's been that thing that's happened with the Sham Army – I would hate to be in Pursey's position. I think that the nice thing with The Specials, apart from the fact that there's no violence in our music, is that we don't live in London, and we have nothing to

First releases on 2-Tone

JULY 14

Coventry band The Specials turn label impresarios, with a debut single from Madness.

THE SPECIALS HAVE announced the first releases on their own 2-Tone record label. The debut single is from London band Madness on August 10, called "The Prince", coupled with "Madness".

The Specials release a second single in August and a debut album in September. Their current single, "Gangsters", is now being distributed by Chrysalis. Another signing to the label is Coventry-based band The Selecter, who go into the studio next month to record a single for September release.

The Specials will reopen the newly soundproofed Electric Ballroom on July 21 with a special 2-Tone Night. Confirmed to appear are The Specials, Dexys Midnight Runners, Madness and The Selecter. Doors will open at 7.30pm and tickets will be available from agencies and Rock On Records priced £2.

More Specials dates for August include the Bilzen Festival, Belgium (17), Manchester Fun House (10) and a benefit for one-parent families at the Hammersmith Palais (21) with Linton Kwesi Johnson.

A major UK tour is planned for September and some extra European dates in August. **MM**

do with the territorial hierarchy that dominates the skin thing. One of the skins told me that what they needed was a band from outside."

Now that The Specials have found both an audience and a responsive industry, they're keen to develop their 2 Tone label.

"Once that's established, we want to start recording other bands who complement us, people like Dexys Midnight Runners and Madness, the two or three bands in the country who are playing the same sort of music.

"That way it'll come over as more of a movement, which it is, and I think people are more interested in a movement than a particular group. I suppose I could be pessimistic and say the interest in this sort of music is coming about because there's nothing left to revive, but really that isn't it. The reason for us is solely our involvement in black and white music." **MM**

▶ The Specials in action, 1979: in the foreground, Neville Staple and Jerry Dammers, with drummer John Bradbury and bass player Horace "Sir Horace Gentleman" Panter

Transfixing

FEBRUARY 2 · MOONLIGHT CLUB, LONDON

A Pretenders show makes minor history.

NO APOLOGIES FOR following Mark Williams' review of The Pretenders at the Moonlight last week with an instant replay. Now is the time to catch them, before success (which is inevitable) and the consequent expectations modify them in any way.

Last Friday night's event had the edge that feels like minor history being made: lots of interested faces from unexpected quarters, jammed into the Railway Arms' small room, lent a vibrancy to the atmosphere, and The Pretenders delivered.

I thought they'd goofed when they opened with "The Wait", the B-side of their Real Records single, the best thing of its kind I've heard since the MC5's "Looking At You". They hadn't, though: almost every subsequent song was its equal (and, in at least one case, its superior). It was one of those sets which build to the point where, when it's over, you're cursing the fact that you didn't have a cassette machine in your bag and a microphone up your sleeve, because you want to hear it all over again, right away.

Chrissie Hynde deals with rock'n'roll like no woman I've ever seen. She avoids the pop nuances of Debbie Harry while, unlike Siouxsie Sioux or Poly Styrene, making an instrumental contribution (on rhythm guitar) of a weight equal to any of the three men in the group. Although she looks tuff (by Keith Richards out of Veronica Bennett), there's an uncondescending charm about her introductions and asides which establishes the performer/audience rapport at a very interesting and constructive pitch.

She also happens to be the best new singer in ages: razor-phrasing abets a pushy delivery, and she doesn't have to stop playing while she sings (or vice versa). She can spit out "The Wait" or drawl a Lou Reed-soundalike song about anonymous phone calls (better than anything Reed's written in years), and she transfixes the listener both ways.

The band matches her extraordinary power, most notably on "Married Life", the only decent white reggae song I've ever heard, and they cope beautifully with the dense pop textures of Ray Davies' "Stop Your Sobbing" (the A-side). Some of the originals have quite complex rhythmic substructures: I think it was "I Can't Control Myself" which had alternating bars of 4/4 and 7/8 in the verses, attacked very confidently by the rhythm section.

Anyway, the theme of this message is See Them Now. Maybe in Northampton tomorrow night (Friday), where the "House Full" notice will doubtless go up early again. But, pretty soon, it won't even be that easy. **MM**

Chrissie: Why Pretend?

MARCH 3

So Chrissie Hynde of the Pretenders doesn't want to become the front lady of the band. Thanks to Mark Williams and the *MM* photographers, she's halfway there.

In the Pretenders feature that Williams penned for the *MM*, he states, "Unfortunately, the system has a tendency to single out any girl in an otherwise male group, making her star of the show."

Dead right!

He continues to say that because Chrissie is a good guitarist she's more a part of the band than just a front for it. So what? Debbie Harry is a good vocalist and her voice is an integral part of Blondie's music. Williams then states that Chrissie "won't let it happen". If it is the system that idolises females in otherwise male groups, then how can she stop it – split up the group?

Besides this, the majority of the interview revolved around Chrissie, her previous work in other groups, etc, and how long it took her to form the Pretenders. To complement this, Chrissie's photo appears on the front page, titled The Great Pretenders – despite the fact that they're not there.

On the first page of the interview, another big photo of Chrissie appeared, again titled as the group's name, but they're absent – again. Anyone who merely glanced through the Pretenders feature would soon grasp the fact that Chrissie Hynde has a backing group called the Pretenders.

Also, when the *MM* reviewed the recent Pretenders single, accompanying the review was a photo of Chrissie Hynde minus the Pretenders yet again. So despite the fact that Chrissie claims (via Mark Williams) that she doesn't want to steal the limelight from the rest of the group, the *MM* are doing it for her.

JIM JACKSON, Home Farm, Beningsbrough, York. **MM**

▶ A 1979 portrait of the Pretenders'
Chrissie Hynde, taken in the UK by
photographer Fin Costello

A Jekyll -and-Hyde personality

RIP, SID VICIOUS (May 10, 1957–February 2, 1979)

JOHN SIMON RITCHIE, better known as Sid Vicious, died in New York last week after taking an overdose of heroin at a party held to celebrate his release from jail on $50,000 bail pending his trial on a charge of murdering his girlfriend, Nancy Spungen, some four months ago.

The party was held at the flat of Sid's current girlfriend, Michelle Robinson, and among those present was his mother, Mrs Ann Beverley, who had been campaigning for his release since the Spungen death.

Following his arrest for murder, Sid was initially released – on $50,000 bail and conditions which included treatment for his heroin addiction – but he was arrested again after an assault on Patti Smith's brother Todd in a New York disco. This time he served 55 days.

While in prison, Sid was put on a detoxification course to "clean out" his addicted system. Without the "tolerance" built up by regular usage of heroin, even Sid's normal dose was potentially fatal.

The precise circumstances of the lethal dose are not known. What is evident is that around midnight Sid was given heroin at the party and that shortly afterwards he collapsed and went into a seizure, his skin and lips taking on the blue/grey tinge associated with heroin overdose.

◀ Sid Vicious singing in typically defiant pose, beer in hand and without his bass guitar

He was covered with blankets and his pulse checked until, some 40 minutes later, he revived. Guests spoke of seeing him walking around at this point. Around 3am the party finished and Sid and Michelle retired to bed. Mrs Beverley stayed the night on the couch in the front room.

The following morning she went into the bedroom to wake the couple and discovered her son dead, naked and lying outside the covers while his girlfriend slept on the bed beside him, unaware of his death. The police were called. Patrolman Robert Zink, the first to arrive, discovered "a syringe, a spoon and what is probably residue near the body".

Later, Dr Michael Baden, who performed the autopsy, said that Sid "died much like a drowning person. There was an accumulation of fluid in the lungs characteristic of heroin."

There remains some dispute, however, on the origin of the dose that actually killed him. Mrs Beverley, once a registered addict herself, admitted in an interview with the *Daily Express* that on the night of Sid's death she had been holding his heroin supply, but claimed that, after the seizure, Sid "didn't have any more that night because I had the packet in my pocket".

She did agree, however, that the heroin he had taken had been unusually pure: "He knew the smack was pure and strong and took a lot less than usual."

The view held by some people is that Sid had another source of heroin and may have taken an additional dose after his mother and Michelle Robinson were asleep. If this was indeed the case, then the overdose may have been tantamount to suicide.

The product of a broken home, London's East End and Clissold Park School, Sid started his rock'n'roll career with the Sex Pistols. As a former crony of Johnny Rotten – the two were at a further education college together – he was one of the small faithful coterie of friends/fans who followed the Pistols' early gigs from late '75 onwards.

It was during this time that he acquired the name Sid Vicious, apparently inherited from Rotten's pet hamster. Later he was to declare that he hated the name, but at the same time did little to shake it off. He was fond of carrying a bike chain as a weapon and was sometimes in evidence at the occasional eruptions of violence at early punk gigs.

Sid was not a "hard man" – not constantly or determinedly aggressive – but there was a violent streak in him. Sometimes this was turned against other people and at times against himself in fits of self-mutilation. Friends and associates spoke of a Jekyll/Hyde disposition. "He seemed to have a lot of demons in his head," said one. "He was tormented."

Whatever, the name stuck.

Sid's first public performance was at the Punk Festival at London's 100 Club in September '76, when he played drums for the hurriedly arranged debut gig of Siouxsie And The Banshees. Later he took up bass and hoped to play with the Banshees, but this came to nothing.

Following Glen Matlock's departure in spring '77, he joined the Pistols as bassman in time to sign with A&M Records and face the sound and fury that accompanied the eventual release of "God Save The Queen" in the Jubilee summer.

His playing was strictly rudimentary but he seemed to learn and practise. All the Pistols agree that for a time his playing got better.

A major change in Sid's life took place when he met Nancy Spungen, a 20-year-old New York groupie who had followed Jerry Nolan of The Heartbreakers to this country and seemed determined to "pull" one of the Pistols. She got Sid.

All agree that Spungen was a bad, if not disastrous, influence on him. His weak character was easy prey for her aggressive, vampish ways. She instigated dissent between him and the other Pistols, and more importantly, introduced him to heroin.

Nonetheless, the couple had an obvious liking for each other, and when Nancy was threatened with deportation, Sid falsely testified that they were married to gain her a visa extension.

Once Sid became involved with heroin, his self-destructiveness and self-mutilation gained momentum, and by the time of the Pistols' tour of America at the beginning of '78, he was taking the stage with

Punk *Is* Dead

FEBRUARY 24

So Sid Vicious is dead, and with him must go the last festering remains of the punk movement which, ironically, Vicious was partly responsible for killing. Had the true face of punk rock been maintained – ie, setting up an alternative culture and pointing out, through that culture, the faults of conventional society – they would still be with us.

But, of course, human instincts caused people like Vicious and various others to take advantage of the movement for personal glory and commercial gain.

So many groups conned us, by using the images created by the Pistols (Matlock-Rotten version) to achieve their present position, and then selling out to record companies in order to maintain that position.

When I saw Sham 69 in January '78 in Brighton, I would have laughed at anybody who said they would produce the crass commercial trash they have recently.

And what has living in a hotel in New York, making massively publicised feature films and printing T-shirts with your face on them, got to do with punk? About as much as Margaret Thatcher. DAVID JONES, Rudwicks Close, Felpham, Bognor Regis, West Sussex. *MM*

◄ Sid Vicious at the Pistols' last ever gig, at the Winterland Ballroom in San Francisco, January 14, 1978

▲ Sid on stage in January 1978, as his brief career with the Sex Pistols came to an end

"Ten days after Nancy's slaying, Sid slashed his wrists in an apparent suicide attempt"

his torso covered in self-inflicted lacerations. He also indulged in some ugly scuffles with the Pistols' American audiences, kicking and using his bass as a cudgel.

He was also taking increasingly large amounts of the drug, alienating himself from the rest of the band and contributing to their decision to split.

Following the Pistols' final gig in San Francisco, he had to be rushed from New York airport to hospital for emergency treatment following an overdose.

Back in London things did not improve. He and Nancy were remanded for possession of amphetamines, but the case was never heard. Attempts to start his own band with the remainder of The Heartbreakers – either as The Flowers Of Romance or, more brutally, The Junkies – were a failure.

The couple then moved to New York, where Sid hoped he would find a new career (he felt his ex-Pistols status gave him more credibility there), but he never got further than the methadone clinic and a few abortive gigs at CBGB with old friends helping out.

Shortly after the CBGB gigs came Nancy Spungen's death, the grisly secrets of which will probably follow Sid into the grave. Whether Vicious killed her or not, once she had gone it seemed only a matter of time before Sid followed. Even before the Pistols' US tour, he had talked to *NME*'s Nick Kent about premonitions of his death.

Talk of an explicit "suicide pact" at the time of Nancy's death may have been exaggerated but there is little doubt that, via their mutual

fascination for hard drugs, knives and violence, the two were on a "death trip" together. There could be only one outcome.

Ten days after the slaying, Sid slashed his arms and wrist in an apparent suicide attempt, and was treated in hospital. Then came the disco attack and he was back in custody.

Inevitably, there will be repercussions from Sid's death, and already there is talk of who was "responsible" for it. Malcolm McLaren, Sid's manager has – with some justification – laid the blame directly on whoever gave Sid the heroin at the party.

Others will doubtless attribute the responsibility to McLaren himself as the progenitor of the punk role Sid acted out.

Others still will blame the whole ethic of punk rock and seek to draw moral conclusions about the music as a whole from Sid's tragedy. Again, some will point a finger at the media that played up and glorified the Pistols and Sid – which must include the music press and *NME* – claiming that his death is the inevitable outcome of elevating a nobody to undeserved heights.

Some might also point to the late Nancy Spungen as the person who gave Sid his fatal fascination for heroin in the first place. Probably there is an element of truth in all of these accusations, but the simple fact remains that it was heroin that killed Sid Vicious; a drug and not a person, a drug that he took of his own free will. That is, in as much as junkies can be said to have a free will.

Certainly on the night of his death Sid Vicious was not under any compulsion from physical addiction to take more of the drug; his detoxification is the guarantee of that.

Finally, his death is mostly a warning about the futility and ultimate fatality of heroin addiction, and the responsibility for that cannot be laid at the door of punk rock, just as the death of Charlie Parker cannot be blamed on jazz or the death of Janis Joplin on '60s rock.

In fact, there are far, far fewer hard-drug users in punk-rock circles – at least in this country – than among the echelons of rock's so called "old guard".

Ultimately, Sid's death has far more to do with organised international crime and its traffic in heroin than rock'n'roll. What rock must not do is to propagate heroin addiction – something which, alongside acclaimed radical literati like William Burroughs, it has sometimes been guilty of in the past.

The equation that Heroin = Death has been enacted enough times for it to be obvious to all. *NME*

▶ Sid Vicious in London, March 27, 1977; in more tranquil times than those surrounding his tragic death

"Desperation – I recommend it"

With their backs to the wall, THE CLASH rise to the challenge – and deliver *London Calling*. Discussions now include: "pokey" lyrics, bat piss, and why in the war against the "grey neu musik" a band must have swing and soul.

INSIDE THE CLASH'S new rehearsal studio, under a railway bridge somewhere in South London, Joe Strummer is singing a slow country blues about rolling boxcars, twisting his head way down under to reach a low mic, perched next to an electric piano. To his right, Mick Jones, dressed in black shirt, vest and trousers, looking like a maverick from a Western B-movie, messes around with a bottleneck; while to his left Paul Simonon slouches on a bar stool, as if posing for the silhouette logo on *Top of the Pops*. Behind them, Topper Headon drops an occasional beat to throw drumsticks for his dog.

This is the new Clash, relaxed and unfettered by the chains – or "bullshit", as Joe would have it – with which some would bind them to their past. They will later worry about the lack of work they're getting done, but undoubtedly the music will be as tough and as tight as it ever was by the time they reach the stage in January. By then, their attack will be strengthened by an influx of new songs from their third album, *London Calling*, which showcases an ardent, much younger-sounding band, for the first time allowing itself the expression of a full range of emotions, rather than just those sentiments we all wanted to hear. The sound is exhilarating, jumping from the loping, lightweight "Jimmy Jazz" to the swinging political punch of "Clampdown", the "white trash" reggae of "Lover's Rock" and the upstart rocking "I'm Not Down" or "Hateful".

The songs' source-material is rock'n'roll, old movies, Raymond Chandler, anything – not just personal experiences or responses, which limited the scope of *The Clash* and *Give 'Em Enough Rope*. Those albums were necessarily narrow, pushing forward the punk message. But life goes on, things change, people grow, and in doing so The Clash have broken out gloriously from their own confines. They've learnt from their mistakes, which were many, and today they're far more cautious in what they say off the record, friendly and helpful, without volunteering the "good copy" they used to deliver, and which they've been forced to live down ever since.

"The trouble is, the newspaper men have forgotten why humans like music," says Strummer. "It's like the fairy tale, when people forget the basic thing because they're too involved with the bullshit. And that's the moral of this fairy tale – they can't see the wood for the trees any more.

"We're just a group and we release records, and that's the face of the situation, but people think they've got to swallow all the bullshit with it. That's why I thought 'Blind Date', which you used to have in your paper (*MM* used to carry single reviews by a guest musician who wasn't allowed to see the label or the artist's name before passing comment) was so good, because the reviewer had to judge it on the tune and the beat – what it should be judged on, you know, not what kind of trousers he's got on."

Easy to say that now, but The Clash – with or without Bernie Rhodes, whom they've acknowledged as being important in establishing the political character of the band at the beginning – formed the blueprint for the whole movement of socio-political punk bands, and thrived on confrontation at all levels: with authority, with their record company (CBS), and with their public – the last category perhaps still to come.

The Clash coming clean will shock those harbouring illusions about them being frontline troops, though the band began the whole mobile-guerilla-unit thing themselves. Even on the new album, on "Spanish Bombs", Strummer glamorises the "artists at war" image.

"I got that from reading – Orwell and people like that," he says. "It's been pretty well covered. But me, I've gone through my *Starsky And Hutch* stage. If there was another one, I don't think I'd rush out there and get in the front line. Who lives by the gun dies by the gun – never was a truer word said."

The emphasis has shifted. The Clash still shoulder responsibilities, like making sure the songs are right and the band are fit to play them and to give their all on stage: "It ain't like sitting on a stool; it's about 300 times more physical than that. I'm now 27 and it's something

The Clash posed outside Notre Dame Hall in Leicester Square on July 6, 1979

"Our ability has widened slightly. You gotta learn…"

you gotta learn by the time you're 25, that before then your body doesn't keep a record of what you do to it. After that you get real sick, sort of burning the candle at both ends – especially doing the stuff we do. All this junkie he's-so-out-of-it rock'n'roll stuff doesn't appeal to me at all. That's the easy way out, you know?"

He adds: "I wrote 'Rudie Can't Fail' about some mates who were drinking [Carlsberg Special] Brew for breakfast. They think nothing of it. Me, I'm past the stage where I can. I can drink Brew for breakfast, but not every day, and that's what made me notice them. I thought it was a hell of a way to start a day."

Their commitment comes in the positive exuberance of the songs, concentration on getting the basics right and helping people in the most direct way they know – cutting the price of the album to the minimum. Eighteen tracks for £5, as the ad goes. Most of them worth having, too.

Ironically, bearing in mind the music's healthy vitality, The Clash were at their lowest when they began planning *London Calling*. Reeling from expensive court hearings, extricating themselves from former manager Bernie Rhodes, then leaving his successor, Caroline Coon, The Clash were going through a radical reappraisal of their whole approach.

First, they took control of their management, only recently relinquishing it to Blackhill Enterprises when they had the album in the can, because "we didn't wanna spend all day on the phone". But they were at rock bottom, and desperately needed to find a way out. Says Strummer: "Economically, we were really tight at the time. This album woulda been our last shot, never mind if we didn't have the spirit for it, which we did.

"I don't know why, but the problem seemed to relax us, the feeling that nothing really mattered any more, that it was make-or-break time.

"Desperation. I'd recommend it. We thought of this idea to create the £2 wall of sound, by recording it on two Teac recorders to keep the costs low, so we could release it cheap. Then the music would have to be fucking good to cover this fucking insanity. We just said to ourselves that we'd never put out a Clash album for six quid.

"But to do that, we knew we'd have to pay for the recording costs ourselves, otherwise CBS woulda told us to fuck off and sent us another list of debts when we asked them to put it out cheap."

They got CBS to agree to the lowest price category, which would also cover a free 12-inch single; they played a festival in Finland – "It was good dough and would pay for the recording costs at Wessex Studios," says Strummer – and recorded between May and August.

"We gave CBS 20 tracks and told them to put eight on the 12-inch single. They freaked out, so we said, 'Look, make it a fiver', and against my expectations they agreed to put it out as a double album. I'd say it was our first real victory over CBS." *MM*

Paul Simonon and Mick Jones on stage at the Palladium, New York on September 20, 1979

ED ZOO
I7 ST. J

GIG REVIEW

"You want to be everything"

APRIL 14 · **PALLADIUM, NEW YORK**

British Invasion! THE JAM undertake a US tour. Sheer commitment wins out over radioactivity and equipment trouble, just about. "In the end, we gotta break through. Everybody's gotta win in the end."

I T WAS ONLY as we drove into Philadelphia that realisation struck. "Isn't this near where they had that nuclear accident?" gasped Angela, Polydor's ultra-efficient press person.

Of course it was! How could we have been so stupid as not to make the connection? How could we have been so stupid as to, er, come...? I instantly studied the cityscape. That bubble of radioactive gas was lodged in the power plant at Three Mile Island, which is just outside Harrisburg, which in turn is just a thyroid gland or two away from Philadelphia. On the atomic scale, 90 miles is a drop in the ocean. Civil disorder had to be round the next corner.

However, everything looked so normal. The headlines screamed panic and talked in terms of the worst nuclear disaster ever. Farmers were apparently worried about contaminated milk supplies; engineers fretted over infected water. So where were the thousands fleeing to safety? Why wasn't there a military curfew to

◄ The Jam outside The Townhouse recording studio in Shepherds Bush, London, 1979. Left to right: Rick Buckler, Paul Weller and Bruce Foxton

"We could never get away with doing anything avant-garde"

prevent looting? Where were the hucksters peddling overpriced Geiger-counters?

All apocalyptic fantasies vanished when the only evidence of any public concern turned out to be a couple of trestle tables manned by protesting students and a downtown cinema showing *The China Syndrome*.

And, obviously, the cinema was not concerned with making any heavy-duty political statement. It was simply cashing in on the current "meltdown" obsession with a thriller that depicts a near-catastrophe at a plant outside LA. As someone remarked when the film was over. "I go to the movies to find out what's happening in the papers."

In fact, nothing much was happening in Philadelphia as we kicked our heels waiting for The Jam to arrive and play the celebrated Tower Theatre. At almost exactly the same time last year they had played the Tower, supporting the Ramones and Runaways. Now they were headlining, and the switch in status indicates how much ground they've covered in the intervening 12 months.

Nevertheless, they still have a long, uphill struggle ahead of them before they crack the massive American market. They may have topped the bill at the Tower, but the place was only quarter-full. Such apathy didn't stop them putting on a superlative set. Indeed, it spurred them to heights which, despite technical hitches, they didn't reach the following evening in New York when the Palladium was sardine-packed with adoring disciples.

The band's reaction is exactly what you'd expect: they view it from a realistic historical perspective. Paul Weller constantly refers back to the British invasion of the States during the '60s, noting the differences and seeing the parallels.

The Beatles, he reckons, had few problems because they were already such a phenomenon in Europe and delivered "nothing really new", whereas "all the really innovative British bands like The Kinks and The Who, it took them a long time anyway".

While you might not agree with his quality judgements, his comparisons with The Who and Kinks in terms of winning transatlantic recognition is perfectly on target. This is the group's third trip over the water and they know that, barring a marketing miracle or a modern-world equivalent of something like the Monterey Pop Festival, there are several more such journeys in store before The Jam become anything like a household name.

Every gig, then, means another round of photographs, another round of interviews when the same questions are asked and the same level of ignorance displayed, plus another round of meeting the

Polydor representatives. At one point Bruce Foxton sighed, "We should give them a tape of our answers. We can't keep coming up with new answers to the same old questions."

To be fair, The Jam really believe that they have nothing new to say to the press. The only aspect that matters to them is playing live and releasing records. Paul said, "We've been talking about this a lot recently... especially the press point of view. They've been trying to find something different to write about us for good copy... like deep meanings about what we're about. What we're about is being on stage and the records... just what we say in the songs. Yet if you say that to someone it just sounds so simple, and then they say The Jam are a bunch of thickies. It's so difficult.

"You want to be everything. You want people to come and dance to us and enjoy it and get off on that level. We want people to listen to what we say, and make their own minds up. We're not preaching from any particular stance. We just strive to be the perfect group, better than any other group is.

"The only people who always get it right are the fans. The thing is, we don't affect your life. We're not going to change your way of thinking. All I'm saying is that the fans are in touch. Most of the time they don't have to ask these things, because they know. Instead of them coming to say, 'What's this song about?' they say, 'I understand that song because it meant this or something has happened in my life', which is exactly the same thing.

◀ Paul Weller in concert with The Jam at
Portsmouth Guildhall, January 1979

▲ Photographed by Richard E. Aaron, The Jam relaxing
backstage during a visit to New York in 1979

▲ The Jam posing confidently with their instruments for photographer Tommy Nutley in 1979

"It's taken four years of hard work and believing in ourselves and not listening to other people saying we're shit or something. It's a question of maturing, growing up fast. I tell you... a great quote I saw in the paper the other day comes from Stevie Wonder's song 'Uptight'. The line says, 'No one is better than I/But I know I'm just an average guy'.

"That really sums it up, as far as I'm concerned. It's a question of saying we're just the same as everyone else, but we have our pride and self-respect and we know we're good. As far as I'm concerned, we're the best... but anyone can do it."

At the moment The Jam are going through a vital transitional period, which is when a band's tensions and contradictions show more than ever. The band don't want to be "big"; they crave it. In Britain their name is made, and they know that they can only go on to consolidate that success.

More importantly, they consider that they achieved this with the minimum of compromise, and they want to do exactly the same in the States. It'll be an awful lot harder; even Elvis Costello allowed CBS to remix and add strings to "Alison" before they put it out as the first single. Consequently, The Jam are almost embarrassingly grateful for every piece of ground that they gain, and never stop showing their determination to get more the honest way.

For example, it was once suggested to them that George Martin produce the next album "in order to get the American market". Paul sighed, "It's just like The Clash getting Sandy Pearlman. They're always suggesting people like that."

Bruce took up the point: "It would just become George Martin, or Phil Spector, or whoever it is. It wouldn't be The Jam any more."

In Philadelphia, Paul barked at the audience, "Last time we said we'd be headlining when we came back. Next time we're here, there'll be fucking queues outside."

In New York, he announced, "I have to say in all honesty this place ain't really us and I'm sure it ain't you either. What we give is what we get." By this time they'd only played four numbers, but Paul – quite rightly – realised that the band were slack. The prestige of a Big Apple gig together with their fanatical commitment never to put on a poor show made them even more desperate.

After a patchy version of "Strange Town", where the guitar solo was strangled and Bruce fluffed his usually brilliant harmonies (on record they're pallid; on stage they're rousing), Paul blurted out, "In the end, we gotta break through. Everybody's gotta win in the end."

But fate was cruel and the situation just got worse. During "Down In The Tube Station At Midnight", Paul's amp blew. He covered up by using his mouth as a harmonica, almost doing permanent damage to it in the process.

Then, as a parting shot, Paul introduced "A Bomb In Wardour Street" with, "This song, we feel, is very, very close to us. It may take you three or four years. We don't know." The song, accompanied on stage with a battered tenement backdrop and exploding smoke bombs (they aren't above a bit of traditional corn) is, of course, all about the Vortex, punk's second home after the Roxy. Predictably, the audience went bananas.

New York is a Jam stronghold, as an incident earlier on in the day confirmed. DJ Mark Simone from Radio WPIX held a competition on air to give away 50 tickets for that night's gig. He would stand at a certain crossroads in New York, and the first 50 people to recognise him would get a freebie. Hundreds of fans turned up and caused a minor commotion. The police appeared and tried to smuggle Simone away in one of their squad cars.

But the traffic was so bad that following the car was easy. So everyone arrived at the police station and started to lay siege to what should have been a place of safety for Simone.

A more major source of change, however, is the band's growing musical maturity. When *All Mod Cons* and the two successive singles came out, critics noted a new depth to Weller's songwriting. He's beginning to deal with a larger and more subtle spectrum of emotions, embodying them as often as not in a wider array of characters. Some artists use characters to hide their own feelings; Weller does the opposite.

"I use characters to express the way I feel. I'd use a character to bring myself out more. It's easier for people to relate to, instead of saying, 'This is just about me and do you dig it?' The whole thing is so ambiguous that they can make up their own minds and inject themselves into it."

As a result, bigger and better things are constantly expected of the band. Everyone seems to be waiting for Weller's masterwork, and more and more Paul finds himself being treated as an "artist" – which brings its own dilemmas. Did he think that such elevation would make The Jam less accessible to fans?

"That's the only drawback. Like having an idea for a song... we could never get away with doing anything avant-garde, or even vaguely avant-garde... even if we wanted to, and I'm not saying that we do.

"The whole punk thing started because people were alienated by crappy music, obscure lyrics and references and everything.

"We don't want to get into that. That's what everyone was fighting about. Some people might not have meant it, but we did. But also we don't want to suppress anything that wants to come through naturally. We've overcome it in the past, so maybe we can keep on doing it. It's difficult. The day that we stop being accessible is the day we die." ***MM***

The show will consist of a brick wall

MAY 19

The new Pink Floyd album has a heavy concept.

THE PINK FLOYD, who are currently recording their new album under utterly punishing conditions in Nice, have settled upon a novel concept for the accompanying stage show. The album, the whisper goes, is called *Bricks* (oh, well – it's only taken them two years). It's being produced by Bob Ezrin, whose presence will have done little to curb their exaggerated grandeur.

The stage show, continuing the kind of modest presentations favoured by the Floyd (as they are affectionately known by their fans), will consist of a brick wall, which will be erected along the front of the stage. Through this remarkable edifice, the audience will be able to see only the hands and the instruments of the internationally acclaimed combo. At the conclusion of the set's third song (three and a half days into the performance), the wall will EXPLODE! Oooooh! The audience will be showered with bricks.

We presume the "bricks" will be manufactured from expanded Polystyrene or loose portions of Roger Waters' brain. Or something similarly soft and harmless. Typical, really, of tax exiles to be able to spend so much time designing such exciting theatrical distractions. ***MM***

The Jam "When You're Young"

AUGUST 17

Paul Weller continues to recreate the perfect heritage, utilising an almost military, stuttering beat to prove he's the undisputed boss of all this quasi-mod stuff. The quirky use of dub to break down the riff mid-stream is amusing, and serves to tone the listener's reflexes for the steely, one-step-at-a-time guitar solo that sneaks in the back and ricochets neatly off the tail of the bass and drums. Classic Jam, what more can I say?
NME

Pink Floyd "Another Brick In The Wall Part 2"

NOVEMBER 16

A decade's rolled by without Pink Floyd releasing a single in Britain for reasons beyond me (probably something to do with the old myth linking selling out with chart success). So it's nice to know they're aware of the switch in emphasis and further that they've been listening to the radio. Because "Another Brick In The Wall" is a great modern single, described aptly by Ian Birch as "an elegant Sham 69 record". Floyd characteristics are there – ominous guitar/keyboards themes, this time fired by a scratchy guitar figure, sardonic "people's voice" singing and a smooth, homogenised production – all effectively streamlined in keeping with the times. The song is an anti-educational rant, the lyrics are playfully illiterate and the killer punch comes when the children's choir is brought in to sneer its way through the chorus, upending the seasonal tradition of cutesy kiddy novelty records. Kids haven't been used so effectively since Lou Reed's *Berlin*. The flip's an oddity called "One Of My Turns", where a taped conversation leads the song into a metallic romp. ***MM***

Guiding spirit of Little Feat

JUNE 29

RIP, Lowell George.

LOWELL GEORGE, the founder and guiding spirit of Little Feat, died in America last Friday after a heart attack. George, whose singing and guitar-playing had been featured with Little Feat from 1971 until their final split earlier this year, died in Arlington, Virginia, during a tour to promote his first solo album.

Following a concert in Washington, DC, on Thursday night, George woke up in the Marriott Twin Bridges Hotel on Friday morning complaining of chest pains. His wife called an ambulance, but George died within half an hour. He was aged 34.

George earned respect and admiration primarily as a slide guitarist, and played on many sessions for other artists – notably Van Dyke Parks, Bonnie Raitt and Robert Palmer.

But it was through Little Feat that he found fame. Among his compositions for the band were several songs which became rock standards, like "Willin'"and "Sailin' Shoes".

The last few years of Little Feat's life had featured several well-publicised internal disputes – but, ironically, once having made the break, George had been receiving highly favourable reviews for the recent concerts with his own band. **MM**

Aimlessly Frenetic

NOVEMBER 10 · **BRIGHTON CENTRE**

Mod is resurgent, but The Who go from stately to stumbling.

THE WHO HAVE always been acutely aware of their own legend – just look at *The Kids Are Alright*. Each landmark is carefully stage-managed and duly recorded, which rather diminishes the supposed spontaneity and secrecy of their return to Brighton.

Naturally, fans heard about it early enough to form long queues days before tickets went on sale. The media were there, the legend thus fuelled. Brighton, a sentimental journey for the band and fans alike: a veterans' run rejuvenated by an influx of new mods. *Quadrophenia* was showing further on up the road, supplying the script to this particular movie.

The Who in Brighton sounds better in retrospect than it did on the night. But it didn't have to be that way, and for half of the concert it was more than that. The return of mod means that The Who no longer have to strain to justify their presence, like they did with the less-easily-pleased punks who preceded them. The first half was relaxed and stately and fine by me. The Who gently caressed the strings marked "audience response", rather than tugging at them as they were to do later on.

"Substitute" and "I Can't Explain" are great pop songs by any standards, and the band played them with lively respect. "Baba O'Reilly", possibly the best of all Who numbers, with easily the most recognisable intro, was astonishingly moving, fusing Townshend's joyful gigs with his own plaintively sung chorus.

The first newish song, "Sister Disco", was solid, lightened by John "Rabbit" Bundrick's airy synthesizer; "Who Are You" had all the classic Who hallmarks: stuttering intro, reticent Townshend chorus and impassioned Daltrey voice. "Music Must Change" sensibly introduced a three-man horn section, leanly used to bolster the song's chorus. Like the Stones, The Who are adept at assimilating newer songs into their set, so with each subsequent hearing they seem more and more like they belong.

The Who were happy together, joking between themselves without forcing the friendship on the audience. Once, Daltrey and Townshend began a chorus of "We were the mods, we were the mods", and later Townshend qualified his relationship to the movement thus: "Naturally, we don't have much to do with the mods today, and we didn't have much to do with them 15 years ago." The irony was probably lost on the audience, but they both seemed pretty pleased with each other's presence.

Quadrophenia was represented by a forceful "Punk And The Godfather" and – perhaps the set's highlight – "Drowned", beginning with rumbling piano and hefty drum rolls. Their other opera representation, "Pinball Wizard"/"See Me Feel Me", combined with heavy floodlighting to prompt the biggest reaction of the night.

But then everything went downhill. The disguised intro of "My Generation" was swiftly recognised, the song turning into a seeming endless rock'n'roll-style medley. "Won't Get Fooled Again" was similarly spoilt. Townshend is just incapable of jamming interestingly, so that Who jams stumble over a crashing, falling rhythm and their leader's aimlessly frenetic riffing, based more on a boredom and relief gamble than tension and release.

The end and the encores: the band's lasers have been replaced with a lighting rig that spells out their name, to much applause. They returned with "Young Man Blues" – an unfortunate choice, as the father figure of the chorus now resembles Townshend too closely: "How did you learn how to fight/spit/shit", etc. Later there's a half-hearted attempt to smash a guitar, and it's all over.

Whether they like it or not, The Who have become an institution – one that would benefit from nationalising and rationalising if it wants to function efficiently in the '80s. *MM*

A Labyrinth That Is Rarely Explored

ALBUM REVIEW

JUNE 15

Joy Division's stark, defiant debut LP is "memorably psychotic".

Joy Division *Unknown Pleasures*

JUST WHEN THE YEAR'S vitality was threatening to be expunged by a non-stop parade of rehashed fashions, "ordinary geezers" with French Riviera yachts and the acceptable face of cuddly popular music, the Manchester band Joy Division snuck in by the back door, quiet and unannounced.

Joy Division's reticent foursome – Bernard Albrecht (guitar), Peter Hook (bass), Stephen Morris (drums) and singer Ian Curtis – have hinted at these "unknown pleasures" in the last 18 months; their contributions to 1978's *A Factory Sample* were intriguingly alien to the prevalent mood. Their own 12-inch sketch "An Ideal For Living" was more to the point – hard-faced, sombre, neanderthal and manic, an inverted shape cast in heavy metal, never conforming to the expected thrust of the beat.

Admirers of this new sound who managed to check out the animal on its live patch were pleased and maybe shocked to hear that Joy Division weren't joking. Never funny peculiar, funny ha-ha or clever-clever – the lot of most of the bands trying to slip into the

current avant-garde – their music clearly fuses all the frayed ends with a new, unforced simplicity, a direction beyond expectancy.

Joy Division's atmosphere is uncomfortably claustrophobic in meaning, but its structures and dynamics are accessible. Although the band and their producer Martin Hannett have constructed something memorably psychotic, I'd hesitate to linger on their background of mental institutions and the vocabulary of the psychologist – for fear of encouraging images of contrived banshee rant and postured metal-machine thrashing, all of which has its place but is not the guiding experience here.

Joy Division music worries and nags like the early excursions of the better known German experimentalists. Investigate these confined spaces, these insides of cages, this outside of insanity. They all bring to mind endless corridors where doors clank open and shut on an infinite emotional obstacle course. "Disorder" and "Insight" start out slow and smooth, echoing Can's *Monster Movie* pattern, but the monotonies and deviations are Joy Division's unique territory. The root causes of Curtis' lyrical "insights" – industrial and urban decay – are ignored in favour of the end result; the noises are human and the effect is shattering, literally. So, the brutal numbness of "Day Of The Lords" bears a slight resemblance to the well-planned spookiness of a Bowie or an Osterberg, except that Curtis' voice conjures up a withdrawal from response and an immunity to anaesthesia. There is "no room for the weak" in this world and no cheap pity either. Joy Division are solitary men, but assured and confident.

All the material bears the mark of obsession and personal experience; it's stark, alarmingly defiant. Curtis delivers his parts with dramatic flatness, as semi-chants, matter-of-fact monologues, pushing out the meaning in spurts. Alongside his compelling vocal, the three instruments sift through gaps on graphic frequencies, producer Hannett distorting the orthodox conceptions of sound level, balance and attack. This fragmented logic is most evident on the closing pieces, "New Dawn Fades" and "I Remember Nothing", where negative stasis confronts the listener with his/her conception of ordered existence. At their most compelling Joy Division invite you to participate in their journeys to the edge of chance. Try the mental hang-gliding of "She's Lost Control", "Interzone" or "Wilderness" (a blood-pulse of a streamlined account of a time traveller who witnesses the agony on the cross face to face).

In many other hands, Joy Division's relentless litanies would appear pompous, tasteless or just plain vicarious; the Sex Pistols, for example, turned out to be all three. But Joy Division are treading a different tightrope; what carries their extraordinary music beyond despair is its quality of vindication. Without trying to baffle or overreach itself, this outfit step into a labyrinth that is rarely explored with any smidgeon of real conviction. By the time they experiment with the dialogues of schizophrenia on "I Remember Nothing", they have you convinced of their credentials.

Unknown Pleasures is an English rock masterwork, its only equivalent probably made in Los Angeles 12 years ago: The Doors' *Strange Days*, the most pertinent comparison I can make. Listen to this album and wonder because you'll never love the sound of breaking glass again.

This band has tears in its eyes. Joy Division's day is closing in. **NME**

◀ Joy Division photographed in Manchester, January 6, 1979.
Left to right: Drummer Stephen Morris, singer Ian Curtis,
guitarist Bernard Sumner and bass player Peter Hook

▲ July 28, 1979: Joy Division in Waterloo Road, Stockport, near
Manchester, in the vicinity of Strawberry Studios where they
recorded *Unknown Pleasures* in April, 1979

◄ Ian Curtis performing live with Joy Division (Stephen Morris and Peter Hook in background) at the Bowdon Vale Youth Club, March 14, 1979

"Don't you ever say that to me!"

After a triumphant London show by LOU REED, members of the press are invited to join him at a restaurant. There, an unseemly spectacle unfolds, as Reed scraps with former patron DAVID BOWIE. What was said? "Ask fucking Lou," says a battered Bowie.

THE WORD WAS THAT Lou Reed wanted to see me back stage after the show. He also wanted to see Giovanni Dadomo, a freelance writer who had recently contributed to *Time Out* an enthusiastic preview of his solitary London engagement.

Howard Harding, the Arista press officer who had been dispatched with the invitations, led us backstage. We lingered a while in the bar, to allow Lou a minute or too to cool down after his performance. We had a drink and lingered. There was no sign of Louis. We had another drink and lingered. There was still no sign of Louis. We lingered a while longer. Harding went off to find Lou.

He returned five minutes later.

"Aaah," he said, "Lou's gone."

Bloody typical, we all agree.

"I'll try to find out where he is," Howard Harding promises.

Lou, he informs us upon his return, is having dinner at a restaurant in South Kensington. He is with David Bowie.

"He says he wants us to go over," Howard tells us.

Dinner with Lou and the Thin White Duke seems an attractive proposition. Howard notes our enthusiasm and agrees to drive us to the restaurant – the Chelsea Rendezvous in Sydney Street.

"They'll be on the pudding by time we arrive," Giovanni Dadomo reflects.

Lou and David are huddled together at the head of their table when we arrive. Lou has his arm around David's shoulder. David is smiling. Lou is laughing, slapping the table. David seems content to play a supporting role. Lou talks. David listens, hands cupped together, elbows on the table.

We are shown to our table. Howard presents himself to Lou, tells him that Giovanni and I have arrived.

"Lou says to go over," Howard tells us.

Giovanni leads the way. Lou takes him firmly by the hand. I play gooseberry.

Bowie looks up.

"Allan," he says, extending a hand.

"David," I say, taking it.

"Nice to see you," says David. "How are you?" Bowie's charm is overwhelming.

"Allan," roars Lou.

"Lou," I reply, less raucously.

He clasps my hand, nearly breaking a finger in the process. He yanks me across the table. I almost end up sprawled in David's lap. I have an elbow in the remnants of Lou's dinner.

"Do you know Allan?" Lou asks Bowie.

"We meet occasionally," he tells Lou.

"Did you see the show tonight?" asks Lou.

"I'm still recovering," I tell him.

"Good," says Lou. "What did you think of it?"

"I felt like I was being given a good pistol-whipping."

▶ David Bowie, pictured on a happier occasion in New York City, in 1979

"You probably deserved it," Lou snaps.

I decided to leave them to their supper.

"Yeah," says Lou. "Go."

I go. Lou turns back to David. They get their heads down. The old pals' act well under way.

Lou gets up and waddles down the restaurant to talk to some people at a table adjacent to ours. He deposits some dirty dishes on the floor, grabs a chair for Bowie who's followed him. There is a considerable amount of mutual backslapping, good times remembered. They exchange dates; contemplating some joint project in the near future, it appears.

Lou orders Irish coffee.

It is delivered.

Lou and David raise their glasses in a toast.

"To friends."

It is a touching scene.

They return to their original places, resume their conversation.

Five minutes later, the place is in uproar.

Bowie has said something to Lou. Lou is not entirely enamoured of the comment. He fetches David a smart crack about the head; fists are flying. Most of them are Lou's and they're being aimed in violence at Bowie. David ducks, arms flying up above his head. Lou is on his feet, screaming furiously at Bowie, still lashing out.

"Don't you EVER say that to me!" he bellows hysterically. "Don't you EVER fucking say that to ME!"

About nine people pile on Lou, wrestle him away from Bowie, drag him away from the table. There's an arm around his throat. He continues to spit insults at Bowie, who sits at the table staring impassively, clearly hoping Lou will go away. Lou shrugs off his

▲ Performing live in San Francisco, California in 1979; Lou Reed's fists are performing a more useful service here

344 •

minders (or are they Bowie's?). There's a terrible silence. People are watching open-mouthed in incredulity. Howard Harding looks as if he might die.

Lou sits down next to Bowie. They embrace. There is a massive sigh of relief. They kiss and make up. We wonder what on earth provoked the argument and Lou's fit of violence.

"Perhaps," suggests Giovanni Dadomo, "David tried to pinch Lou's Bakewell tart."

Meals are resumed. More wine is brought to the tables.

It looks as if the tiff has blown over.

The next thing I know, Lou is dragging David across the table by the front of his shirt and fetching him a few more smart slaps about the face. The place explodes in chaos again. Whatever David said to precipitate the first frank exchange of conflicting opinions, he's obviously repeated. The fool. Lou is beside himself with rage and rains down slaps upon Bowie's head before anyone can drag him off.

"I told you NEVER to say that," Lou screeches, fetching the hapless Bowie another backhander; another flurry of blows follows in hot pursuit. Lou is batting David about the top of his head. David cowers; Lou looks like an irate father boxing the ears of a particularly recalcitrant child for pissing in his slippers. He gets in a few more whacks before the minders haul him away from Bowie. He will not calm down. He tussles and struggles, tries to launch himself again at Bowie.

The silence that follows is ghastly. Lou's party decide to leave. Lou is escorted from the restaurant by an especially large fellow. He has his arm around Lou's shoulders; less in support than restraint. Lou has a look of ferocious blankness; his face is set in a fierce scowl. His eyes looked dead. He leaves with his party.

"Good Lord – what happened?" asks Howard Harding.

Bowie is left at the head of the table. It's a desolate scene. The table is covered with the debris of the meal and overturned wine bottles.

He is joined by two friends (a man and a woman; they are never successfully identified). Bowie sits with his head in his hands. He appears to be sobbing. He seems to be trying to explain what had happened between him and Lou.

I decided to play the fearless reporter and went over.

"I've just come to say goodnight," I said.

"Oh," says Bowie. "Why don't you join us?"

"There isn't a chair," I tell him.

"Then sit on the table," he replies a little testily. I sit on the table.

I tell him that I'm sorry that his reunion with Lou seems to have ended so disastrously. "I couldn't hear what was going on... Lou seemed very upset..." I mutter.

"Yes," says Bowie, wearily. He seems close to tears.

"It was nothing. It's all over," says his female companion.

"It isn't," says Bowie, hands clenched, eyes glaring.

"If it hadn't been for the heavies, they would have bloodied each other's noses and it would have been all over and they'd have been all right," his companion says.

The idea of Bowie bloodying anyone's nose seems remote.

"Are you a reporter?" somebody asks.

"Yes," I admit. "But don't worry – you won't see any of this on the front page of the *Daily Express* in the morning."

This is intended as a feeble joke. No one is amused.

"You'd better go," I am told.

"David's just invited me to stay," I protest quietly. "I was just wondering what happened."

This does it. Bowie leaps to his feet.

"Fuck off," he shouts. He means me. "If you want to know what happened you'll have to ask Lou Reed. Don't bother me with your fucking questions. Ask fucking Lou. He knows what fucking happened. He'll tell you."

"But he's already gone," I remind Bowie.

Bowie, angry, with tears in his eyes, turns on me. He grabs me by the lapels and shakes me and shakes me. I fear he might rip my jacket (recently worn on stage by Mike Oldfield in Berlin, it is of considerable sentimental value).

"Hey," I protest eloquently.

"Just fuck off ," Bowie swears, shoving me back. "You're a journalist – go and fuckin' find him. Ask him what happened. I don't know."

He pushes me again, turns away, knocking over a chair. I am grabbed from behind and dragged away. I return to my table.

"I think you've upset the Thin White Duke," remarks Giovanni Dadomo.

"I think perhaps I have," I reply.

Bowie sits down again. Then he stands up, furniture starts to fly.

"Aaaah fuck" he declares.

He pushes his way down the restaurant, chairs are kicked out of the way. He begins to climb the stairs to the street. Most of the steps on the stairway are decorated with potted plants and small shrubs, and a palm tree or two. Bowie smashes most of them on his way out. He kicks a few, up-ends the others. There is a most terrible mess on the stairs.

The remaining guests are speechless at this further outburst. The waiters look on, astonished. We share their amazement.

The damage, it turns out, is not expensive. I discover later on in the week from the manager of the Chelsea Rendezvous that Bowie has sent "a bodyguard" to the restaurant to pay for replacement of the demolished plants; a cost of about £50.

The cause of the altercation, however, remains obscure. Lou flew out early the next morning to Dublin, cancelling all engagements, including a photo session.

The most popular explanation suggests that Bowie had been discussing with Lou the possibility of producing his next album. Bowie, though, is said to have demanded one thing before committing himself to the project: that Lou clean himself up, and get himself together. If Lou didn't clean up his act, David would refuse to work with him.

Lou, perhaps, was outraged at the suggestion that he was too untogether ("Don't you ever say that to me," he yelled, remember), and replied by belting David. The bully!

A further irony is added to the tale the following morning when it is announced that Bowie's new single is called "Boys Keep Swinging".

Oh, how we laughed. **MM**

▶ Robert Plant of Led Zeppelin struts his stuff on stage in front of a packed crowd at the Oakland Coliseum on July 23, 1977

Index

Credits

The publishers would like to thank the following sources for their kind permission to reproduce the pictures in this book.

4-5. Terry O'Neill/Hulton Archive/Getty Images, 9. Michael Putland/Photoshot/Retna, 10-11. Chalkie Davies/Getty Images, 12. Walter Iooss Jr./Getty Images, 14. TS/Keystone USA/REX/Shutterstock, 15. Tony Russell/Redferns/Getty Images, 16. TS/Keystone USA/REX/Shutterstock, 17. Chris Morphet/Redferns/Getty Images, 18. Michael Putland/Getty Images, 20-21. Henry Diltz/Corbis via Getty Images, 22-23. Jan Persson/Redferns/Getty Images. 24-5. © Barrie Wentzell, 26. Jan Persson/Redferns/Getty Images, 27. Chris Walter/Photofeatures /Retna/Photoshot, 28-29. Jorgen Angel/Redferns/Getty Images, 30. Adam itchie/Redferns/Getty Images, 31. Herve Gloaguen/Gamma-Rapho via Getty Images, 32. Leon Morris/Redferns/Getty Images, 33. © Barrie Wentzell, 35. Evening Standard/Getty Images, 37. James Garrett/NY Daily News Archive via Getty Images, 38. Ron Howard/Redferns/Getty Images, 40. Evening Standard/Getty Images, 42. Jan Persson/Redferns/Getty Images, 43. Fred W. McDarrah/Getty Images, 45. Monitor Picture Library/Photoshot/Getty Images, 46. © Barrie Wentzell, 49. Anthony Barboza/Getty Images, 50. Michael Ochs Archives/Getty Images, 52-54. Peter Stone/Mirrorpix, 55. Earl Leaf/Michael Ochs Archives/Getty Images, 57. Popperfoto/Getty Images, 58-59. Charlie Gillett/Redferns/Getty Images, 60. Reg Lancaster/Daily Express/Hulton Archive/Getty Images, 61. GAB Archive/Redferns/Getty Images, 62. Gijsbert Hanekroot/Redferns/Getty Images, 63. Michael Putland/Getty Images, 64. Chris Morphet/Redferns/Getty Images (top), Gijsbert Hanekroot/Redferns/Getty Images (bottom), 66. Michael Putland/Getty Image, 68. Robert Knight Archive/Redferns/Getty Images, 69. Koh Hasebe/Shinko Music/Getty Images, 70-71. Ilpo Musto/REX/Shutterstock, 72. Michael Putland/Getty Images, 73-75. Estate Of Keith Morris/Redferns/Getty Images, 76. Araldo Di Crollalanza/REX/Shutterstock, 77. © Barry Plummer, 78. Michael Ochs Archives/Getty Images, 80. Jorgen Angel/Redferns/Shutterstock, 81. Jorgen Angel/Redferns/Getty Images, 82. David Redfern/Redferns/Getty Images, 82-83. Michael Ochs Archive/Getty Images, 84-85. Henry Diltz/Corbis via Getty Images, 86-87. Michael Putland/Retna/Photoshot, 88-90. © Bob Gruen, 91. Michael Putland/Getty Images (left), Aylott/Daily Mail /REX/Shutterstock (right), 92. Michael Ochs Archives/Getty Images, 95. Michael Putland/Getty Images, 96. Gijsbert Hanekroot/Redferns/Getty Images, 98-99. Michael Putland/Getty Images, 100. Gijsbert Hanekroot/Redferns/Getty Images, 101. Gijsbert Hanekroot/Redferns/Getty Images, 103. Ed Caraeff/Getty Images, 104. Michael Putland/Getty Images, 106-107. Fin Costello/Redferns/Getty Images, 108-110. Brian Hamill/Getty Images, 111. © Bob Gruen, 112. Michael Putland/Retna/Photoshot, 115-118. Gijsbert Hanekroot/Redferns/Getty Images, 119. Baron Wolman/Iconic Images/Getty Images, 121. Michael Putland/Getty Images, 122. Michael Ochs Archives/Getty Images, 123. Alan Messer/REX/Shutterstock, 124. Gary Merrin/Keystone/Getty Images, 125. Alan Messer/REX/Shutterstock, 127. Ginny Winn/Michael Ochs Archives/Getty Images, 128. Alan Dister/Retna/Photoshot, 129. Ginny Winn/Michael Ochs Archives/Getty Images, 130. © Bob Gruen, 131. Michael Putland/Getty Images, 132-135. Ginny Winn/Michael Ochs Archives/Getty Images, 137-140. David Gahr/Getty Images, 141. © Bob Gruen, 142. Michael Ochs Archives/Getty Images, 143. Steve Wood/Express/Getty Images, 144-148. © Bob Gruen, 149. Ron Pownall/Corbis via Getty Images, 150-151. Sunshine/Retna/Photoshot, 152. David Redfern/Redferns/Getty Images, 153. Ron Galella/WireImage/Getty Images, 155. © Bob Gruen, 157-159. David Warner Ellis/Redferns/Getty Images, 160. Waring Abbott/Getty Images, 161. Maureen Donaldson/Getty Images, 162. Richard McCaffrey/Michael Ochs Archive/Getty Images, 164. Richard McCaffrey/Michael Ochs Archive/Getty Images, 165. Michael Putland/Getty Images, 166. Ron Galella/WireImage/Getty Images, 167. Frank Edwards/Archive Photos/Getty Images, 169. Michael Putland/Photoshot/Retna, 171. Mick Gold/Redferns/Getty Images, 172. Gijsbert Hanekroot/Redferns/Getty Images, 174. Martyn Goddard/Corbis via Getty Images, 176. © Barrie Wentzell, 179. Howard Barlow/Redferns/Getty Images, 180. Andrew Putler/Redferns/Getty Images, 181. Koh Hasebe/Shinko Music/Getty Images, 182-185. © Bob Gruen, 187. Brian Hamill/Getty Images, 188-189. Ron Galella/WireImage/Getty Images, 191-192. Julian Yewdall/Getty Images, 193. Fin Costello/Redferns/Getty Images, 194. © Bob Gruen, 195. Michael Putland/Getty Images, 196-198. © Bob Gruen, 199. James Fortune/REX/Shutterstock, 200. Michael Ochs Archives/Getty Images, 201. Michael Ochs Archives/Getty Images, 202. © Barrie Wentzell, 203. LFI/Photoshot, 204-205. Peter Mazel/Sunshine/REX/Shutterstock, 206. Jazz Archiv Hamburg/ullstein bild via Getty Images, 207. Gijsbert Hanekroot/Redferns/Getty Images (top), Gijsbert Hanekroot/Redferns/Getty Images (bottom), 208. Barry Schultz/Sunshine/REX/Shutterstock, 209. © Bob Gruen, 210. Larry Hulst/Michael Ochs Archives/Getty Images, 213. Michael Putland/Getty Images, 215. David Gahr/Getty Images, 216. Larry Hulst/Michael Ochs Archives/Getty Images, 217. Michael Ochs Archives/Getty Images, 218. David Gahr/Getty Images, 219. Michael Ochs Archives/Getty Images, 220. Terence Spencer/The LIFE Images Collection/Getty Images, 222-223. © Bob Gruen, 225. Hulton-Deutsch Collection/CORBIS/Corbis via Getty Images, 226-228. © Bob Gruen, 229. Moviestore Collection/REX/Shutterstock, 230. Michael Putland/Getty Images, 231-234. Michael Putland/Retna/Photoshot, 235. © Bob Gruen, 237. Waring Abbott/Getty Images, 238-239. Martyn Goddard/Corbis via Getty Images, 241. Gijsbert Hanekroot/Redferns/Getty Images, 242. Larry Hulst/Michael Ochs Archives/Getty Images, 245. Ian Dickson/REX/Shutterstock, 246-247. Howard Barlow/Redferns/Getty Images, 248. Ebet Roberts/Getty Images, 249. Chalkie Davies/Getty Images, 250. Ron Bull/Toronto Star via Getty Images, 251. Chalkie Davies/Getty Images, 252-253. Alan Dister/Dalle/Retna Pictures/Dalle, 254. Chris Walter/Retna/Photoshot, 255. Brian Cooke/Redferns/Getty Images, 256. LFI/Photoshot, 257. Idols/Photoshot, 258. Elisa Leonelli/REX/Shutterstock, 259. Terry O'Neill/Hulton Archive/Getty Images, 260. Estate Of Keith Morris/Redferns/Getty Images, 263. Barry Schultz/Sunshine/REX/Shutterstock, 264-265. Michael Ochs Archives/Getty Images, 266. Gus Stewart/Redferns/Getty Images, 267. Peter Still/Redferns/Getty Images, 268-270. Kevin Cummins/Getty Images, 271. Ian Tyas/Keystone Features/Getty Images, 272. GAB Archive/Redferns/Getty Images, 273. Alain Le Garsmeur/Getty Images, 274. Richard E. Aaron/Redferns/Getty Images, 276. Paramount/Getty Images, 277. Michael Ochs Archives/Getty Images, 278. Paramount/Kobal/REX/Shutterstock, 279. Michael Putland/Getty Images, 280. Allan Tannenbaum/Getty Images, 281. Clayton Call/Redferns/Getty Images, 282. Ebet Roberts/Redferns/Getty Images, 284-285. Echoes/Redferns/Getty Images, 286-289. Beverley Goodway/REX/Shutterstock, 291. Michael Ochs Archives/Getty Images (top), Denis O'Regan/Getty Images (bottom), 293-294. Gijsbert Hanekroot/Redferns/Getty Images, 296-297. Ray Stevenson/REX/Shutterstock, 298. Gus Stewart/Redferns/Getty Images, 300-301. Ray Stevenson/REX/Shutterstock, 302-303. Martyn Goddard/REX/Shutterstock, 304-305. Martyn Goddard/Corbis via Getty Images, 306. Fin Costello/Redferns/Getty Images, 307. George Wilkes/Hulton Archive/Getty Images, 308. Paul Slattery/Retna/Photoshot, 310-311. Chalkie Davies/Getty Images, 312-315. Ray Stevenson/REX/Shutterstock, 317. Fin Costello/Redferns/Getty Images, 318. Sheila Rock/REX/Shutterstock, 321. Michael Ochs Archives/Getty Images, 322. Peter Stone/Mirrorpix, 323. Charlie Ley/Mirrorpix, 325. Virginia Turbett/Redferns/Getty Images, 326-327. Ebet Roberts/Redferns/Getty Images, 328. Janette Beckman/Getty Images, 330. Denis O'Regan/Getty Images, 331. Richard E. Aaron/Redferns/Getty Images, 332-334. Tony Nutley/REX/Shutterstock, 336. Andre Csillag/REX/Shutterstock, 337. Ebet Roberts/Redferns/Getty Images, 338. Kevin Cummins/Getty Images, 339. Paul Slattery/Retna/Photoshot, 340-341. Martin O'Neill/Redferns/Getty Images, 343. Robin Platzer/Images/Getty Images, 344. Richard McCaffrey/ Michael Ochs Archive/ Getty Images, 346-347. Ed Perlstein/Redferns/Getty Images

Every effort has been made to acknowledge correctly and contact the source and/or copyright holder of each picture and Carlton Books Limited apologises for any unintentional errors or omissions that will be corrected in future editions of this book.